INSTITUTIONAL LITERACIES

INSTITUTIONAL LITERACIES

Engaging Academic IT Contexts for Writing and Communication

STUART A. SELBER

The University of Chicago Press
Chicago and London

The University of Chicago Press, Chicago 60637
The University of Chicago Press, Ltd., London
© 2020 by The University of Chicago
All rights reserved. No part of this book may be used or reproduced in any
manner whatsoever without written permission, except in the case of brief
quotations in critical articles and reviews. For more information, contact the
University of Chicago Press, 1427 E. 60th St., Chicago, IL 60637.
Published 2020
Printed in the United States of America

29 28 27 26 25 24 23 22 21 20   1 2 3 4 5

ISBN-13: 978-0-226-69920-2 (cloth)
ISBN-13: 978-0-226-69934-9 (paper)
ISBN-13: 978-0-226-69948-6 (e-book)
DOI: https://doi.org/10.7208/chicago/9780226699486.001.0001

Library of Congress Cataloging-in-Publication Data

Names: Selber, Stuart A., author.
Title: Institutional literacies : engaging academic IT contexts for writing and
communication / Stuart A. Selber.
Description: Chicago : University of Chicago Press, 2020. | Includes bibliographical
references and index.
Identifiers: LCCN 2020008791 | ISBN 9780226699202 (cloth) |
ISBN 9780226699349 (paperback) | ISBN 9780226699486 (ebook)
Subjects: LCSH: Education, Higher—Information technology. | Web-based
instruction.
Classification: LCC LB2395.7 .S44 2020 | DDC 378.1/7344678—dc23
LC record available at https://lccn.loc.gov/2020008791

♾ This paper meets the requirements of ANSI/NISO Z39.48-1992 (Permanence of Paper).

For Kate: My first source of inspiration

CONTENTS

PREFACE

This book conceptualizes how colleges and universities treat information technologies and why this matters to writing and communication and to the teaching of writing and communication. The discussion interweaves theories and practices of institutions, literacies, and technologies in a rhetorically sensitive fashion, providing a durable approach to enacting change in local settings.

In my first local setting for teaching college-level writing, I was a master's student at Northeastern University in Boston, a large private school where I studied technical writing from fall 1988 to spring 1990. As a student, I used a mainframe computer to write and compile code for my programming courses (in Pascal and C++) and a computer lab to print out the code and assignments for other courses. I used equipment from a university recording service to make an instructional video in VHS format for a course in professional presentations. And for several different courses in my degree program, I used my own personal computer, a Macintosh Plus, to compose essays in Microsoft Word, design functional documents in PageMaker, and create hypertext applications in HyperCard. As a teacher of first-year writing and technical writing, I used an overhead projector and transparencies to focus student attention and a mimeograph machine to duplicate handouts. I required students to word process their assignments, print them out for peer review, and hand them in to me or put them in my English department mailbox. If students wanted to communicate with me outside of classroom or office hours, they could try my office phone. I may be forgetting a few details, but this was the basic technological scene for literacy instruction and practice.

There were several notable developments in my second local setting for teaching college-level writing. From 1990 to 1994, I was a doctoral student studying rhetoric and technical writing at Michigan Technological University in Houghton, a small public school that emphasizes engineering and sciences. Students and teachers could use a dial-up modem from home to access an email system that ran on BITNET or to access extrainstitutional resources; my favorite was the Cleveland Freenet. I was able to teach in a department-controlled computer classroom, which was also used to support electronic conferencing in graduate seminars: students would check out their course disk from the front desk, read the file from the top, add their entries, and then return the disk to the front desk. This approach was a version of "sneaker net" in which people hand-carried files in order to overcome the limitations of a computer system. Students and teachers could also use the Daedalus Integrated Writing Environment (DIWE) and Mosaic, one of the first graphical web browsers. Running on a local-area network, DIWE provided a platform specifically designed for teaching writing courses. And teachers used Mosaic to help them create course websites that could be accessed over wide-area networks. In my dissertation, I had to define home pages and links.

Although a lot has changed over the past several decades, even early institutional experiences with academic IT foretell current scenes and issues. Today, teachers of writing and communication remain preoccupied with the affordances and constraints of production platforms and delivery media, approaches to composing processes and collaboration, and questions of access and control. For example, a social-justice turn in the field has renewed and expanded questions about the political obligations of people who design and support production platforms. Teachers remain alert to the reality that personal and institutional spheres entwine and entangle in teaching and learning contexts. For instance, in addition to bringing personal computers to campus, students now arrive with smartphones and other types of digital devices, which they expect to be able to integrate into everyday experiences, educational and otherwise. And teachers remain sensitive to the fact that institutions, literacies, and technologies are constantly moving targets, evolving and changing with time. For example, DIWE was discontinued a long time ago, but some of its key pedagogical ideas are recognizable in modern software programs. The present usually reveals traces of what are considered bygone practices of distant times.

These days, what is distinctive and more noteworthy is the extent to which and the rate at which colleges and universities invest in the development and support of information technologies and how much students and teachers have come to rely on them, including student information systems, course-management systems, asynchronous and synchronous communication systems, tutoring platforms, writing environments, visual design environments, publishing platforms, videoconferencing systems, wide-area networks, computer classrooms and labs, makerspaces, file-sharing and storage services, help systems, training materials, acceptable use policies, and more. These investments are financial but also political and social, and they have both short-term and long-term consequences. Financial investments in information technologies often require a considerable initial outlay of institutional funds, and additional money is needed for maintenance and support. In an era of shrinking resources, colleges and universities face hard budgetary choices, funding certain initiatives and not others. Politically, funded initiatives become sanctioned and therefore legitimized in the eyes of students and teachers. Teachers may very well find an investment to be suitable for writing and communication instruction, but in any event, that investment will help condition what is possible or impossible to do. Social investments become obvious in the stories institutions create about themselves and the role of information technologies in improving the quality and character of higher education. In concrete and direct ways, information technologies have become thoroughly integrated into the world of colleges and universities.

This integration, in large measure, is overseen by academic IT units. Academic IT units are centralized campus units responsible for planning, implementing, managing, and evaluating information technologies for institutional purposes. There are academic IT units that support business and administrative operations, start-up and research enterprises, and teaching and learning activities. These areas often converge and can all be present to some degree in a specific project or initiative, leading to a natural overlap of responsibilities. The units charged with supporting teaching and learning activities are particularly consequential for the field, for they play a major part in shaping the ways students and teachers both think about and do their work, from invention to delivery. In very broad strokes, the planning conducted by academic IT units involves identifying relevant, reliable, and fruitful systems and services for students and teachers of writing and communication. Implementation involves setting up and configuring the systems and services, which must be able to function within overarching sociotechnical infrastructures. Managing involves establishing policies, creating various forms of user assistance, and troubleshooting problems; and evaluating involves measuring the success of the systems and services against stated purposes and goals. I am glossing over many tasks and responsibilities, but the point is that academic IT units organize and regulate the end-to-end process of institutionalizing systems and services for writing and communication and the teaching of writing and communication.

The good news is that there are systematic approaches to engaging academic IT units and influencing their thinking and actions. Furthermore, teachers of writing and communication are well positioned to play a crucial role in institutionalization processes because of their enduring interests in investigating and contextualizing information technologies. The systematic approaches offered in this book leverage the fact that all academic IT units share certain dimensions in common, and these dimensions can be analyzed and acted on to affect institutional directions. The two universities I mentioned earlier, Northeastern and Michigan Tech, are very different types of schools, and yet their academic IT units contend with the same sorts of historical, spatial, and textual dimensions, which on some level condition and influence nearly everything in their purview. Not surprisingly, these dimensions are also of concern to writing and communication teachers, who have an established habit of asking historical, spatial, and textual questions about information technologies to judge their value and worth for teaching and learning activities. The common ground here is a vital inventional resource for addressing high-stakes institutional domains. My hope is that teachers will approach this common ground rhetorically, in the manner I am suggesting, to make an impact and a difference in their own schools.

Many people assisted me with this book project, and I would like to thank them for their generosity and kindness. I am fortunate to work in a department with so many productive colleagues who challenge me to be my best academic self. I would especially like to thank Jack Selzer, Cheryl Glenn, Debbie Hawhee, Keith Gilyard, Mark Morrisson, Garrett Sullivan, Daniel Tripp, and Leslie Mateer for their ongoing support and friendship. I have also benefited from research assistance from Antonio Ceraso, Michael Faris, Kristopher Lotier, Jason Maxwell, and Nathan Voeller. Outside the English department, I have received invaluable support from my dean, Susan Welch, and from the Center for Humanities and Information. The research for this book would not have been possible without encouragement from my academic IT colleagues. Cole Camplese, now vice president for information technology and chief information officer at Northeastern University, opened his office to me and allowed me to shadow his daily routines, providing the access I needed to write this book. Other helpful academic IT colleagues include Terry O'Heron, Jennifer Sparrow, Kyle

Bowen, Chris Millet, Ryan Wetzel, Markus Fürer, Bart Pursel, Chris Lucas, Derick Burns, Brad Kozlek, Allan Gyorke, John Harwood, and Kevin Morooney. Thank you all. For interesting and insightful discussions, I thank the various members of the following academic IT groups at Penn State: the Faculty Advisory Committee on Academic Computing, the e-Education Council, the MOOC Strategy Group, the Student Technology Advisory Committee, and the Learning Innovation Forum Team. I learned a great deal from participating in these groups. Mary Laur, Mollie McFee, and the staff at the University of Chicago Press deserve special recognition for their editorial efforts, as do two anonymous reviewers and David Morrow. My longtime collaborator, Johndan Johnson-Eilola, is a continuous presence in the intellectual work I do. My sons, Avery and Griffin Selber, were good sports about my writing schedule and spending too much time in the office with me. And in the end, always, there is Kate, to whom I dedicate this book. She is my first source of inspiration.

1

SITUATING ACADEMIC IT

Twenty years ago, IT for the most part was the domain of IT specialists. Today, no one in the academy can avoid taking some responsibility for its impact.
POLLEY A. MCCLURE (2003)

Scenes of literacy on university campuses inevitably involve information technologies (IT) supported by the academic institution. "Academic IT," as I will refer to it in this book, has become a key aspect of the teaching-learning complex that students and teachers negotiate routinely. For that matter, academic IT is instrumental to writing and communication activities in off-campus contexts, including spaces devoted to vernacular practices. Institutions, literacies, and technologies are entwined and interlinked in a concrete fashion, and their dynamic relationships present opportunities and challenges for the field.

The shaping power of academic IT is hard to exaggerate. It has a significant bearing on the fundamental endeavors of students, teachers, and administrators and on the prospects for change in literacy education. Academic IT is a component part of intellectual transactions and other social interactions, of production and reception activities, and of collaboration and communication activities. It is also a thoroughly integrated element in the design of campus landscapes, making an indelible mark on how physical spaces are organized and used. In a relatively quick manner—the span of a few decades, really—the imprint of academic IT has gained a steady foothold in a culture otherwise known for its resistance to change, and its effects are dramatic and not to be minimized.

In addition to its immediate and tangible presence, academic IT has also become a factor in discussions about planning in higher education.

Early on, academic IT comprised initiatives for administrators and faculty with high-performance computing needs. Participants especially worked on student data systems, library databases, and science and engineering projects. Although these areas continue to be important, they have been conjoined with a host of additional vital directions. At my institution, there are five primary units for academic IT, the titles of which are somewhat self-explanatory: Business Intelligence, Strategic Operations, Enterprise Service Management, Infrastructure, and Teaching and Learning with Technology (TLT; many of my examples will involve the TLT unit). On a national scale, this expanded purview has been formalized at the highest levels of university administration, making it routine for the head of academic IT to hold the post of vice president or vice provost in a presidential cabinet. Such a position presupposes involvement in more general discussions of planning, discussions in which the overall goals of an institution both reflect and leverage the capabilities of and hopes for information technologies. Academic IT has become a strategic asset for institutional design and development.

This new normal is evident to students. I will not cite growth statistics from the Pew Research Center or EDUCAUSE, two leading organizations that track technology use on university campuses, because such statistics become outdated quickly. Generally speaking, however, survey after survey shows that college students have growing expectations for and from academic IT, as they spend more and more time online, rely more and more on online resources, and contribute more and more content to online environments. Many researchers claim that such trends are a function of generational phenomena, that students who have been exposed to technology their entire lives are necessarily good at using it (Prensky 2001). Digital natives, so the argument goes, have a knack for technology that their elders do not, producing an inverse relationship between age and expertise that is not typical in classrooms.

Setting aside for now the colonizing nature of certain academic IT metaphors, I am skeptical of generational arguments for several reasons: people of the same generation do not share a single interpretation of cultural phenomena, do not share a single approach to learning or communicating, and do not enjoy the same level of access to digital technologies. In fact, there can be as much variation within generations as between them, resulting in mixed pictures of students' literacy abilities. On the other hand, one can reject claims of expertise in generational arguments and still recognize rising participation rates. Students today are living in a new and different time, one in which technology is ubiquitous and inseparable from education itself. Regardless of their skills and abilities, students have increasingly encountered this reality in their daily lives.

For their part, teachers of writing and communication have been persistent investigators of academic IT. Ellen Nold (1975) published the first article on the role of computers in college writing classes. Her view was that teachers should become creators of software so that computers could better serve the needs of students learning to write. This early vision emphasized invention and teacher engagement, and it acknowledged that technologies can be configured and interpreted in multiple ways. Since then, the field has consciously worked to situate academic IT in disciplinary contexts, advancing a rich agenda for literacy education. One can glimpse the scope of this agenda by considering critical questions that arise while teaching and learning with academic IT: What can history contribute to a rhetorical understanding of technological contexts? How do issues of technology intersect with issues of identity, subjectivity, and agency? With race, class, gender, and ability? With other contemporary theory issues and categories? Who owns writing classes in an age of user-generated content? What might literacy narratives reveal about the nature of the digital divide? What might computer games reveal about the nature of learning? Is programming writing? Are soundbeds texts? What are the ethical, professional, and institutional issues raised by technology and its current contexts? These sorts of questions both accommodate and resist status quo thinking in the field and position academic IT as a warranted element of rhetorical situations.

Although teachers of writing and communication have attended to certain institutional aspects of academic IT, they have tended to do so at the level of courses and programs and for disciplinary initiatives. My stance is that teachers also need to involve themselves in the working lives of academic IT units, which condition the fields of possibilities for technology development and use on college campuses. A first-order task for this agenda is conceptualizing how academic IT works as a unit, product, service, event, or other institutional formation. Teachers can then imagine thoughtful approaches to action and problem solving.

This chapter launches an investigation into the character and culture of academic IT in higher education. I begin by reviewing the work the field has done to address academic IT units, making the case that teachers of writing and communication need to do a great deal more in this important domain. I then consider the institutional, educational, and commercial contexts that shape the aspirations and practices of academic IT units. The final section of the chapter explains my working assumptions about institutions, literacies, and technologies and introduces a heuristic for conceptualizing the academic IT landscape. The heuristic reflects my overall argument that all academic IT units have historical, spatial, and textual dimensions and that teachers everywhere should work to understand and influence these dimensions in professionally valuable ways to help enact positive change in university settings.

INSTITUTIONS AS DISCIPLINARY SITES OF STUDY

In technological contexts for writing and communication, approaches to institutional critique have coalesced around several overlapping themes, including computer labs and classrooms, networked pedagogies, electronic portfolios, tenure and promotion policies, and copyrights and intellectual property rights. Projects falling under these themes demonstrate a sensitivity to institutional dynamics, at times suggesting, though not actually pursuing, the types of encounters with academic IT units that I am proposing.

Computer labs and classrooms are fitting places to start because they have preoccupied teachers for as long as anything else. Indeed, the field has a substantial track record of designing and administering computer labs and classrooms, producing decades of evidence-based advice for novices and experts alike. In his review of the extensive literature in this area, Sean Williams (2002) traces a disciplinary conversation arguing that teachers should aim to develop partnerships with academic IT units. The motives for this argument are economic and pragmatic, as Williams explains: "We must build partnerships to maintain technology and to secure funding to keep our facilities running because, simply put, we can't do it alone" (345). For programs that operate their own facilities, this suggestion stems from a particular reality on the ground: computer labs and classrooms are dynamic learning spaces that must be maintained if they are going to remain relevant. It is one thing to acquire initial support to build a classroom or lab and quite another to secure access to a regular stream of resources that can ensure operational success. If academic IT partnerships are crucial to the state of computer labs and classrooms, however, how might these partnerships be created and nurtured? What are the critical elements and considerations? Compared to the why of academic IT partnerships, the how and the what have not been addressed so thoroughly.

Networked pedagogies are a crucial counterpart to computer labs and classrooms, for such pedagogies appropriate academic IT environments for the purposes of writing and communication instruction. Although pedagogies and technologies are dialectical pairings involving reciprocal relationships, the field has tended to foreground instructional frameworks, which are a professional strength. In its formative years, the field was preoccupied with designing computer labs and classrooms, programming software to support composing processes, studying word processing practices, using local-area networks for conversations and file exchanges, and training teachers (Holdstein and Selfe 1990; Selfe, Rodrigues, and Oates 1989). In this early period, teachers relied on a variety of academic IT resources, including servers and technical specialists, but the somewhat stand-alone activities of teachers encouraged a disproportionate sense of self-sufficiency. This feeling of autonomy was tempered by the popular emergence of wide-area networks and the internet, which literally wired together the pedagogical and the institutional in new and different ways, extending centralized university assets to classrooms and offices. As a result, the field began to explore the physical and metaphorical dimensions of networks for literacy education.

The first wave of research articles maintained the inclination to foreground instructional frameworks, an understandable impulse for teachers who were considering an emerging literacy technology. Many of these articles first articulate the social turn in writing studies and then examine the ways computer networks might support that turn by connecting people to people and to institutional resources, enhancing phases of composing processes, and providing alternative forums for conversations and collaborations (Faigley 1992; Kemp 1992). Teachers often discuss academic IT as either a barrier to or an enabler of change. It can be both, of course, and simultaneously.

The split view surfacing from initial responses to networks was useful because it enabled the field to continue to develop a critical stance that is alert to both promises and perils. This split, however, has now been complicated by developments in theory and practice that attend to the full ecology of institutional activities in technological contexts. In discussing the dynamics involved in implementing an iTunes University channel at SUNY Cortland, Alex Reid (2008) confounds the literacies-technologies dyad that organizes numerous discourses in the field, formulating instead a conceptualization in which institutions are repositioned as elements comparable to literacies and technologies in rhetorical situations. A key facet of his project traces a series of networked interactions through the "bureaucratic labyrinth" (66) of the university, characterizing how students, teachers, technologies, and institutions co-construct the spectrum of potentialities for teaching and learning. The institutional components include committees, curricular structures, approval workflows, college policies, and support systems. Reid encourages teachers to see such components as a consequential part of the "compositional process" (63).

Another thematic area that exhibits a sensitivity to institutional issues is electronic portfolios. E-portfolios are a natural outgrowth of the practices and pedagogies of print-based portfolios, which have long been used to situate and assess writing and communication processes and products and to represent such activities for multiple audiences, including teachers, employers, and external review boards. This outgrowth has come to depend on academic IT because e-portfolios are often created using dedicated systems such as myEfolio and Pathbrite, which are meant to be administered by academic IT units for an entire university population. In addition, such systems can be connected to larger efforts on a campus to create enterprise-level, data-driven structures in which a variety of areas— e-portfolios, student records, course evaluations, benchmarking statistics, outcome measures, and more—are tied together and mined for planning and assessment purposes. In lieu of dedicated systems, which can be home-made, open source, commercial, or a hybrid of these options, universities promote website development platforms as authoring environments for making e-portfolios. There are also third-party deployments that host e-portfolios, although people often prefer internal solutions because they carry the imprimatur of a school. My school has not built or bought an e-portfolio system. Rather, it asks students and teachers to use a WordPress installation for their communication projects. This approach depends on custom templates, university networks, and institutional support systems.

E-portfolio authors' reliance on academic IT has been mentioned in at least two position statements from the Conference on College Composition and Communication (CCCC). The "CCCC Position Statement on Teaching, Learning, and Assessing Writing in Digital Environments" (2004) offers guidelines to help teachers and program administrators think rhetorically in technological environments. One section notes that writing programs should work "in concert with their institutions" (788) to achieve two goals: to assess student readiness for and access to digital environments and to foster approaches that enable students to become critical designers of extensible e-portfolios, which can be redesigned for a variety of contexts and evolved over time. According to this position statement, a fundamental role for writing programs and institutions is collaborating to build the necessary infrastructure for e-portfolio development. The "CCCC Position Statement on Principles and Practices in Electronic Portfolios" (2007) elaborates on this collaborative assignment. Each of the principles in the position statement is accompanied by a list of "supportive best practices" for four groups of people: teachers, writing program directors, technology staff, and university administrators. The best practices for technology staff include creating and maintaining accessible archives of e-portfolios, designing and testing templates, providing workshops and training materials, establishing credentialing and privileging systems, contributing to the creation of open standards and initiatives, and staying abreast of new software programs. Technology staff are advised to inflect these activities with instructional principles that guide sound e-portfolio practices. Both CCCC position statements considered institutional infrastructure an indispensable part of college writing today.

Stepping back from professional position statements, teachers might wonder about the risks associated with making time for academic IT endeavors. For those in tenure-stream appointments, a tremendous risk is losing tenure, and the field has been alert to this hazard for some time now. At issue are a number of intractable questions with considerable importance to education. Some of the questions derive from a more general concern over the boundaries and rigor of academic work: Is database design an intellectual activity? Is remix production sufficiently original? Is usability testing a serious form of research? Although answers to such questions should depend on the character and quality of the work, it can be difficult for those outside the field, including colleagues in English departments, to judge the tenure value of projects involving academic IT.

Other matters reflect a desire to demystify tenure by encouraging stakeholders to be as lucid as possible about processes, expectations, and contributions and to be proactive and strategic. Rebecca Rickly (2000) focuses on tenure candidates, advising them to "work hard to present what we do in terms of what the institutions we are associated with value. That is, we need to understand our rhetorical situation, and adopt the language of that discourse community as we describe what we do with technology" (23). Rickly proposes an accommodative stance that makes sense in a high-stakes context. Michael Day (2000) approaches the task of demystification from a different angle. He asks administrators to make explicit their approaches to evaluation, especially criteria for judging teaching effectiveness, to account for the complexities of online environments. For everyone involved in the tenure process, Cynthia Selfe (quoted in Young 2002) emphasizes the value of dialogue. Selfe moderated an online discussion of several fictional tenure cases for people working with information technologies; the deliberators included deans and faculty members. In one case, most of the participants agreed that the candidate deserved to be denied tenure, for the publishing record was thin, and also that administrators should have done more to communicate expectations: the tenure process is nothing if not a shared institutional endeavor. Is there a role for academic IT units in this endeavor? Although it is hard to imagine a scenario in which academic IT units would cast a tenure vote, it is easy to see the considerable impact of their priorities on the imaginative lives of teachers.

Let me provide a final example of the nature of institutional awareness in the field. Copyrights and intellectual property rights incorporate issues that are fundamental to the production and consumption of texts. In discursive contexts, relatively settled questions over who owns what and why and what can be used and how have been reopened by the ways digital technologies treat texts, by networked modes of authorship, and by revenue models for internet content. By and large, the field has championed liberal stances on copyrights and intellectual property rights by working to explicate the tenets of the Fair Use Doctrine (Rife 2007), maintain access to texts in a shrinking public domain (Gurak 1997), participate in alternative copyright designation systems that facilitate sharing and collaboration (Ratliff 2009), critique consumerist rhetorics that undermine the value of student writing (Ritter 2005), critique approaches to writing that sustain traditional notions of intellectual property (Johnson-Eilola and Selber 2007), understand the impact of social networks on rhetorical delivery (Porter 2010), clarify when a university can claim ownership over intellectual property (Galin 2009), and propose new strategies for publishing that reconcile the differing interests of authors and commercial publishers (Galin and Latchaw 2010). These activities have also been accompanied by concrete actions in the public sphere: the Intellectual Property Caucus of the CCCC has lobbied Congress to rein in corporate influence over copyright laws and intellectual property rights.

In the work I cited, several units within a university are either discussed or implied, with academic IT units being a notable exception. Academic IT units, of course, do not make intellectual property policies for universities, nor do they usually play a leading role in copyright administration and management. These responsibilities are coordinated efforts involving high-level institutional personnel in legal departments, copyright and intellectual property offices, graduate schools, research libraries, research and development offices, technology transfer offices, and the like. Academic IT units, however, assist with implementation and support. At my institution, academic IT units provide educational materials on legal uses of digital media, tutorials and quizzes on plagiarism, tutorials on remixing media, guides for determining fair use, annotated links to open-source media sources, and workshops where people share project experiences with copyrights and intellectual property rights. These resources interpret and illustrate policies and laws for students and teachers, but they also function to structure thought and action. For example, Turnitin.com has become an institutionally sanctioned response to plagiarism in writing and communication courses despite the fact that the writing program was not consulted about its efficacy or utility. IT units play a considerable role in the formation of campus approaches to copyright laws and intellectual property rights.

In sum, teachers have investigated institutional dimensions in a variety of areas important to writing processes and systems, but those investigations tend to ignore or gloss over the shaping power of academic IT units. Their influence, however, is anywhere and everywhere in higher education, and it increasingly matters to teaching and learning, to writing and communication, and to administering programs—that is, in contemporary college scenes, literacy activities can no longer be considered islands unto themselves, operating outside of academic IT contexts. The next section discusses these contexts in more detail.

CONTEXTS FOR ACADEMIC IT UNITS

Academic IT units operate within contexts that serve constitutive and regulative functions. The constitutive functions configure and enable actions and activities; the regulative functions maintain the status quo. These contexts, in addition, are internal and external to university settings, with a portion bridging both regions, sometimes simultaneously. This section discusses three contexts that are particularly salient to the development and use of academic IT: institutional, educational, and commercial. For my purposes, institutional contexts refer to rhetorical dynamics in the larger university settings within which academic IT units operate, educational contexts refer to perspectives that inform the work of academic IT units, and commercial contexts refer to relationships that academic IT units have with third-party vendors. I use examples from my own school and others to illustrate these contexts.

Institutional Contexts

In her article on innovation and change in organizations, Barbara Curry (1991) advances a model of change with three recursive phases: mobilization, in which organizations are readied for change; implementation, in which innovations are introduced into organizations; and institutionalization, in which innovations are stabilized by organizations. The third phase of this process addresses the larger university settings for academic IT units. According to Curry, innovations achieve an appreciable level of stability once they have become integrated into the everyday structures, procedures, and cultures of organizations. Structural integration involves developing formalized support systems for innovations and realizing significant moments in which innovations are merged with established organizational formations. Procedural integration involves routinizing the activities associated with innovations, developing workflows, and adapting innovations to existing ways of working. And cultural integration involves accepting (or at least tolerating) the norms and values associated with innovations and attempting to use them for principal job activities. The conditions associated with these phases can domesticate innovations but also engender alternatives and new possibilities.

At my school, the institutional contexts for academic IT are visible to students and teachers. Penn State is a large land-grant university with twenty-four campuses, over one hundred thousand undergraduate and postgraduate students, and over eight thousand academic staff. A twenty-fifth campus, the World Campus, serves more than 10 percent of the student body through online courses and programs. So scale matters at Penn State—a great deal. As a land-grant institution, Penn State aims to balance teaching, research, and service in seventeen colleges, branding itself a comprehensive, student-centered research university. This characterization is explained in strategic plans and other vision documents, which circulate widely and function to coordinate planning efforts in both academic and nonacademic units. The university strategic plan lists seven goals and thirty-eight concrete strategies for achieving them. The goals include enhancing student success, advancing academic excellence and research prominence, maintaining affordability and enhancing diversity, and controlling costs. In theory and oftentimes in practice, plans from the various institutional levels nest within one another, with the goals of the overall plan guiding the way toward a shared vision of the future.

One of the main goals centers on academic IT: to use technology to expand access and opportunities. The associated strategies aspire to enlarge and diversify the online offerings of the World Campus and improve its instructional and managerial approaches, invest in flexible infrastructures, protect the security of infrastructures, and improve efficiencies. These strategies, which are meaningful to students and teachers, not only reflect institutional preferences and realities but also reveal something about how upper-level administrators tend to think about academic IT.

Enlarging and diversifying online offerings would allow an already crowded campus to attract and enroll new students; provide additional options and experiences for traditional, on-campus students, who are encouraged to enroll in online courses; and provide additional options and experiences for nontraditional, off-campus students, who represent a growing segment of the university population. Improving the instructional and managerial approaches of the World Campus would allow it to concentrate on developing faculty capacities for online teaching, designing consistent interfaces for online courses, consolidating and centralizing technical support, and simplifying the models for revenue sharing with academic colleges.

Investing in flexible infrastructures would allow academic IT units to evolve their support for the ways digital texts are created, used, and stored. Procedures for working with digital texts are not static or identical everywhere. Although such procedures are maturing and becoming increasingly standardized—examples are the ePub file format for publishing e-books and HTML5 for creating websites—an enormous challenge for universities is anticipating the digital future of higher education. Tantamount to hedging technological bets, investing in flexible infrastructures would provide tangible support for teaching and learning without overcommitting the university to particular approaches or environments.

Protecting the security of infrastructures would allow Penn State to redouble its commitment to providing safe conditions for the study and practice of digital literacies. By safe, I mean environments for writing and reading in which identities, artifacts, and activities are shielded from exploitation in ways that still empower people to take risks, stretch themselves, and grow. Balancing security with usability is a ceaseless obligation, regulatory and otherwise, and a constant source of struggle, not a one-time decision for academic institutions. To put the challenge in perspective, in one year at Penn State, more than one thousand university computer accounts were compromised, over twenty-five hundred computer systems were compromised, and more than twelve million hostile probes attacked university servers daily (Kimball 2011). And such attacks are becoming all the more sophisticated as people turn to social media and personal mobile devices for accessing university systems. For higher education leaders, concerns over protecting the security of campus infrastructures are on par with top academic issues.

Finally, improving efficiencies would allow the institution to do more with less in tough economic times. On nearly every college campus, the demands on academic IT are growing faster than IT budgets, which are subject to multiplying pressures from competing stakeholder interests. In part, campuses are responding to this new normal by encouraging internal and external partnerships that reduce costs, leverage capabilities, and promote sustainable practices. Although reinventing the wheel can be useful to learning, productive partnerships are a metric of business value and a platform for academic IT work. The efficiencies of partnerships are particularly significant when they produce opportunities that would not be possible otherwise.

Targeted growth, flexibility, security, and efficiency—these university priorities constitute an influential backdrop against which processes of institutionalization unfold and evolve. Structurally, academic IT has become integrated with registrar systems, library systems, advising systems, evaluation systems, storage systems, testing centers, tutoring centers, and many other systems and centers. For example, from within our course-management system, I can access dynamic class rosters and submit new course proposals to the Faculty Senate. Procedurally, academic IT has become integrated with institutional and personal workflows. For example, in our faculty assessment system, there is a critical workflow for preparing annual merit reviews. And culturally, academic IT has become integrated with the norms and values of campus life. In fact, it is impossible to participate in many aspects of campus life without an academic IT account. Slowly but surely, questions about whether information technologies are good or bad have been replaced by questions about how and when to use them to advance university endeavors. Information technologies have become so prevalent in academia, so much a part of the common sense of students, teachers, and administrators, that people now expect technologies to be involved in their professional and personal lives. This situation has not always been the case, of course: the institutional contexts for academic IT reflect the realities of a rapidly changing world.

Educational Contexts

The educational contexts for academic IT specialists include two dimensions: formal degree programs and professional development activities. Many people in academic IT units hold degrees in education, instructional design, or computer science or engineering. As far as I can tell, the nearest approximation to formal degree programs in academic IT are education programs with technology tracks and IT programs with education tracks.

IT programs are historically new additions to the degree portfolios of universities; one of the first programs was established in 1992 at the Rochester Institute of Technology (Subramaniam 2005). Although IT programs are emerging at all levels of higher education, some universities—including Penn State, George Mason University, Carnegie Mellon University, and the Georgia Institute of Technology—have created IT colleges or schools in an effort to overcome "the traditional territorialism of academic departments" (Denning 2001, 19). Peter Denning (2001) notes that the IT schools movement arose from two realizations: programs in computer science or engineering are not broad enough to address many of the emerging areas within IT, and universities are investing in IT programs to create competitive advantages in the higher education marketplace. As alternatives to programs in computer science or engineering, IT programs tend to require fewer math and programming courses, focusing instead on blending technical abilities with perspectives from business management, organizational communication, industrial psychology, human factors, and other areas that foreground contexts, practices, and users. Assuming attentive advising and planning, IT programs could support the study and practice of academic IT in concrete ways.

As I suggested in the previous section, a first principle of academic IT is that the strategic plans of universities should govern the aspirations and actions of campus IT units. Perhaps it goes without saying, but this principle implies knowing more than a little about university settings. Brian Hawkins (2006), a past president of EDUCAUSE, one of the leading associations for IT professionals in higher education, contends that understanding the working atmosphere of universities is "essential to being perceived as a partner in the academic enterprise rather than just as some bureaucrat who has responsibility for the IT environment on campus" (58). Developing such an insight, and such an ethos, is a formidable task for academic IT specialists because universities are heterogeneous workplaces with multiple cultures and audiences and because the audiences can have different and even conflicting interests. Hawkins discusses habits of successful academic IT specialists that should be nurtured in universities. Several of these habits are rhetorically minded. For example, he encourages academic IT specialists to become "multilingual" professionals who can "effectively communicate with faculty, with students, with vendors, with trustees, and with other administrators" (57); generalists who can "tackle problems that cut across specialized and professional boundaries and silos" (64); and curious readers who can "develop a broader view of the environmental factors that are affecting the technology, the campus, and higher education as a whole" (58). Although the educational contexts for academic IT specialists are varied and ever-developing, a challenge for everyone is the tension between the big and small pictures. In mediating this constant tension, Hawkins advocates erring on the side of the big picture.

At Penn State, the educational contexts for academic IT specialists in the TLT unit reflect a full spectrum of global and local possibilities. I will begin with formal degree programs and then turn to professional development activities. Academic IT specialists in the TLT unit are responsible for imagining, architecting, and managing pedagogical infrastructures and assisting the students and teachers who use them. Chapter 3 will discuss institutional hierarchies, but it is useful to know here the two major structural divisions in the unit: innovation, which includes subunits that support learning spaces, production studios, assessment initiatives, instructional design activities, faculty engagement programs, and creative learning initiatives; and operations, which includes subunits that support computer classrooms and labs, networks and infrastructures, teaching and learning platforms, accessibility initiatives, and marketing and communications. Each division has a director, and the subunits have managers. The managers report to directors, the directors report to a senior director, and the senior director reports to the campus chief information officer (CIO), a vice president. The two divisions within TLT employ over one hundred people (in total, there are around fifteen hundred IT professionals at Penn State).

As might be expected for a complex unit, the educational degrees of employees are all over the map, but not in a random fashion: there are different valid pathways to a career in academic IT. William Aspray and Peter Freeman (2002) provide a scheme for classifying academic IT workers that correlates job roles and educational degrees. Although Aspray and Freeman emphasize that "none of the relations between training, education, and particular IT occupations are hard and fast" (9), they nonetheless argue that their scheme "applies reasonably well to all kinds of IT workers in all sectors of the economy, including universities" (6). It certainly applies to the TLT unit, at least in broad strokes. The scheme distinguishes four types of roles—conceptualizers, developers, modifiers or extenders, and supporters or tenders—and the levels of degrees that people in those roles are most likely to have earned. Considering levels of degrees is one way to account for generalized versus specialized knowledge: the higher up the organizational ladder academic IT workers climb, the greater their need for broad-based preparation and experience.

The job of conceptualizers is to imagine and describe the fundamental characteristics of IT systems and services. Conceptualizers can be researchers or designers, but their institutional understandings exceed their technical understandings. Directors in TLT tend to be conceptualizers, inventing new systems and reassessing old ones from new and different angles. Their institutional understandings have been informed by graduate programs in adult education, instructional systems, educational technologies, and public administration. Directors without graduate degrees have significant on-the-job experience or an unusual talent for seeing the big picture.

The job of developers is to advance the plans for academic IT systems and services in concrete ways. In TLT, managers tend to function as developers. For example, if conceptualizers from Classroom and Lab Computing were to imagine a web-based application for helping students locate available computers on campus, then developers would create specifications and scenarios to guide the design process. Developers, as designers, programmers, or testers, would also be involved in the design process itself. As this example illustrates, the technical understandings of developers exceed or at least match their institutional understandings. The technical understandings of developers in TLT have been informed by graduate and undergraduate programs in computer science, operations and information systems management, instructional technologies, and engineering.

The job of modifiers or extenders is to adjust or augment existing academic IT systems and services. In my example of a software application for finding available campus computers, an extender or modifier could create a mobile version of the software for smartphones. Modifiers or extenders tend to have the same levels of degrees and educational profiles as developers, but their role in the design process is more limited and specific, emphasizing programming or database administration. The TLT unit employs numerous modifiers or extenders. Not surprisingly, many of them have undergraduate degrees in technical fields.

The job of supporters or tenders is to maintain and document academic IT systems and services. In my ongoing example, workers in this role could update the mobile application as new labs and classrooms are opened or as old ones are updated, create online help texts, or troubleshoot user problems. According to Aspray and Freeman (2002), supporters or tenders do not need to hold graduate degrees and could even hold high school diplomas or associates degrees. And among the four roles, they have the least amount of use for institutional understandings. This characterization of supporters or tenders can certainly ring true: replacing a motherboard or updating a server hardly requires a sense of the larger university setting, and in fact undergraduate workers at Penn State perform such tasks all the time. But the scheme begins to break down with supporters or tenders who function as help desk specialists, customer support specialists, documentation writers, and software trainers.

It is ironic that Aspray and Freeman (2002) diminish the need for institutional understandings for the very workers who are in routine contact with actual users. Although the scheme provides a useful approach to mapping the employment landscape, the elements and dynamics of particular projects will help determine the extent to which and what conceptualizers, developers, modifiers or extenders, or supporters or tenders need to know about institutions. Thus as opposed to thinking about these roles in discrete and static ways, it might be more productive to imagine them as complimentary subject positions that any type of academic IT worker could inhabit (with varying levels of intensities) in a simultaneous fashion. This identity formulation acknowledges the inevitable slippage that occurs among roles—modifiers and extenders can reconceptualize projects, for instance, and conceptualizers can depict use cases and create other types of instructional materials—and affords the possibility for supporters or tenders who work with students and teachers to develop a greater degree of institutional awareness.

The professional development activities for academic IT workers are external to the institution and job-embedded. Gene Spencer and Jeannie Zappe (2006) explain that an important agenda for professional development activities is to prepare people for "unanticipated and complex situations," which requires "agility, curiosity, service orientation, empowerment, collaboration, self-motivation, leadership, accountability, and a willingness to embrace change and take appropriate risks" (2.2). Their concerns about the intricacy of academic IT problems, the rate of sociotechnical change, and the uncertainty of tomorrow are reflective of the concerns of the IT community at large. Although budget appropriations for professional development appear to be trending lower for the future, investing in an academic IT workforce remains as crucial as ever: since 2012, professional development has regularly appeared on EDUCAUSE lists of priority issues.

In the TLT unit, two of the main sources of external professional development are professional associations and peer institutions, especially universities in the Committee on Institutional Cooperation (CIC), which includes Big Ten schools and the University of Chicago. Professional associations provide data services, publications and publication opportunities, conferences, workshops, special interest groups, mentoring opportunities, and numerous other initiatives. The major professional associations include EDUCAUSE, the Association for Computing Machinery Special Interest Group on University and College Computing Services (ACM SIGUCCS), and the Sloan Consortium.

According to the EDUCAUSE website, more than 1,900 universities belong to this professional association. Because EDUCAUSE offers institutional rather than individual memberships, all academic IT workers at a member institution can participate in professional development activities. Academic IT workers in the TLT unit read *EDUCAUSE Review*, the practitioner magazine, and the annual *Horizon Report*, which identifies key trends in academic IT; present papers at meetings; serve on committees; and participate in leadership and management programs as students or teachers. Their professional development derives from consuming multimodal informational texts, engaging in sociotechnical interactions, and assuming leadership positions (TLT workers have served on the committee that coauthors the *Horizon Report*).

ACM SIGUCCS, which was founded in 1963, also has a conference, workshops, mentoring opportunities, and social networks. Its conference proceedings, however, are a particularly vibrant resource: bibliometrics from the ACM Digital Library show that over 2,800 papers were published between 1965 and 2018 and that papers have been downloaded over half a million times. TLT workers have published papers on learning communities (Lucas and Huntsinger 2009), desktop conferencing systems (Heckel 2009), software deployment processes for computer classrooms (Tyndall 2012), training IT student employees (Moeller 1999), and more.

The Sloan Consortium has a comparable suite of professional development activities, but it focuses on online teaching and learning. Its core function is to help universities create and evaluate academic courses and programs. In fact, a start-up capital grant from Sloan was crucial to the establishment of the World Campus. Academic IT workers in TLT use frameworks from the Sloan Foundation to design online interactions, create accessible websites, and develop faculty capacities. A popular resource is the Sloan-C Quality Framework, which advances five "pillars of quality" for online teaching and learning: learning effectiveness, cost-effectiveness and institutional commitment, access, faculty satisfaction, and student satisfaction (Moore 2005). For each of the pillars, the framework provides concrete goals, practices, metrics, and progress indices. Kee Meng Yeo and Frank Mayadas (2010) advise academic IT workers to extend the scope of the pillars so that individual courses and programs can be "evaluated in the context of the organization as a whole" (46). Their holistic approach addresses a widespread coordinating problem for institutions—the left hand should know what the right hand is doing—and challenges academic IT workers to be cognizant of their surroundings and the ways "separate programs interact with one another" (46). Coordination of problems can be aided by professional development activities.

Academic IT workers also learn from their counterparts at peer institutions. Schools with conference or other types of affiliations collaborate on projects and share knowledge, experience, and assets. The CIOs of the CIC have ongoing strategic relationships: they leverage resources for both the greater good and individual institutional gain, building shared services, maximizing cost benefits and economies of scale, and cultivating leadership talent. Their relationships have resulted in federated management systems that enable people to access digital resources at other CIC schools and ultra-high-speed networks and data storage systems that support collaborative projects across the CIC. In addition, the CIOs have invested in initiatives that target leadership competencies, and they organize committee structures that encourage CIC schools to work together on common interests.

I attended a meeting of the CIC Learning Technologies Committee held at Penn State. At this meeting, representatives from CIC schools discussed academic IT priorities at their home institutions. These priorities were then organized into themes so that people could more easily see who was working on what. The University of Illinois, Indiana University, University of Michigan, Michigan State University, and Purdue University were all making major changes to their course-management systems; Penn State and the University of Iowa were investigating issues in learning analytics; and Ohio State University and Indiana University were restructuring their organizational approaches to distance education. There was also a committee report on learning spaces, a discussion of digital badges, a tour of Penn State media production facilities, and breakout sessions on pressing topics. I attended a breakout session in which participants considered strategies for engaging faculty members. They shared experiences and brainstormed solutions to academic IT problems; those with established faculty engagement programs explained their working parameters. All in all, the meeting presented an array of opportunities for peer-to-peer learning in an extended professional community.

For academic IT workers in the TLT unit, the external professional development activities of professional associations and peer institutions are complemented by job-embedded activities, which include periodic and continuous programs. Although both types of programs address global and local issues, a value-added proposition for job-embedded professional development is that it can more thoroughly situate global issues in local terms and thus more thoroughly illuminate local contexts. Two periodic programs at Penn State are Learning Design Summer Camp and the Symposium for Teaching and Learning with Technology. Learning Design Summer Camp is an informal summer conference that invites campus learning designers to present their projects. The phrase "learning designer" is intentionally broad, encompassing workers who have some role in building, delivering, or supporting instructional experiences that involve educational technologies, including faculty and staff from academic departments and Penn State libraries and centers. In addition to project demonstrations, the conference includes hands-on workshops, panel discussions, small-group discussions, lightning rounds, networking opportunities, and social events. It leverages open-ended boundaries—college campuses are replete with various people who can reasonably claim to be learning designers of some stripe—in order to facilitate information sharing that transcends university silos. The Symposium for Teaching and Learning with Technology is an annual spring event that attracts over five hundred attendees, including people from across the Penn State system. It is more than three times the size of Learning Design Summer Camp and a bit more formal: recent symposia have had four time slots with seven to ten concurrent sessions and also two keynote speakers. Past keynote speakers include Jane McGonigal, Clay Shirky, Michael Wesch, Danah Boyd, Lawrence Lessig, and Henry Jenkins. Although the symposium covers broader ground than Learning Design Summer Camp, it serves a comparable function, providing opportunities for TLT workers to learn about activities in their institutional surroundings.

As with external professional development, it can become commonplace to think of job-embedded professional development as a special mode of action, for attending local conferences, renewing technical certifications, or enrolling in university courses are activities that are less than seamless with normal workflow procedures (TLT employees often enroll in Penn State courses, taking advantage of a popular tuition benefit). Professional development programs, however, are available to TLT workers on an everyday basis, and their continuous presence in local contexts can routinize professional development and aid short-term problem solving.

A good example is on-demand training. Penn State owns a site license for Lynda.com, which provides thousands of video-based courses on many relevant subjects—among them website development, programming, interaction design, graphic design, user experience, e-learning, and project management. TLT workers can design and share playlists of courses to help them manage learning goals; they can also earn completion certificates. The courses themselves range widely in length and scope: a course on learning to build websites is six hours, while a course on creating online surveys is fifty-five minutes. The courses also vary in their level of ambition, sometimes discussing underlying concepts, sometimes not. In all the courses, users can bookmark their places and return to them at a later time, making it easier for users to learn at their own pace and access information for problem-solving purposes. On-demand training is often framed as a cost-savings approach, but its embeddedness in local settings can blur the lines between professional development and work activities, emphasizing the daily dividends of lifelong learning.

Academic IT is a relatively new field, especially compared to traditional disciplines. Many applicable degree programs can support IT careers in universities, and the curricula for these programs are often less rigid than those for computer science or engineering. This emergent educational landscape opens up thinking in fruitful ways but can also produce fragmentation and promote a kind of intellectual separatism in job roles. Academic IT workers therefore use professional development activities to help create coherence in both global and local projects and shrink the gap between what they know and what they need to know about how institutions function. In these ways, educational contexts are constitutive of academic IT units.

Commercial Contexts

It is no news to report that commercial contexts are an influential force in universities and that boundaries between the commercial and the educational are permeable. Teachers of writing and communication have been vocal participants in discussions of schooling that interrogate the means and ends of education, thereby questioning the shaping power of commercial contexts on the directions of academic institutions (Giroux 2011; Ohmann 1985). These discussions oppose instrumental and critical approaches and contend that an essential project for literacy educators is to prepare students to be citizen-workers who can identify, analyze, and en-

professional cultures of teachers and academic IT specialists. The reasons are not really a function of commercial inclinations.

To further illustrate the relationship between commercial contexts and academic IT units, let me return to the example of Lynda.com. The Training Services group has the formidable responsibility of providing educational opportunities for students and teachers who want to learn about the software at Penn State. It is not unusual for Training Services to offer hundreds of training sessions to thousands of users; the total number of participant hours in a year can exceed twenty thousand. The different types of training sessions—workshops run by Penn State trainers, workshops run by commercial vendors, and tutorials in on-demand environments—address both in-house and third-party software. The financial puzzle for Training Services is to figure out how to pay for everything and still meet their objectives: teachers do not expect to be charged for training for their courses, especially for software encouraged by the institution. So where does the money come from? A good deal of it comes from student IT fees, which yield tens of millions of dollars per year. Training Services, however, is a partial cost recovery unit, meaning that it must recoup a portion of its expenses in order to help fund unit operations. This is where Lynda .com and its kind fit in. Training Services outsources a large quantity of on-demand training for third-party software to Lynda.com, Learning Tree International, Net Objectives, HDI, and a few other commercial vendors, allowing Training Services to focus on in-house software. Partnering with commercial vendors has saved Penn State millions of dollars, but these partnerships also generate internal revenue that subsidizes training sessions for students and teachers. For example, if multiple units at Penn State are interested in the same Oracle database training course from Learning Tree International, Training Services will negotiate a reduced price for volume purchasing but then add a charge for coordinating the training sessions. The overall expenses for individual units are still far lower than they could realize on their own, and the additional fees are used to help offset the cost of providing training sessions for students and teachers. This approach is the work not of a corporate university but of a pragmatic institution supporting its own initiatives.

The institutional, educational, and commercial contexts I discussed are more than just a backdrop against which the work of academic IT units plays out or unfolds. Instead, these contexts help constitute processes of institutionalization, bringing meaning and value to academic IT environments and organizing the perspectives and experiences of everyone involved. The challenge for teachers is to enter into processes of institutionalization in direct and meaningful ways and take an active role in consequential deliberations and decision-making.

A HEURISTIC FOR CONCEPTUALIZING ACADEMIC IT

I now turn from laying the groundwork for my arguments to introducing a heuristic for institutional action. In providing this heuristic, I recognize that there are different valid ways to operate academic IT units and that local circumstances will be a determining factor for institutions. I also recognize that any approach will evolve over time: establishing an effective model for operating academic IT units is not a one-time proposition but rather a continuous management function, an ongoing process tied to both the past and the future. Academic IT units are constantly renewing themselves.

In addition, I make certain assumptions about the nature of institutions, literacies, and technologies. I align myself with teachers who understand institutions as complex rhetorical systems capable of being changed from within. James Porter, Patricia Sullivan, Stuart Blythe, Jeffrey Grabill, and Libby Miles (2000) explain the perspective I have adopted: "Though institutions are certainly powerful, they are not monoliths; they are rhetorically constructed human designs (whose power is reinforced by buildings, laws, traditions, and knowledge-making practices) and so are changeable." "In other words," they continue, "we made 'em, we can fix 'em. Institutions R Us" (611). From this perspective, change is not easy or automatic but possible if people conceptualize institutions as rhetorical systems, pay attention to their contexts, and participate in knowledge-making activities. Importantly, conceptualizing institutions as rhetorical systems presupposes a view of causality in which no single factor determines the histories, developments, and practices of institutions (or literacies or technologies). Such a view shifts the focus away from oversimplified cause-effect relationships, often between just two variables, and toward systems-oriented conceptions in which causation is considered to be a mutual, multiple, and contingent phenomenon, one that can be difficult to pin down at any particular moment. Institutional change is a function of numerous interlocking determinants.

The rhetorical nature of institutions becomes especially visible in projects that involve new implementations. Tablet devices are a good case in point. When the iPad arrived in 2010, commentators engaged in a dualistic line of questioning that always seems to drive their thinking about the capabilities of new technologies: Will the iPad help or harm student learning? Will it increase or decrease academic achievement? Although teachers should pursue a positive agenda for change when investigating the promise of new technologies for writing and writing instruction, answers to such evaluative (and Manichaean) questions can never be generalized to all institutions or classrooms. Institutional practices are not universal but based in time and space, configuring and reconfiguring in concrete expressions that inhabit specific situations. To a significant extent, then, the effects of the iPad in any particular setting will be a function of the arrangements and intensities of the causal factors in that setting. For example, in my study with Michael Faris, we identified a complex array of causal factors that have a bearing on how the iPad gets treated in technical writing courses at Penn State (Faris and Selber 2013). These factors include file storage methods, default settings, literacy histories, writing processes, instructional approaches, curricular relationships, textbook designs and uses, workflow procedures, and app update protocols. Such factors, in particular (and contingent) combinations and configurations, construct my institution as a mutable rhetorical system that shapes academic IT and enables and constrains the possibilities for educational transformation. Other schools will exhibit their own variations on this theme.

My assumptions about literacies have to do with the meaning-making role of language in institutions. I understand institutional discourses to be epistemic, by which I mean that the literacy practices of academic IT specialists help construct the social knowledge and reality of both developers and users. Language is not some transparent window into an independent objective world but rather a mediating tool, a technology, that shapes understanding, action, and experience (Ong 1988). As Carolyn Miller (1979) argues, "Reality cannot be separated from our knowledge of it; knowledge cannot be separated from the knower; the knower cannot be separated from a community" (615). And of course, all of this cannot be separated from the means by which and through which people come to know things. Miller is responding to colleagues who hold a logical positivist view of technical and scientific practices, including communication about those practices; they understand the goal of functional writing in objectivist terms as "subduing language so that it most accurately and directly transmits reality" (610). Although Miller notes that such an arhetorical view is "no longer held by most philosophers of science or by most thoughtful scientists" (615), academic IT specialists are certainly capable of treating language as a neutral conduit for information exchange.

A persistent example can be found in attempts to create artificial intelligence software that can grade student essays. Attempts to produce a grading machine that can evaluate writing quality have been reenergized by concerns over efficiency: In MOOCs, how can teachers provide worthwhile feedback to thousands of students at a time? The answer offered by MOOC provider EdX is free essay-grading software, which trains itself by analyzing the practices of human graders: "This is machine learning and there is a long way to go," said the president of EdX, an electrical engineer, "but it's good enough and the upside is huge" (Agarwal, quoted in Markoff 2013). At issue for teachers are the perspectives on language underlying machine learning, which insist on formal rules and surface features rather than rhetorical considerations. Doug Hesse (2013) discusses the ill-defined problem of responding to student writing and elaborates on meaningful criteria for evaluation that compel graders to understand a rich panoply of contexts, including those associated with audiences, purposes, motivations, and argumentation strategies. He also stresses that grades are not really useful to students without explanations from a "trusted reader and coach" who understands "individual students, their interests, abilities, needs, and trajectories." Hesse is but one voice in a chorus of opposition that is attempting to educate people about the limitations of essay-grading software: the National Council of Teachers of English (NCTE; 2013) released a position statement on machine scoring that articulates the most intractable problems, and thousands of teachers have responded by signing an online petition (at http://humanreaders.org). The message to academic IT specialists is that computers are ill-equipped to assess the rhetorical dimensions of language use.

The meaning-making role of language use is addressed by innumerable perspectives in the field. I am drawn to ecological views because they treat institutions, literacies, and technologies in a dynamic and interwoven manner. Marilyn Cooper (1986) was among the first to discuss what ecological views of writing might entail; she was responding to cognitive models that equate writing with thinking and social perspectives that are limited to the relatively immediate contexts of writers. This early articulation and her updated approach (Cooper 2010) inform my assumptions about literacies in institutions. In "The Ecology of Writing," Cooper (1986) equates writing with action and argues that writing activities are "dependent on social structures and processes not only in their interpretive but also in their constructive phases" (366). She makes a distinction between perspectives that acknowledge social dimensions of writing and those that see writing as "an activity through which a person is continually engaged with a variety of socially constituted systems" (367). According to Cooper, "the ideal image the ecological model projects is of an infinitely extended group of people who interact through writing, who are connected by the various systems that constitute the activity of writing" (372). These systems, which are formed and transformed by writers on an ongoing basis, both suggest and structure openings for invention and engagement. For Cooper, writing is at once a process of making and being made by systems of culture. People participate in this process through discursive interactions with ecologies of ideas, purposes, individuals, institutions, norms, genres, and more, entering into concrete human experiences and negotiating the complex web of overlapping social structures that comprise human activities.

In her updated approach, Cooper (2010) shifts the argument from an epistemological to an ontological realm, refining her points about ecosystems and positing humans as "natural born cyborgs" for whom literacy practices are inseparable from being itself: "Neither language nor technology is foreign to our nature; tools and words are us, not things we create and use" (18). This view reenvisions writing as an open-ended process of responding to others, to texts, to contexts: a many-sided, conditional process that is a function not so much of intended plans or actions but of coordinating and mobilizing resources in settings of relevance to writers. The meanings and uses of literacy emerge from human interactions with social and physical environments and are part of the cognitive ecologies elaborated by humans in acts of discourse. As a result, people experience writing as part of their "bodies and brains" (19) continually participating in a "process of stimulus and response" organized and regulated by "dense interactions" (20) with the constellations of structures and activities that constitute (and are constituted by) their social worlds of work. These interactions draw on many different aspects of institutions, literacies, and technologies.

My assumptions about technologies foreground their constructedness and the arguments and values they encode and help naturalize. Although teachers have employed any number of metaphors to characterize academic IT environments, I find it profitable to think of them as "articulations" of sociotechnical forces that rationalize—however temporarily and for whatever reasons or ends—institutional structures and systems. The notion of technologies as articulations is a rejoinder to decontextualized approaches and to those that embrace contexts but are vague or nebulous about what they entail or how they work. This rejoinder is an application of articulation theory, which teachers have used to describe how technologies come to be imbued with meanings. As discussed by Jennifer Slack (1989), there are a few basic ideas behind articulation theory, which I will summarize at the risk of oversimplification: technologies in and of themselves do not have preset or absolute meanings; technologies come to be imbued with meanings and purposes through specific connections with other social and technical forces (in articulation theory, *forces* is a shorthand term for practices, systems, and ideologies both material and discursive); these connections, or articulations, create tentative unities that can appear to be monolithic, but there are no necessary associations among the forces that constitute articulations; the forces that constitute articulations exhibit varying strengths and intensities, producing asymmetrical influences within articulations; and articulations can be rearticulated, shifting the meanings and purposes of technologies and opening up other possibilities for understanding and action (330–31).

I use articulation theory as a platform for establishing certain predicating assumptions about technologies. First, although technologies can be physical and virtual artifacts, they can also be processes, procedures, systems, structures, or practices. Library databases are indeed technologies, but so too are the rules and procedures that impose a rationalizing order for cataloging texts. Second, the forces that constitute technologies can derive not only from technical contexts but also from social, political, and economic contexts. Consider the practice of website design in a writing program, which involves software programs, style guides, institutional policies, collaborative methods, budgets, and more. Such forces coalesce in particular ways from project to project, exhibiting varying degrees of intensity across time and space: budgets matter more to some projects than others, for example, and can become more or less important at different moments across projects. Third, technologies embody and reflect human values. Designers of technologies instantiate their perspectives, which are themselves articulations of professional, institutional, and other forces, in concrete features that provide shape to writing environments. Users, in turn, employ these environments in specific situations, accepting or rejecting the features or hacking them to fit their own needs. This open-ended negotiation is really about values: technological designs speak to users when the matches in values outweigh the mismatches, when the perspectives of designers and users tend to align, or can be made to align, in the context of meaningful activities. Technologies are therefore social all the way down to a fundamental level. Acknowledging that technologies embody and reflect human values does not have to be viewed as critical in a negative sense, however: design biases are inevitable, even necessary, and an element of articulations that should be explored and leveraged.

TABLE 1.1 Heuristic for framing academic IT

Heuristic dimensions	Dimension elements
Histories	Standards
	Legacies
	Conventions
	Rituals
Spaces	Hierarchies
	Processes
	Methods
	Bodies
Texts	Metaphors
	Subjectivities
	Genres
	Stories

As might be apparent, my assumptions about institutions, literacies, and technologies derive from frameworks with overlapping interests. In one way of thinking, rhetorical systems, ecologies, and articulations simply provide different slants on the same task: contextualizing the processes and products of culture. But these approaches involve assumptions that can function together as a coherent set of propositions. The propositions are increasingly social and spatial, situating institutions as rhetorical systems, tying rhetorical systems together into larger functioning ecologies, and describing how those ecologies come to articulate meanings. None of the approaches alone is adequate enough to establish a full range of assumptions for academic IT.

This all leads me to my heuristic, which provides a framework teachers of writing and communication can use in their own institutions. Employing the heuristic, teachers will be able to order their thinking about what academic IT units do, how they are arranged, how they accomplish work, what drives and shapes them, and where interventions might be made to improve things. Teachers will then be able to formulate plans and actions that can contribute to campus IT directions in professionally useful ways. As table 1.1 shows, the heuristic includes three dimensions: histories, spaces, and texts. These dimensions function as prisms for rhetorical analysis, and their elements ground the heuristic for practice. In addition, the dimensions function both independently and collectively, enabling teachers to oscillate between the prism views themselves and a more holistic perspective in which the dimensions are seen in the totality of their relationships. Heuristics, by definition, have blind spots and are selective in their explanatory scope. My framework is meant to be suggestive rather than definitive and illustrative rather than comprehensive. It is, above all else, an apparatus for invention.

More specifically, the heuristic reflects the reality that academic IT units are complex, multilayered units with historical, spatial, and textual dimensions. The historical dimension, which I discuss in chapter 2, addresses the role of histories in the formations, decisions, and dynamics of academic IT units. Although their work can appear to be ahistorical and blind to matters of the past—nothing is more future-facing than technological enterprises—standards, legacies, conventions, and rituals all play a major part in shaping academic IT initiatives. The spatial dimension, which I discuss in chapter 3, addresses the role of spatial structures, material and conceptual, in arranging, regulating, and implementing academic IT environments. This dimension focuses on relationships and how academic IT units navigate institutions by appropriating and managing a variety of spatial structures. I am referring to the hierarchies that organize institutions, the processes that guide work, the methods that produce knowledge, and the embodied spatial practices that constitute human-machine interactions. Considering these elements provides different spatial vantage points from which to view happenings on the ground. The textual dimension, which I discuss in chapter 4, addresses the role of texts and textual practices in representing and shaping academic IT units. Academic IT units generate an enormous number of texts. These texts document activities and inform audiences, but they also aid invention, persuade audiences, regulate activities, and promote values. I consider how metaphors, subjectivities, genres, and stories contribute to culture formation and to stasis and change in institutions. The final chapter provides an integrated discussion of the dimensions of the heuristic and focuses on implementation, applying the heuristic in pedagogical and programmatic contexts that involve a university makerspace and portfolio of online courses.

The historical, spatial, and textual dimensions of academic IT units do not exist in an intellectual vacuum, of course, nor are they particular to my own setting. The heuristic is widely applicable precisely because the dimensions reflect both conventional perspectives in academic IT units and enduring questions in the field. The body chapters first explain how academic IT units tend to imagine and approach histories, spaces, and texts. I then provide a critique of how conventional perspectives shape

TABLE 1.2 Enduring field questions about academic IT

Enduring historical questions	Enduring spatial questions	Enduring textual questions
What are the sociocultural roots of information technologies?	What is spatial about using information technologies for writing and communication processes?	How are information technologies like texts?
How do rhetorical theories and practices illuminate or fail to illuminate the design and use of information technologies as writing and communication environments?	What are the implications of information technologies for the "where" of writing and communication?	What are the assumptions in textual depictions of information technologies?
What is the role of technological experiences in learning to write and communicate?	How should instruction about information technologies be organized for students who are learning to write and communicate?	What are the textual practices involved in developing information technologies?
How and when do information technologies become obsolete?	How is power exercised in the spatial contexts for information technologies?	How should information technologies be documented for users?

institutional landscapes. (Because I apply the analyses from these opening sections in my final chapter, the conclusions for body chapters are more synthetic than analytical.) The enduring field questions serve as disciplinary commonplaces for invention, investigation, and discovery. Table 1.2 lists the enduring questions I address. For example, in terms of histories, what are the sociocultural roots of information technologies? How do rhetorical theories and practices illuminate or fail to illuminate the design and use of information technologies as writing and communication environments? In terms of spaces, what is spatial about using information technologies for writing and communication processes? What are the implications of information technologies for the "where" of writing and communication? In terms of texts, what are the assumptions in textual depictions of information technologies? How should information technologies be documented for users? These and other enduring questions unite the concerns of writing and communication teachers and academic IT specialists. The heuristic addresses shared institutional territory with high-stakes consequences for everyone involved.

Using this shared territory as a starting place and a resource, I encourage teachers to develop institutional counterparts to the faculty engagement programs that already exist in academic IT units. Academic IT units have a rich history of offering formalized programs that support teaching and learning with technologies. It is time for teachers to work from the opposite direction, to develop academic IT engagement programs that enable them to meet academic IT specialists in a robust middle space where issues of institutions, literacies, and technologies can be treated as one and the same. Such programs are essential to a future in which information technologies will become ever more a part of the lives of students and teachers.

2

HISTORICIZING ACADEMIC IT

We look at the present through a rear-view mirror. We march backwards into the future. MARSHALL MCLUHAN AND QUENTIN FIORE (1967)

In "Researching Your Institution's Computer Past," Russell McMahon (2007) discusses his recovery project of writing an institutional history of academic IT at the University of Cincinnati (UC). The project began in an undergraduate course in the history of computing: McMahon asked students to interview people in computing fields about the nature of their work. As an assignment for documenting professional activities, the project brought computing history to life for students who had been raised on the internet. History writing, however, can serve multiple purposes and ends. The project took on additional meaning and symbolism when university administrators encouraged McMahon to develop the project as an institutional resource.

The findings revealed several interesting moments in the history of academic IT at UC. For example, in 1964, UC created the first program that trained students with disabilities to become computer programmers. According to a university press release, "Eleven visually impaired students from across the nation enrolled in that groundbreaking program in its first year" (University of Cincinnati 2008). In addition, the project traced the careers of UC graduates and discovered a number of notable accomplishments: 1942 graduate Viola Woodward, a female pioneer in information technologies, programmed code for the first all-electronic computer, the Electronic Numerical Integrator and Computer, or ENIAC; 1949 graduate Arnold Spielberg, the father of filmmaker Steven Spielberg, created the first point-of-sale computer system and patented the first electronic library system; and 1977 graduate Vinod Dham, often referred to as the father of the Intel Pentium chip, played a major role in the development of microprocessors that improved the speed and efficiency of computers.

McMahon also recounts the circumstances around which UC secured its internet domain name (www.uc.edu): "We were lucky to grab our URL before the universities of Colorado, Connecticut, or any of the California schools did" (University of Cincinnati 2006). The luck McMahon is referring to can be made by early adopters who are willing to explore technological possibilities without making firm institutional commitments. Although the benefits of URLs' navigational and semantic qualities have become increasingly clear over the years, in the 1980s, academic IT specialists were just beginning to consider the emergent technical standards for the internet. As Joe Landwehr, a onetime director of telecommunications at UC, explained, "We had a Bitnet connection, a daisy-chain connection to Ohio State which, in turn, had a connection to the next institution. It was good enough for sending e-mails, but that was about it" (University of Cincinnati 2006). Predicting the future of academic IT remains an uncertain business but can never be independent of interinstitutional relationships.

McMahon dedicates a portion of his article to research methods, for he wants to encourage people to write computing histories of their own institutions. He discusses how to use search engines, university archives, and cameras and voice recorders and shares his approach to conducting interviews with professors and administrators. The article also includes URLs for computing histories that have been initiated or written at Carnegie Mellon University, Stanford University, Michigan State University, and many other places. These histories document the development of computer science or engineering as a discipline on campus or the development of campus computing systems. The tenor of these histories is epideictic in nature, commemorating individual achievements and institutional milestones. In fact, McMahon is primarily interested in history writing as a mode of epideictic rhetoric for institutional positioning and identification. Although McMahon notes that other types of value can be extracted from histories, he emphasizes the contributions a history can make to marketing and community building: "It can be a way to connect present day students with their institution's own achievements and it can be a mechanism for recruiting young people into your institution" (University of Cincinnati 2006, 191). The benefits of making accomplishments visible are obvious and significant enough to warrant institutional investments in history writing.

In addition to epideictic rhetorics, I am also interested in deliberative aspects of histories that have a bearing on the plans and actions of institutions. McMahon moves in this direction at two different points. He concludes his article by stating that "recognizing the importance of an institution's computing past can help lead to its computing future" (University of Cincinnati 2006, 194). And in the section on rationale, he notes that "there is value in knowing 'useless' knowledge because it allows for an understanding of where we came from, how we got to where we are today and it can help in the decision making process for the future" (191). These statements acknowledge ahistorical attitudes while also exhibiting useful perspectives. The ahistorical attitudes about "useless knowledge" are often implicit in application: academic IT specialists are preoccupied with future-facing agendas and constantly searching for new solutions to teaching and learning problems. On the other hand, McMahon recognizes that histories can and do matter to decision-making. Although he expresses an overly rational perspective, he nonetheless admits histories into academic IT settings and understands historical elements to be consequential to future actions. This sort of recognition opens the door to crucial conversations about the influence of institutional conditions from past times.

In this chapter, I contend that considering histories is essential to understanding how academic IT units function as institutional formations. I begin with a discussion of how academic IT units tend to think about and treat histories. I then offer my own view of how histories ought to be imagined in institutional contexts for teaching and learning with information technologies. Next, I explore a series of enduring historical questions that make my heuristic applicable across a range of institutions. These questions address the sociocultural roots of information technologies, the rhetorical theories and practices of teachers, the technological experiences of students, and institutional notions of obsolescence. The final section explicates the historical elements of my heuristic: standards, legacies, conventions, and rituals. I define these elements and provide examples that address the ongoing concerns of writing and communication teachers.

HISTORICAL PERSPECTIVES ON ACADEMIC IT

I have a colleague in academic IT who is fond of saying that "time only moves in one direction." There are at least three contexts for this popular axiom. One is the overlapping areas of resource and project management. Ash Maurya (2012) depicts time as a priceless asset for IT organizations: "Of all resources, there is no resource more valuable than time. Time is more valuable than money. While money can fluctuate up or down, time only moves in one direction" (176). He argues that wasted and misspent time are leading causes of failure in IT organizations and that these problems, which are rooted in the experiences of yesterday, break innovation efforts. The solution to leveraging the stream of time, says Maurya, is using applied techniques to continuously evolve action plans before resources, including time, run out. This iterative process hinges on a willingness to revisit assumptions about audiences, work processes, and other institutional elements that teachers of writing and communication would consider to be rhetorical in nature.

A second context for the axiom is change management. John Mansfield (2010) notes that one function of time, as a historical concept, is to illuminate moments of cultural change: "We exist in four dimensions: the three dimensions of space and the dimension of time. Time only moves in one direction—forward—and it is because of time that we are aware of change" (3). Mansfield addresses situations in which people misconstrue the nature of change in sociotechnical systems, mistaking correlations for cause-effect relationships and overlooking the fact that a change in one part of a system can affect all the other parts. For Mansfield, change is a mirror of human and nonhuman activity: to talk of sociotechnical systems is to imply movement and interaction, which take place in time and space. A first principle in change management, then, is that change is a constant process that creates both solutions and problems. This dynamic is familiar to academic IT users.

A third context for the axiom is institutional management, particularly the management of public institutions in democratic societies. Journalist Sasiwimon Boonruang (2013) worries about reactions of the Thai government to activists' uses of social media: "Time only moves in one direction: forwards. Information and communications technology has evolved at a rapid pace, from analogue to digital, from PCs to tablets, from feature phones to smartphones. Users have adapted well to these advances, but our government still seeks to wield its power as if television were still the most sophisticated medium available to the general public." At issue here is government interference with YouTube and Facebook, which citizens use to express discontent and organize themselves for political purposes. Boonruang paints a picture of an institution that is out of step with the realities of contemporary life: attempts by the Thai government to control social media have only backfired, further fueling oppositional movements. Institutional practices conditioned by technological antecedents are not always relevant or effective.

These contexts—resource and project management, change management, and institutional management—all reveal something instructive about how histories tend to be treated in academic IT units. From the perspective of resource and project management, histories are deprioritized as actionable elements in work situations. If time is a priceless asset for IT organizations, histories hold little immediate value for managers who are charged with delivering projects on time and within budget: people in the throes of resource and project management are most interested in things that appear to be controllable and unfolding. From the perspective of change management, change is the only constant feature in an ever-changing world in which time is forever turning the present into the past and the immediate future into the present. What is important here is the perceived rate of change in sociotechnical systems. All too often in academia, institutional change is considered to be imminent at nearly every twist and turn: my discussion of the hysteria surrounding the rollout of MOOCs is an obvious case in point. Although the Gartner hype cycle provides a longitudinal method for representing the life cycles of technologies (Fenn and Raskino 2008), in daily experience there is often a mismatch between the forecasts for change from academic IT specialists and the dynamics of change in universities. In part, this mismatch is born of an inclination to underestimate the abilities of histories to appropriate and domesticate innovations. And from the perspective of institutional management, histories can mire institutions in old-fashioned ways of doing business, segmenting technological developments into discrete phases and creating the illusion of hard breaks between the boundaries of the phases: according to Boonruang, the television age holds little relevance to the world of today. Many of the university computing histories cataloged by McMahon reflect this mode of thinking, organizing institutional time lines as a progression of increasingly sophisticated technical achievements.

In academic IT units, the desire to deprioritize, underestimate, and atomize histories is an understandable impulse: academic IT projects are constituted by numerous moving parts, and people are always trying to get a handle on where things are heading and why. Moreover, academic IT projects are pressured by deadlines, budgets, and other time-oriented constraints that emphasize future plans and actions. This impulse, however, is not a totalizing one. Histories are accounted for in attempts to learn from past experiences, to avoid going mindlessly into the future. These attempts are formalized in workflows as reflection and assessment activities.

Reflection is a standard component of academic IT work. Its definition varies from one location to another, but the objective is to encourage higher-order thinking about the practices of histories. Such reflection-on-action (versus reflection-in-action), as Donald Schon (1990) would put it, is summative in nature, occurring toward the end of workflow phases or projects. An unmistakable moment for reflection is the annual performance review: workers assess themselves, and are assessed by others, using institutional criteria for evaluation. Reflective moments are also initiated by conference trip reports, progress reports, and project debriefings. In addition, development activities include routine occasions in which people actively reflect on the work they are doing. Agile approaches to project management, for example, dedicate weekly time to the task of retrospection. As Chris Sims and Hillary Johnson (2011) explain, "The retrospective allows learning and insights to be captured while experiences are fresh, and before negative patterns have a chance to harden in place. The goal is simple: to identify one or maybe two specific things to improve, and to create an action plan to implement those changes" (91). Advancement over past time periods, or continuous improvement, is an institutional ideal that drives reflection as a built-in process.

Reflective activities in academic IT settings are shaped by the immediate contexts of the work at hand in relatively contracted intellectual spaces. Joelle Jay and Kerri Johnson (2002) construct a typology that is useful in helping explain this phenomenon. Their typology involves three dimensions of reflection: descriptive, comparative, and critical. Descriptive reflection bounds and characterizes the domain, enabling reflective activities to be focused and structured. Programmers use functional specifications as descriptive tools for reflecting on software development projects, checking projects against specifications and specifications against projects in order to gauge progress. What is happening? Is this working? How do I know? What am I pleased about? What do I not understand? Such fundamental questions (from Jay and Johnson 2002, 77) are the basis for descriptive reflection, which elicits system-centric dialogues about the relationship between the present and the past: in my example, the target of descriptive reflection is the execution of implementation plans (at any phase) for academic IT systems.

If descriptive reflection is system-centric, comparative reflection is human-centric, widening the frame for reflective activities by encouraging people to relook at problems from divergent perspectives. According to Jay and Johnson (2002), "Comparative reflection involves seeking to understand others' points of views, which may be incongruent with one's own" (78). An example of comparative reflection occurs in pair programming, where two people sit together at a computer. One person works to implement the code while the other reflects on the code in light of alternatives and implications. What is more, the roles and pairs are not fixed: programmers move back and forth between the two roles and also pair up with other programmers. The grist for comparative reflection includes not only alternative individual viewpoints but also the published perspectives of other academic IT units.

The third dimension of reflection is context-centric in scope. Critical reflection considers the broader "historical, socio-political, and moral" issues associated with academic IT (Jay and Johnson 2002, 79). Some of the more talked-about issues include accessibility, intellectual property, workforce diversity, and the cost of higher education. Although all three dimensions of reflection are discernible in academic IT settings, the descriptive and comparative dimensions monopolize the everyday routines of workers, overshadowing critical approaches. In the realm of reflective activities, histories are largely mined as aids to functional task performance.

Conducting assessment activities is a second way academic IT units recognize a generative role for histories. Assessment activities are research efforts that evaluate the outcomes, costs, and benefits of IT initiatives. Although academic IT units are typically categorized as service units, they must nevertheless conduct research that attempts to make some sense of teaching and learning with technologies. These efforts are formal and informal and employ surveys, questionnaires, interviews, use cases, usability tests, learning analytics, and more. They can also be collaborative, involving partners from the disciplines and from other centralized units, such as libraries and learning centers.

In part, the decision to engage in formal research is influenced by the level of institutional investment. Systems that represent a considerable investment are likely to be assessed in a formal fashion, but nearly every endeavor incorporates at least an informal assessment practice to address the demand for accountability. Also motivating formal assessments are re-accreditation procedures and initiatives to survey the national landscape. My school is accredited by the Middle States Commission on Higher Education (MSCHE). In numerous areas of the self-study for reaccreditation, Penn State cannot avoid discussing the role of technologies in teaching and learning, for academic IT systems have become synonymous with student and teacher support services, which are major points of emphasis for the MSCHE. In fact, one of our recent self-studies mentions technologies no fewer than fifty times in 165 pages. The national initiatives for data collection are organized by professional associations. A popular initiative is the EDUCAUSE Center for Analysis and Research Study of Undergraduate

Students and Information Technology. This annual report includes data from tens of thousands of students from more than 150 universities. The data provide insights into how technologies are used on campuses nationwide, informing shared agendas in higher education.

Assessment activities—especially those that are sensitive to the full range of contexts within which technologies are developed, used, and supported—can yield meaningful snapshots of past experiences, capturing insights and assembling arguments that have driven the directions of academic IT units. Assessments that triangulate methods or emphasize multiple perspectives often produce robust institutional accounts of what has been done with technologies and to what effect. More often than not, however, assessment activities are weakly positioned as guides to past experiences and thereby fail to give sufficient attention to contexts that lend meaning and significance to technologies. Brian Hawkins and Carole Barone (2003) explain that three of the more prevalent assessment approaches—satisfaction surveys, input measures, and self-assessments—actually tell institutions very little about the issues that matter the most to them, such as "how technology is enabling new and better research, whether or how technology is enhancing teaching and learning, or whether administrative functions are easier to access or less expensive to operate" (133). Their diagnosis suggests a structural problem bearing on assessment: rather than situating technologies as an enabling function, it is not unusual for institutions to classify academic IT units as cost centers whose returns on investment are measured in operational terms, such as the number of accounts on software platforms or the number of hits on a website. Although universities align academic IT operations with broader purposes, many assessment approaches decontextualize technologies by eliding the richness and complexity of classrooms. This situation inhibits institutions from learning from histories.

For teachers of writing and communication, foregrounding historical forces in academic IT units is imperative to understanding their aims and projects and making interventions that build bridges across university silos. The perspective that I am advocating can be thought of as a mode of seeing the institutional situatedness of technologies. It is composed of a series of arguments about histories and technologies that emphasize certain dynamics in higher education. The first argument is that the continuity of technological histories is both perpetuated and disrupted by institutional practices. One can find numerous instances of continuity in academic IT settings, but these instances do not emerge or exist in a linear fashion. Instead, they are associated through recursive linkages that point both backward and forward in time. Michael Mahoney (1996) explains why continuity itself is such a discernible phenomenon in academic IT projects: "Nothing is entirely new, especially in matters of scientific technology. Innovation is incremental, and what already exists determines to a large extent what can be created" (773). Although innovations are typically presented as wholly new or different techniques or products, their realizations are the result of gradual developments shaped by past circumstances. In other words, the road to innovation is path dependent, involving cumulative and noncumulative trajectories. In fact, many innovations in academic IT combine existing knowledge structures in novel ways, using very little or perhaps no new knowledge. The relative stability of institutional contexts is best suited to adapt to incremental changes or modifications of existing systems.

My second argument is that the weight of institutional histories is on the side of technological conservatism. I have already alluded to the tensions between stasis and change in university settings, which are never made but always in the making, always partial and incomplete, and thus open to transformation. Although academic IT has become increasingly central to the never-ending process of institutional formation, institutions themselves can become agents of the status quo, using histories, unwittingly or not, as a basis for technological conservatism. A central tension in the performance of (re)making institutions is between the mentalities of start-up enterprises and the responsibilities of universities. Academic IT units are assuredly not start-up enterprises, being situated squarely within the contexts of larger institutional structures. But their imaginations can be animated by a high-tech ethos that values experimentation, risk taking, disruption, and even failure. These values, however, can be at odds with institutional or regulatory expectations that tend to eclipse everything else. For example, thousands of people at Penn State use Piazza.com as an alternative to the communication features in our course-management system. But because Piazza is unwilling to assume liability for security breaches that could threaten the confidentiality of student information and thus threaten a violation of the Family Educational Rights and Privacy Act (FERPA), Penn State is unwilling to support it despite the groundswell of use across a wide range of courses. Universities are conditioned by historically established laws, policies, assets, and routines, and such conserving elements can be impossible to ignore, oftentimes for good reasons. To claim, then, that the weight of institutional histories is on the side of technological conservatism is not to make an absolute value judgment about stasis or change: neither is inherently better or worse without reference to particular situations.

My third argument is that comparative historical analyses can be informative, but technologies must always be considered on their own terms. In attempting to explain the affordances of technologies, there is an understandable tendency to want to compare the systems of today with those of yesterday: reasoning by analogy is a useful method for organizing arguments about developing components of the world (Hofstadter and Sander 2013). Comparative historical analyses of technologies that rely on analogical thinking are prevalent and not confined to academic IT specialists. For example, James Kalmbach (1996) advises writing teachers to "stay in touch with history" and submits that "one of the best ways that teachers can cope with new technology is by relating innovative uses of technology to old uses of technology" (57). Comparative historical analyses can serve as coping mechanisms for change if they illuminate familiar underlying issues that transcend the scope of time.

Kalmbach employs comparative historical analyses as invention frameworks for relating old and new contexts, drawing analogies, and making suggestions for thinking about the nature of change in computer classrooms. His methods are informative precisely because he avoids the trap of making claims that are too sweeping or overdrawn to be sensitive to the specificities of production and reception activities. This common trap is addressed by Christina Haas (1996), who admonishes teachers to be wary of overrelying on historical analogies for insights into current phenomena. In evaluating ongoing comparisons between the so-called print and computer revolutions, Hass argues that "historical analogies are seldom accurate and usually obscure as much as they clarify; that is, analogous qualities of situations are highlighted while differences are ignored" (207). To make her case, Haas points out problems with comparing the development of print and digital literacies, particularly in work that fails to account for the material aspects of technologies. For instance, while acknowledging Elizabeth Eisenstein's important contributions on the implications of the printing press, Haas notes that "the problem with invocations of Eisenstein's work in arguments about computer technology is that she is an historian, not a technologist. Consequently, she does not treat the technology of the printing press itself in any detailed way" (210). In academic IT units, the inverse of this problem tends to be the case, with people focusing primarily on feature details and technical interdependencies. Although Kalmbach demonstrates how comparative historical analyses can be informative as invention frameworks for teaching and learning, the contexts for technologies involve the interests of both technologists and historians, necessitating a reevaluation of one-dimensional methods. Haas emphasizes methods other than those that view situations as part of either a repeating cycle of history or a series of historical advances. In such approaches, histories provide interpretations of past experiences, but applications and settings of use are instrumental to their relevance and meaning.

Academic IT specialists can be mindful of the constitutive roles of histories: reflection and assessment are vital activities in many projects. But beyond these areas, histories are often deprioritized, underestimated, and atomized regularly in large part because people are focused on future-facing agendas. Academic IT specialists, however, do not operate in a temporal vacuum, and in any case, institutional learning tools are inseparable from institutional histories themselves. As Michael Mahoney (1996) explains, "It is not a matter of learning the 'lessons of history' or exploring 'what history can teach us,' as if these were alternatives or complements to practice. We are products of our history or, rather, our histories; we do what we do for historical reasons" (778). In academic IT units, these reasons are shaped by institutional forces that perpetuate and disrupt the continuities of histories, encourage conservatism, and imbue histories with significance and a sense of pertinence (or not). The effects of institutions on histories are carried out daily and as a matter of course in academic IT projects.

ENDURING HISTORICAL QUESTIONS

Teachers of writing and communication work at every type of institution in higher education, and universities necessarily differ in their approaches to academic IT. In this diverse landscape, one of the common threads that binds teachers together is a set of enduring historical questions that involves the entanglements of institutions, literacies, and technologies. These questions are significant for their answers but also for what they suggest about priorities and practices, institutional and pedagogical. What are the sociocultural roots of information technologies? How do rhetorical theories and practices illuminate or fail to illuminate the design and use of information technologies as writing and communication environments? What is the role of technological experiences in learning to write and communicate? And how and when do information technologies become obsolete? Although these historical questions are not the only ones that have been raised by the field, they address critical areas that unite the concerns of all teachers.

What Are the Sociocultural Roots of Information Technologies?

Teachers have expressed an abiding interest in the sociocultural roots of information technologies because they help set terms of engagement. By sociocultural roots, I mean social and cultural drivers (not determiners) that influence how people understand and construct their experiences as students and teachers. These roots are not causal structures or origin points for histories but sociocultural elements that have a bearing on how institutions treat academic IT. The sociocultural roots of information technologies are discernible in academic and industrial settings, and elements from both are relevant to students and teachers. Such elements, in fact, interpenetrate one another across the boundaries of settings, forming something of an academic-industrial complex of sociocultural roots.

Histories of the internet, hypertext, and copyright law provide lucid examples of sociocultural roots that are consequential to students and teachers. Lester Faigley (1997) dedicates a considerable portion of his CCCC chair's address to the task of examining "how the Internet developed over several decades and what actually is new about its widespread use" (36). What is new—or rather, potentially new—are reconfigured lines of authority in the classroom, increased opportunities for civic participation, and additional forms of literacies. As Faigley cautions, however, positive educational outcomes are not guaranteed by historical trajectories that involve Cold War ideologies, differential patterns of access, and privatization measures. Likewise, in reviewing this same historical terrain, especially the sociocultural roots of ARPANET (the precursor to today's internet), Myra Moses and Steven Katz (2007) interrogate "the military genesis" (80) of email systems and their underlying values of "efficiency, speed, and productivity" (82). Moses and Katz illustrate how the early contexts for email continue to promote a technological mindset that treats asynchronous messaging practices as tools for advancing instrumental (versus educational) aims.

In terms of hypertext histories, Robert Johnson (1995) contends that hypertext "developed from an apractical romantic viewpoint that remains a very strong driving force" (11) in writing programs. This viewpoint was romantic in that it imagined a universal system that could interlink all the texts in the world, an ambitious project that promised to address a wide range of issues for researchers. The problem for Johnson is not the vision per se but that early work on hypertext failed to test its capabilities in actual situations of use, favoring instead theoretical accounts of liberatory changes predicated on the imaginative ideas of a few "great men" (19). Scott Lloyd Dewitt (1996) unpacks these romantic theoretical accounts and reviews their claims and evidence, concluding that "in an area that has grown at such a phenomenal pace, it is surprising that so little empirical research has been reported on the use of hypertext in the context of the writing classroom" (70). Aided by the sociocultural roots of histories, theory can override or eclipse practice (and vice versa), even in applied fields where the linkages between practice and theory are considered to be essential to students and teachers.

In terms of copyright histories, Andrea Lunsford and Susan West (1996) examine a complex knot of sociocultural roots that "honor creation as the inspired act and property of an autonomous genius" (389), disregarding the collective dimensions of language use deeply bound up with sense making in human endeavors. This traditional notion of authorship and ownership, which has been "perpetuated effectively by teachers of writing (and educational systems in general)" (387), is reinforced by copyright laws themselves, commercial interests, citation practices, publishing systems, and more. Arguments about the gravity of the issues are constant components in fieldwork on copyright histories, which ask principal questions about who owns what and why, who has access to what and why, and who benefits and why.

The previously mentioned work identifies field practices as part of the academic-industrial complex of sociocultural roots for information technologies, but none of it really considers the role of academic IT units despite the inherently collaborative nature of infrastructure development, use, and governance. Michael Roberts (2006) reminds people that "higher education in the United States played an important role in launching and expanding the Internet. Faculty teams did much of the original research; campus computing organizations prototyped early technology and later applied it in campuswide production networks" (22). Although the dynamic Roberts describes has not remained so linear or segmented, everyone is affected by the shaping forces of instrumental ideologies, public-private partnerships, privatization efforts, differential patterns of access, romantic visions, and legal notions of authorship. The effects of such elements (for better and worse) are not simply a thing of the past—sociocultural roots can be reexperienced and reconfigured anew in succeeding historical situations—but are alive and well in higher education, forging connections across institutional types and divides.

How Do Rhetorical Theories and Practices Illuminate or Fail
to Illuminate the Design and Use of Information Technologies
as Writing and Communication Environments?

An enduring historical project for teachers is establishing the relevance of rhetorical studies for contemporary students. As an umbrella term for the field, *rhetoric* is capacious and capable of accommodating innumerable perspectives and issues, encompassing aspects of persuasive communication that help construct the identities, belief systems, and knowledge-making practices of individuals and cultures. Like technologies themselves, rhetorical theories and practices are not static or unmoving. On the one hand, teachers are constantly interpreting and reinterpreting established approaches; on the other, teachers are constantly developing new approaches that attend to the dynamics of technologies and their contexts. Sharing a commitment to the investigation of writing and communication situations, these two directions are not mutually exclusive or even in conflict with each other.

A hallmark of initial forays into working with academic IT was the direct application of established rhetorical approaches to the design of software. Teachers used frameworks from Aristotle, Kenneth Burke, and others as software specifications in creating modules to aid prewriting and invention activities. Applying historically received conceptions of rhetoric to the uncertain world of academic IT provided a much-needed anchor for theories, practices, and studies, enabling teachers to proceed in a manner that was congruent with disciplinary norms. It also allowed teachers to imagine how academic programs might best incorporate technical concerns. There are still a variety of occasions in which applying historically received conceptions of rhetoric can be productive. For example, John Jasso (2013) draws on the language arts curriculum of classical schooling to develop a method for teaching the literacies of media convergence. Michelle Eble (2009) employs the rhetorical canons as a heuristic for designing course-management systems. And Craig Condella (2010) uses Aristotelian notions of friendship to interrogate the nature of social relationships on Facebook. It should not be difficult for teachers to imagine other applications for established rhetorics.

These forays were succeeded by a wave of thinking that wondered about the capacity of rhetorical traditions to illuminate the features and contexts of technologies. James Zappen (2005) surveys the nascent discourses of digital rhetoric, tracing discussions of tensions and contradictions in established conceptions of persuasion, identity, and community. From his analysis, Zappen determined that digital rhetoric is an "amalgam of more-or-less discrete components rather than a complete and integrated theory in its own right" (323)—that is, as opposed to applying Aristotle's topoi, Burke's pentad, or another settled scheme to academic IT environments, teachers began to remix existing rhetorical elements into new frameworks, initiating an amalgamation method that remains popular today. Joyce Locke Carter (2003), for example, invents a rhetoric of hypertext by bringing together and adapting informal logics, stasis theories, spatial metaphors, and reader-oriented strategies for structuring texts. The result is a rhetoric that attends to the features and possibilities of node-link relationships, which have become fundamental to internet-based writing and reading.

If one response to questions about the capacity of historically received rhetorics is to remix their elements into novel frameworks, another is to create new approaches that focus on the distinctive qualities of technologies. At the heart of this second direction is the realization that there are very real differences between print and digital texts. In her review of the disciplinary work on new approaches, Barbara Warnick (2005) asserts that many researchers have come to realize that "critical approaches based on theories of print-based criticism do not always apply well to new media because there are dimensions of hypertext, Web-based media, visual communication, interactive environments, and adventure games that print-based critical tools simply miss" (328). Researchers in this camp are not so much hostile to received rhetorics as unconvinced about their abilities to address a full spectrum of issues. For example, Johndan Johnson-Eilola (2010) develops an approach for thinking through the rhetorical issues that arise when texts become semiautonomous, networked objects capable of collecting and using the data produced by online readers. And James Brown (2012) develops an approach for thinking through the rhetorical issues that arise when speed becomes a manipulable aspect of composing and publishing processes. The complexities of these investigations are new and different and no small matter for teachers of writing and communication.

Teachers, then, are united by the project of applying, remixing, and inventing rhetorical theories and practices that illuminate the design and use of technologies as writing and communication environments. This project, however, will never be complete, entirely certain, or merely positive. Academic IT is a moving target, and so too are rhetorical theories and practices, institutional contexts, and other elements of writing and communication situations. I am not suggesting that teachers work in a rudderless world but that the efficacy and durability of rhetorical theories and practices must be routinely evaluated and defended. The outcome of this process will sometimes show that the past is indeed prologue. At other times, the past will exert a more subtle (albeit still important) influence on the future.

What Is the Role of Technological Experiences in Learning to Write and Communicate?

Theoretical turns in the 1980s opened the door to social perspectives on composing. Lester Faigley (1986) contrasts the commitments of three competing theories of process—expressive, cognitive, and social—and argues that the focal point of a social view "is not on how the social situation influences the individual, but on how the individual is a constituent of a culture" (535). Although the field has since complicated the theoretical lines reviewed by Faigley, it has also worked to enrich the concept of cultural constituency as an inescapable element of all social approaches. In attempting to understand what it means to write and communicate in cultural settings, including institutions, researchers have considered the ways cultures are defined and organized, how they operate and function, how they evolve and change, how they interact with one another, and the ways discourses structure and shape values, knowledge-making practices, and social interactions. A useful insight has been that writing is an accretive process that involves varied historical experiences from multiple cultures.

Deborah Brandt (1995) observes that everyday-life settings, such as schools, workplaces, and homes, are tangled together and "layered with discarded and emergent forms of literacy and their histories," which "give a complex flavor even to elementary acts of reading and writing today" (651). To learn more about the "accumulating" nature of literacies, Brandt conducted interviews with a stratified sample of the US population. Her goals were to elicit accounts of literacy development and understand the roles of institutions, technologies, and human agents in that process. Through these interviews, Brandt discovered that literacies accumulate in vertical and horizontal directions. Vertically, literacies accumulate or "pile up" as "materials and practices from earlier times often linger at the scenes of contemporary literacy learning" (652). For example, in my study of the Sony Reader with Michael Faris, several students attempted to re-create systems for writing and reading not included in first-generation e-book devices, thereby reverting to historically familiar routines of note taking and text marking for comprehension strategies (Faris and Selber 2011). Horizontally, literacies accumulate or "spread out" as the proliferation of technologies "affects the occasions and motivations for learning to read and write" (Brandt 1995, 653). Simply put by Brandt, the stakes for literacy have risen to a point where "the ability to earn a living has become increasingly bound up with the ability to read, document, and traffic in symbol systems generally" (652). As a result of this fact of postindustrial life, teachers are reconceptualizing writers as knowledge workers who extract value and meaning from the abundance of information now available in cultures (Johnson-Eilola 1996). Brandt discusses other ways literacies accumulate, but these examples situate technological experiences at the heart of learning to write.

Teachers have adopted literacy narratives to dissect the effects of technological experiences. Sally Chandler and John Scenters-Zapico (2012) discuss the overlapping purposes of this approach: instructing students, training teachers, collecting data on composing processes, analyzing cultural phenomena, and encouraging social change (185). Although literacy narratives serve multiple purposes, they are predicated on the assumption that people can "claim ownership of their experiences, making connections and coming to new understandings of their histories" (Kirtley 2012, 194). These new understandings are enlightening for individuals and institutions and reveal meaningful observations about process and setting: the gateways that introduce people to literacy practices are formative of their attitudes toward technologies (Ruecker 2012); technological experiences in schools often lack a sense of relevance, and (in contrast) motives for technological engagements are often social and experimental (Ching and Ching 2012); technological experiences can be used to mediate the theory-practice split that exists between high school and college writing instruction (Bradbury 2014); and cultural assumptions about technologies can have a negative bearing on the development of critical literacies (Duffelmeyer 2000). James Porter (2003) encapsulates the broad findings of such studies: "The technological past matters. It shapes the writer and writes the body in significant ways—etching itself on the writer's consciousness and body, influencing how the writer learns to compose and how the writer communicates in a social milieu" (389). In addition, Porter continues, "our ideologies about writing, about composing, about rhetorical situation are formed in these various technological pasts, etched by various technologies" (389).

In teaching and learning contexts, technological pasts are not add-on or parallel experiences living alongside literacy experiences but part and parcel of the history and ongoing development of literacy itself.

In another prominent site for considering the role of technological experiences, researchers have drawn analogies between the worlds of writing and computer gaming. A first connection is that playing computer games often involves a fair amount of writing and that this type of writing is central to the prospects for agency and change in virtual environments (M. Johnson 2008). Another connection is that there is a close and natural alignment between the activities of learning to play computer games and those of learning to write: computer games can obligate users to analyze audiences, solve problems, and collaborate (Sabatino 2014); contend with issues of authority and visuality (Alberti 2008); and ask and answer questions about identity and subject formation (deWinter and Vie 2008). A third connection is that computer gaming can help the field imagine the future shape of writing instruction, which is being pressured from both the outside in and the inside out. According to "Teens, Video Games, and Civics," a report from the Pew Internet and American Life Project (2008), "Video gaming is pervasive in the lives of American teens—young teens and older teens, girls and boys, and teens from across the socioeconomic spectrum. Opportunities for gaming are everywhere, and teens are playing games frequently." In fact, as the study reports, 97 percent of teens ages twelve to seventeen play video games of one type or another, creating pressure from the outside in as students develop expectations from previous technological experiences for multimodal platforms and practices in schools. From the inside out, teachers are starting to take seriously the capacities involved in gaming practices, recognizing them as emergent forms of literate activity. As Jonathan Alexander (2009) argues, "Incorporating a strong consideration of gaming into composition courses may not only enliven writing instruction for many of our students, but also transform our approach to literacy" (37). As with texting and microblogging, computer gaming experiences are not erased by processes of institutionalization.

Previous technological experiences are forged in an assortment of everyday lifeworlds that are increasingly inseparable and interdependent. My examples spotlight the accretive nature of writing and communication as cultural routines that incorporate these experiences in fundamental ways. For teachers of writing and communication in any program, an enduring task is working to understand this ongoing process—a process that shapes the future of the past, the here and the now, as much as anything else in classrooms.

How and When Do Information Technologies Become Obsolete?

In teaching and learning with information technologies, a recurring challenge is transitioning from older systems to newer ones, from historically familiar features and habits to different ways of working. The rapid evolution and turnover of technologies, vendors, and approaches are no longer irregular or periodic occurrences but a constant reality in universities, requiring people to possess a certain degree of flexibility in the literate makeup and processes of their institutional lives. Transitions from one system to another also require an understanding of what is driving the change, for obsolescence can be as much a social construct as a technical or material one, conditioned by historical practices and facilitated, at least in part, by academic IT units. Giles Slade (2007) addresses the notion of planned obsolescence, a systematic and widespread business strategy in which products are manufactured to have an artificially short life span. In an example of the social construction of obsolescence, Slade considers cultural practices and value systems that enable this business strategy: "Deliberate obsolescence in all its forms—technological, psychological, or planned—is a uniquely American invention. Not only did we invent disposable products, ranging from diapers to cameras to contact lenses, but we invented the very concept of disposability itself, a necessary precursor to our rejection of tradition and our promotion of progress and change" (3–4). Value systems and cultural practices are intimately wrapped up with the question of how and when technologies become obsolete.

A principal area in which teachers have had to confront issues of obsolescence is computer classroom and lab administration. Anyone who is responsible for managing a computer classroom or lab must worry about the space becoming obsolete. As I noted in chapter 1, it is one thing to receive start-up resources to establish facilities to support digital pedagogies and quite another to garner long-term commitments that can secure future development. But what I want to note here is that answers to this enduring question almost always involve institutional dimensions that shape understandings of obsolescence. Although there are occasions in which newer technologies replace and outdate older ones or create compatibility problems, obsolescence as a state of hardware and software is often determined in relation to particular activities and contexts. Christina Haas (1999) substantiates this claim by showing how a simple system of printed files in a work culture accrued more power and importance than digital information technologies. For teachers, this situation is akin to attempting to keep up with industry expectations in technical writing, which involve specialized and costly software programs with a steep learning curve. As opposed to chasing industry expectations, a decision that initiates an ongoing cycle of technical obsolescence, teachers can design institutionally sustainable facilities that support rhetorical approaches, providing infrastructures for learning the conceptual fundamentals that underlie skilled abilities (cf. Purdy and DeVoss 2017). In pedagogical and institutional terms, the latest and greatest technologies are not always the necessary or even right choice for students and teachers.

A second area in which teachers have confronted issues of obsolescence is technological access. As Shannon Madden (2014) explains, "As a site for critical inquiry, obsolescence aligns with the field's attention to access issues and disparities of privilege surrounding literacy technologies, and extends the research on how socioeconomic contexts shape and limit opportunities for digital literacy" (31). More specifically, the field has acknowledged the fact that personal device ownership is correlated with income and that device ownership is a determining factor in developing and sustaining productive moments in which students can engage in the study and practice of writing and communication.

But the dynamics associated with personal device ownership are beginning to shift in ways that confound the usual role of academic institutions in matters of obsolescence. It used to be the case that high-tech companies focused their efforts on partnering relationships with academic institutions, outfitting campuses with the latest technologies and providing students and teachers with educational versions of software. Although partnerships remain important to both companies and schools, companies are now appealing directly to students and teachers as consumers in the marketplace, turning the tables on the usual procedures for specifying technologies for universities. As opposed to academic institutions defining the parameters for hardware and software that are compatible with campus systems, students and teachers are pressuring academic IT units to support a dizzying array of internet services and personal digital devices. Tracy Schroeder (2014) unpacks some of the reasons behind this mounting pressure: "Consumerization has brought to students and faculty the capability to connect, collaborate, and compute at a level of quality and intensity that has rendered some campus-based services obsolete and has often overwhelmed campus networks" (18). Although the consumerization movement has been empowering for users, enabling access to a wider and cheaper range of technologies, it is also helping usher in a transitional period in which academic IT units are rethinking their relationships with both university communities and vendors. This rethinking involves searching for solutions that offer students and teachers greater freedom to use popular consumer applications while giving institutions the control they need to support students and teachers, protect data and information, and realize institutional objectives. Of course, academic IT units cannot possibly admit each and every device and service from the high-tech marketplace, so institutions will need processes of exclusion for making judgments about what is in and what is out, about what is accessible and what is not, for writing and communication activities. Such processes will render many new technologies obsolete.

In an important sense, then, obsolescence is a relative phenomenon in institutions, taking on meaning and relevance within the context of specific situations. It is a cultural invention and social construct with material implications that persist over time. In the never-ending cycle of technological invention and consumption, newer technologies do not always drive out older ones, nor do they always integrate well into existing infrastructures and routines, especially those deeply tied to the histories of institutional actions. But the cycle creates endlessly shifting definitions for what institutions consider to be obsolete, for what counts as institutional obsolescence. These shifting definitions are always lingering in both the background and foreground of the relationship between literacies and technologies.

The enduring questions discussed in this section have significant historical dimensions that are consequential to teaching and learning. The sociocultural roots of information technologies, such as instrumental ideologies, privatization efforts, and legal notions of authorship, are manifestations of culture that continue to have an impact on how people think about education and promote learning. Rhetorical theories and practices, as they have been historically mapped out, both illuminate and fail to illuminate the design and use of information technologies as writing and communication environments, creating an imperative for ongoing investigations into the applicability of historical perspectives for theories and practices today. Technological experiences are also central to rhetorical theories and practices, for familiarity and previous exposure to technologies are significant aspects in the accretive process of literacy development. And notions of obsolescence bring meaning and relevance to the always transitional applications of information technologies, helping determine their institutional status and roles. These historical areas transcend individual institutions and reflect the collective interests of writing and communication teachers.

HISTORICAL ELEMENTS OF THE HEURISTIC

Let me now turn to my heuristic for academic IT (table 2.1). The historical elements I discuss—standards, legacies, conventions, and rituals—exert effects that are diachronic and developmental in nature, spanning the boundaries and time frames of individual initiatives. In my discussion, I concentrate on dynamics and issues that these historical elements engender and avoid making abstract judgments about their efficacy or value. Although the elements themselves transcend time and space, their meanings and implications shift and change along with changes in institutional circumstances.

Standards

Standards enable processes or systems—semiotic-discursive and physical-material—to be interconnected and shared within and across institutions. They accomplish their purposes by establishing specifications and procedures that serve as the basis for development activities in technical and

TABLE 2.1 Historical elements of the heuristic

Dimension elements	Historical elaborations
Standards	Academic IT units adopt open and closed standards to enable processes and systems to be interconnected and shared by users, both local and distributed. Standards choices become historical antecedents that shape future institutional developments in teaching and learning.
Legacies	Academic IT units contend with the fact that all information technologies will eventually become outdated legacies. Decisions to abandon, maintain, reengineer, or replace legacy systems and services are closely tied to ways of thinking and working that were established at earlier moments of institutional renewal and change.
Conventions	Academic IT units adopt conventions that both constitute and regulate rules and norms for coordinating work activities and developing systems and services. Conventions choices help to define and delimit what it means to do institutional work in the first place, what is possible for people to do and what they cannot do, and how the work will be evaluated.
Rituals	Academic IT units participate in institutional rituals that express values and interests, serve socializing functions, and embody knowledge practices. Rituals as historical elements impose order and continuity on teaching and learning and can help people manage the demands of sociotechnical change and professional development.

pedagogical areas. An obvious example of standards in academic settings is grading standards, which allow teachers to express expectations for student outcomes but first inform the design of learning objectives, assignments, and more. Another example is standards for e-books and instructional materials on the web, which determine accessibility and condition reading experiences.

Central organizing bodies are involved in the creation of national and international standards, including government agencies, membership organizations, and professional associations. The intentions of these groups are to formalize specifications and procedures that support their policies, enhance user experiences, enable systems to interoperate, and leverage economies of scale. The International Reading Association and the National Council of Teachers of English (2009) collaborated to produce national standards for the assessment of writing and reading that are consistent with their perspectives on how language and literacy ought to be taught in classrooms. The standards are meant to guide efforts to create locally meaningful assessment regimes that are defensible in larger terms: the standards themselves have been user-generated and crowdsourced, incorporating a wide range of research in the field. I use NCTE as an example to emphasize that standards have political dimensions, reflecting ideologies and shaping possibilities.

Although standards are prevalent in both technical and nontechnical domains, they are not without controversy or problems, especially when it comes to creation and implementation methods. The debates surrounding the Common Core standards, which establish unified national expectations in English and mathematics for K–12 students, illuminate issues that are germane to the institutional contexts for literacies and technologies. In a speech to the Modern Language Association about the Common Core standards, Diane Ravitch discusses why and how the standards were created, the commitments they represent, and the stakes for students and teachers (reprinted in Strauss 2014). In addition to pointing out problems with standardizing tests and paying for the initiative in an era of deep cuts to public education—according to a *Los Angeles Times* article mentioned by Ravitch, the city of Los Angeles committed to diverting a billion dollars from its facilities budget to purchase iPads for student testing—a major focus of the speech addresses process issues and how the standards are imagined and understood.

Ravitch points out that the team assembled to create the Common Core included very few educators, that the standards were never piloted or tested in schools, and that there are no mechanisms for providing feedback or revising the standards. The development process, in other words, was undemocratic, bureaucratic, and inadequate, favoring private over public interests—the big winners are educational technology companies and educational testing companies—and short-term expediencies over deliberative methods that involve iteration and collaboration. Ravitch also points out that the standards themselves are considered to be universal to all students and schools, regardless of setting and historical specificities, leaving teachers without the ability to make adjustments to suit their particular environments. As she argues, "It is good to have standards. I believe in standards, but they must not be rigid, inflexible, and prescriptive." Using language from software development, the distinction Ravitch is getting at is between closed and open standards.

Closed (or proprietary) standards are created by private companies with little to no outside input from users. They certainly have their advantages, but systems based on closed standards are not adaptable to contexts. For example, the underlying source code for Blackboard and Desire2Learn, two popular course-management systems, is not accessible to academic IT specialists or teachers, and licensing agreements can constrain how the systems are administered and used. In contrast, open standards are created by consortia of stakeholders who are interested in a public approach. Private companies do adopt open standards, which introduce their own challenges, but the idea is that open decision-making and sharing will result in more accessible, affordable, sustainable, and innovative initiatives. For example, over 250 academic institutions have adopted Sakai and its open standards for organizing course content and learning events (Dolphin 2014). In a voluntary and cooperative fashion, the academic IT units in these institutions function as a community of distributed developers who work together to enhance the capabilities of the platform and solve problems, all for the purpose of implementing Sakai in particular teaching and learning contexts. The contrast between open and closed standards requires institutions to grapple with the basic question of who has a say in how academic IT environments are designed and implemented.

The decision to adopt open or closed standards is not a one-time decision for all systems, and in fact academic institutions can adopt both types of standards at the same time, even within a single project. The important point is that standards choices always help set the stage for future activities and projects, which is to say that standards choices become historical antecedents that influence institutional actions. For example, a university that commits to complying with the standards for accessible design articulated in the Americans with Disabilities Act (ADA), a decision that should be made by all universities receiving federal funding, is committing to retaining technical specialists (or services) who can caption instructional videos. Likewise, a university that commits to aligning standards decisions for technologies with accreditation standards for academic programs is committing to allowing accreditation standards to drive the academic IT enterprise. Although technologies are essential to wide-scale assessment and reporting activities, the increasing interest in institutional analytics and assessment tools should not determine the selection of software for writing and communication.

All technologies involve standards of some stripe, and standards choices serve as predicates for institutional actions. Although standards are frequently revised and updated, they require ongoing commitments to their procedures and specifications. What is more, standards are mixed up with the enduring historical questions that unite all teachers: knowingly or not, previous technological experiences are built on encounters with standards choices, and standards choices help determine notions of institutional obsolescence (new technologies could be deemed obsolete if they do not work with existing standards). Standards are fundamental institutional components that must be accounted for in academic IT environments.

Legacies

Legacies are systems that have been outdated and surpassed by technical improvements but still serve to support institutional initiatives. Legacies are abundant and widespread in institutional contexts. The US government, for example, spends the majority of its IT budget on maintaining legacy systems, leaving just 30 percent for new systems development (Konkel 2012). Although comparable figures for higher education are difficult to pin down, legacies are prevalent in teaching and learning contexts.

Penn State recently replaced its student information system. This multiyear project, which was budgeted at sixty-five million dollars, replaced a legacy system that was over thirty years old. The project was overdue, but there are compelling reasons why legacies have staying power: they are reliable for the purposes for which they were instituted; they can be upgraded by academic IT units, extending capabilities and permitting the systems to function in current environments; and they have mature support structures for aiding users. Moreover, the upfront costs of developing new systems represent a sizable (if not prohibitive) outlay for many universities, and introducing new systems can create disruptions in institutional workflows, including those for teaching and learning. The histories of legacies provide arguments for siding with the status quo. It is important to note that legacies encompass more than just software and hardware systems. More accurately, they are articulations of sociotechnical forces that involve a wide range of institutional practices and structures. When it comes to student information systems, the nontechnical areas that receive the greatest amount of attention are related to business and administrative processes and regulatory compliance. Although these areas provide a framework on which student information systems are developed, they also exert considerable influence in teaching and learning applications by participating as elements in a crowded mix of sociotechnical forces.

In addition to replacing its student information system, Penn State also recently replaced a course-management system implemented in 2001. The requirements for the new system reflect an array of institutional and instructional concerns. For example, the system supports around-the-clock work from students anywhere in the world, complies with ADA standards, provides learning and administrative analytics, supports robust content authoring, and supports a mixture of pedagogical approaches for face-to-face, hybrid, and online courses. The suitability of the new system was assessed using technical criteria that exceed the specifications and features of the legacy system. For example, the new system is optimized for mobile devices. The new course-management system was also assessed using institutional and instructional criteria that are both backward and forward looking. Looking backward, the new system inherited many of the historical practices embodied and embedded in the legacy system. In fact, a typical requirement for new systems is that they are capable of migrating content from old systems: for all kinds of reasons, institutions want to sustain continuity between past and present actions. Looking forward, the requirements for the new system attempt to future-proof it against problems that lie ahead in the new century. Attempts at future-proofing are not exercises in predicting the future but perspectives that privilege adaptability and flexibility as conscious characteristics of systems design, supporting experimentation in stable and secure institutional environments. Adopting open standards—educational or technical—is an example of future-proofing, as is employing processes for generating system requirements that actively solicit use scenarios from students and teachers, who can help anticipate new directions in literacy education. The relationship of tendential forces in sociotechnical articulations can be Janus-faced, pushing and pulling in different temporal directions.

Another area that expresses institutional practices and structures has to do with how legacies are modified and maintained over long periods of time. Legacies are subject to the vagaries of institutional fragmentation, which are, at least in part, a byproduct of the uneven and unpredictable rhythms of change in universities: academic IT specialists come and go, and they can be reassigned to other areas or projects or be promoted; projects and units themselves can be reorganized into new institutional configurations, shifting roles and responsibilities; and projects can be updated in bits and pieces as time and money allow. The result of institutional fragmentation (whatever the cause) is that academic IT specialists who are in charge of legacy systems rarely have a coherent picture of their development trajectories and the reasoning frameworks that guided decision-making. Such gaps in history can inhibit learning from past experiences and confound efforts at contextualizing institutional actions. For example, when I became director of the Penn State writing program, I inherited a print handbook that contains information about the program for our teachers. This handbook has been revised over the course of many decades by numerous different past directors and graduate teaching assistants. As I converted the print handbook to a website, I attempted to evaluate the relevance of the legacy content: Why is this entry in the handbook? Who prepared it? When was it last updated? Does it need to be updated, or should it be deleted? Is the legacy content sufficient? These questions were often impossible to answer or ignore, but not having answers encouraged a content-conserving method that favored inertia over action and tinkering over substantive iteration for fear of deleting histories, weakening or deleting useful aspects of texts, and creating problems for teachers. The long periods of time over which legacy systems are modified and maintained by changing institutional actors and arrangements invariably fragment historical understandings and diminish historical empathies, making it challenging for workers—academic IT specialists and teachers—to explain why institutions have done what they have done and why things are as they are today.

All technologies will eventually become legacies, and dealing with this reality consumes a great deal of time in academic IT units. Academic IT units must decide whether to abandon, maintain, reengineer, or replace legacies. These options, however different or discordant, are closely tied to ways of thinking and working that were established at earlier moments of institutional renewal and change. The decision to abandon legacies is a decision to abandon what were once considered ideas worth developing to a conclusion. For example, Penn State had a portal system that students and teachers used to define and organize their starting places for online activities. Although it was stable for many years, the academic IT unit that was responsible for the portal simply stopped supporting it: their project reflections indicated that students and teachers preferred to use personal and search portals. The decision to maintain legacies is a decision to continue to invest in historically legitimated institutional ideas. Penn State maintained an outmoded student information system for many years because the system was still able to facilitate fundamental business and administrative processes. As the objectives and functions of those processes evolved and changed, however, the justifications for a new system intensified and grew more persuasive. The decision to reengineer legacies is a decision to alter or redirect historically legitimated institutional ideas. Legacies are often reengineered to be more efficient or effective, but reengineering usually inhabits a middle ground between maintenance and replacement approaches, extending the life of a system by instantiating new ideas as feature capabilities. A good example comes from Bucknell University: they reengineered the university website to enable users to customize their browsing experiences. The new design is controversial from a usability design perspective (see Sherwin 2014), but it is meant to signal that Bucknell is an institution that values risk taking and challenging the status quo. Finally, the decision to replace legacies is a decision to begin anew with institutional deliberations. Such deliberations use historical experiences as a resource for considering future possibilities. The deliberations associated with replacing the Penn State course-management system involved widescale reviews of draft requirements documents, focus groups, pilot classes, heuristic evaluations, and more. The conclusions drawn from these investigations were refracted through the lenses of institutional histories: people naturally compare what they have had with what they think they want or need from technologies.

My formulation of approaches to legacies is a bit too neat to be entirely accurate: ideas from abandoned systems can live on in other projects, and new systems tend to incorporate aspects of legacies. My argument, however, is that all the approaches are indebted to precedent and received notions of institutional practice in ways that align with the enduring historical questions of teachers: previous technological experiences influence decisions about what to do about legacy systems, for example, as do institutional understandings of technological obsolescence (new systems can create as many problems as they solve). Legacies and the teaching and learning activities they support are bound by a complex lineage of historical associations.

Conventions

Conventions are social rules or norms that guide institutional actions. They signify accepted approaches to doing things on local or global scales. An academic IT unit might very well decide to adopt a set of conventions for documenting programming code, such as those discussed by Pete Goodliffe (2006) in *Code Craft: The Practice of Writing Excellent Code.* The reason for stipulating conventions is to help coordinate collaborative work and make explicit the metathinking of programmers for those who inherit their projects. Conventions are institutional instruments for making meaning that go beyond the realms of individuals and particular versions of projects. On a global scale, an academic IT unit might very well decide to adopt a set of conventions for reporting institutional data and information. EDUCAUSE provides an extensive guide that helps institutions employ EDUCAUSE conventions for working with their core data services, which produce national data points for over one hundred topics. By following these conventions, institutions can benchmark themselves against peer universities and identify areas for improvement. Conventions normalize representational approaches to reporting institutional data and information, enabling longitudinal historical analyses by individual institutions and professional organizations.

I should clarify my distinction between standards and conventions. Standards can include conventions and conventions can include standards, but to distinguish them, I emphasize their roles in academic IT processes. As mentioned in the section on standards, standards enable systems and services to interoperate across contexts and industries. Standards are sociotechnical building blocks for academic IT systems, representing initial starting points for development activities. Conventions, in contrast, are deployed farther down the chain of production and are situated as design layers that sit on top of standards. In my preceding example, EDUCAUSE adopted database and survey research standards to support its core data services. These standards allow hundreds of member institutions to contribute a wide range of data to the database no matter their particular commitments to administrative structures or technologies. The form of the database output, however, is governed by conventions, by certain accepted approaches to representing data, such as using numerical tables and bar and pie charts. In addition, users have the option of outputting raw data from the database so that they can use their own institutional conventions for analyzing and reporting purposes. Flexible data handling is itself a technical standard that acknowledges the shaping power of conventions, of social rules and norms.

Andrei Marmor (2014) discusses several characteristics that help depict the nature of conventions. I will discuss three of them for my objectives here. First, conventions are arbitrary constructs—that is, people always have alternative choices when employing conventions that serve the same function or goal (9). Goodliffe's book of conventions for documenting programming code is a sensible choice for academic IT units, but so too are books by Dustin Boswell and Trevor Foucher (2011), Peter Eeles (2009), and Donald Knuth (1992). There are more than a few valid convention sets for documenting code. Second, conventions are compliance dependent. By this, Marmor means that people must follow conventions in order for them to exist (3). The number of people is unimportant—a small group of workers could agree on a set of conventions for their own purposes—but conventions can atrophy or die from neglect of use. An academic IT unit could decide to end the practice of documenting code and instead embrace the goal of producing what is oftentimes called self-documenting code, which is written in as simple and straightforward a manner as possible. Conventions are subject to social agreements that can change with time. And third, conventions are constitutive of institutional activities. Conventions function as responses to complex problems of coordination and regulate actions, but they also shape understandings of problems and the values in problem contexts (36). If conventions for documenting code present rules or norms for explaining the routines of software, they also define and delimit what it means to write documentation in the first place, what is possible for writers to do and not to do, and what the criteria are for evaluating the effectiveness of explanations. As Marmor says, conventions "always have a dual function: the rules both constitute the practice, and, at the same time, they regulate conduct within it" (36). Constitution and regulation are inextricably linked when it comes to enacting social rules and norms in institutions.

This complex linkage has significant historical dimensions. Charles Kostelnick and Michael Hassett (2003) investigate how conventions operate in technical writing, offering a rhetorical-historical framework that attends to the visual aspects of information and technologies. They are careful to avoid assigning conventions an overly deterministic role in rhetorical situations, acknowledging the numerous factors that help govern the reception and interpretation of texts, technologies, and user actions, but also provide a robust account of how conventions both advance invention activities (constitution) and hamper adoption or integration activities (regulation). The point Kostelnick and Hassett underscore about constitution is that conventions "invite adaptation and improvisation and allow designers to tailor them to specific situations" (6). Conventions exert a stabilizing influence in institutions, but stability is not an inherent property of conventions, which "are constantly in flux—emerging, evolving, mutating, and declining" (6). In working on design problems in specific situations, people confront opportunities in which to create versions of conventions that can speak to particular audiences and concerns; they also confront opportunities in which to defy conventions. For example, the WordPress publishing system at Penn State provides hundreds of templates that represent possible starting points for website projects. Although the templates feature different elements, actions, and goals, there is no option for starting with a blank screen: invention always begins as an encounter with a set of predetermined conventions. Conventions are unavoidable, and no less so for being ignored.

In terms of regulation, Kostelnick and Hassett emphasize that conventions can slow the implementation of a new technology, which "invariably surrenders some of its design potential when it operates within the realm of conventional practices" (188). They provide historical examples of this phenomenon: the introduction of the typewriter was hindered by the "handwriting industry" and its "legions of scriveners and writing masters who practiced and taught the orthodox styles," and the introduction of computer-aided design software was hindered by the "entrenched drawing techniques of pencils and T-squares" and other then-popular literacy technologies (187–88). Contemporary technologies, likewise, are not immune to the regulating functions of conventions: software for visualizing data and information tends to reproduce and proliferate old modes and forms of representation and organization (188). The tensions between the conventional forces of constitution and regulation run through institutional histories and affect academic IT in central ways.

Conventions have been studied in efforts to explain how genres function as a means of communication. In many of these efforts, conventions are recognized as historical aspects of texts that enable writers and readers to share assumptions and understandings across similar types of rhetorical situations. Conventions, however, are also integral to the enduring historical questions that unite all teachers and conjoin them with the domain concerns of academic IT units. For instance, the historical examples Kostelnick and Hassett discuss implicate the sociocultural roots of technologies, particularly the communities of practice that helped naturalize handwriting, drawing, and visual ways of representing institutional data and information. And in my example, institutional publishing systems encourage rhetorical theories and practices that attend to conventional design templates and their histories as inventional resources for imagining website projects. Conventions, as potent expressions of social rules and norms, influence and are worked out through institutional practices.

Rituals

As with conventions, rituals help construct the social life of institutions, serving constitutive functions when organizing actions and activities. But one of the main things that distinguishes rituals from other historical elements is the symbolic role they play in expressing values and interests in concrete moments of institutionalization. Nick Couldry (2003) reviews three perspectives on rituals that are prominent in investigations of sociotechnical contexts: habitual actions, formalized actions, and actions involving transcendent values. For institutional settings, Couldry dismisses the simple equation of rituals with habitual actions, with "any habit or repeated pattern, whether or not it has a particular meaning" (3). Although I check my email first thing in the morning, merely calling this activity a ritual "adds nothing to the idea of regular action or habit" (3). Rituals and habitual actions are not interchangeable terms.

The other two perspectives are more useful to understanding how rituals operate in institutions. Rituals as formalized actions extend beyond habits in that the patterns involved in formalized actions imbue them with meaning and relevance (3). My email reading in the morning is not comprehensive but entails identifying work messages that require immediate attention. This routine is one of several rituals that defines my relationship with email. In the third perspective, rituals reflect wider institutional patterns and beliefs, shifting "the emphasis *away* from questions of pure form and *towards* the particular values that ritual action embodies" (3). My email routine was born out of growing administrative responsibilities in a writing program that serves over twelve thousand students per year. These responsibilities require me to be readily available to students, teachers, and administrative leaders. They also obligate me to document projects and problems and archive program work. Responsive communication and record keeping are expected institutional practices that are symbolized and enacted by rituals.

Harrison Trice and Janice Beyer (1984) provide a taxonomy for categorizing the different types of rituals in organizations. The taxonomy includes six types of rituals and the social purposes they serve: rituals of passage, degradation, enhancement, renewal, conflict reduction, and integration (657). To paraphrase them quickly, rituals of passage initiate people into institutional cultures; an example is running orientation programs for new graduate students. One purpose of rituals of passage is to inculcate people into appropriate work roles. Rituals of degradation disestablish social identities in institutions; an example is reorganizing institutional units and replacing leadership personnel. One purpose of rituals of degradation is to publicly acknowledge institutional dilemmas. Rituals of enhancement strengthen social identities in institutions; an example is awarding annual prizes for teacher performance. One purpose of rituals of enhancement is to motivate employees. Rituals of renewal rejuvenate institutional practices; an example is strategic planning. One purpose of rituals of renewal is to bolster existing power structures. Rituals of conflict reduction diminish discord and strife in institutional relationships; an example is using university ombudsmen to mediate institutional problems. One purpose of rituals of conflict reduction is to restore stability in moments of institutional crisis or change. Finally, rituals of integration inspire or restore shared institutional sentiments that bond employees together; an example is holding all-employee meetings. One purpose of rituals of integration is to break down silos that exist within large, complex workplaces. Rituals serve a variety of socializing functions that impose order, coherence, and meaning in institutions.

Stephen North (1987) considers the role of rituals from a different angle, arguing that ritualized activities embody institutional lore, an important body of knowledge for teachers. Lore has a socializing function, but it addresses practical questions of what to do on the job. The solutions generated by lore are a product of experience and pragmatic considerations, not formal research. Thus, lore has its own set of rules for the inclusion and validation of knowledge. For instance, any and all practitioners can contribute to the lore of institutions, the contributions themselves can be contradictory and even self-canceling, and practitioners appropriate and transform lore for their own objectives and situations (25–26). An example from my school is the lore associated with managing student email. From a practical viewpoint, our teachers have developed a rich body of knowledge about what to do and how, ranging from technical solutions, such as making filters and using separate email accounts; to social solutions, such as establishing expectations and parameters for asynchronous online exchanges; to hybrid solutions, which involve both technical and social aspects. Although their approaches are all over the map, the practices are grounded in concrete experiential encounters with teaching and learning situations. This mode of knowledge making is invaluable to teachers.

Before considering how the historical elements of rituals influence academic IT units, I want to address a criticism of the construction of lore as a body of professional knowledge. Richard Fulkerson (2011) takes North to task for granting lore a status similar to the results produced by empirical research methods, especially methods on the quantitative end of the descriptive-experimental continuum. To encapsulate his reservations, Fulkerson is skeptical that "evaluative causal claims" based on "experiential narrative" can be applicable to the field as a whole (53). In focusing on the rules for producing lore that North outlines (and that I paraphrase above), Fulkerson asserts that "what North needed but could not find or develop was some fair way of distinguishing credible lore from incredible" (52) — that is, a method for validating lore as generalizable professional knowledge. Although Fulkerson values lore on some level, he does not treat it either as a method for making professional knowledge or as professional knowledge itself. The point I want to make is that lore is never produced in an institutional vacuum by isolated teachers working on idiosyncratic problems. Instead, institutions are a primary shaper of pedagogical patterns of uniformity and variation, of what is generalizable from a situation and what is specific to it.

North (1987) acknowledges this reality when he notes that "the heart of the Practitioner community derives from a shared *institutional* experience" (28). He goes on to explain that "while it is true that each Practitioner's version of lore will assume a peculiar experiential structure, it is also true that for most Practitioners this version will be formed under conditions and circumstances that are widely shared, in the face of what are in many ways common demands" (28). In his criticism of North, Fulkerson does not contemplate the institutional dimensions of lore, and I would add that North does not develop this piece of his argument in enough detail. I suspect Fulkerson would remain unpersuaded by my point: lore becomes professional knowledge not only when it furnishes ending positions such as generalizable conclusions but also when it enables teachers in institutional situations facing institutional tasks to explore those tasks using the shared experiences of others as inventional starting points for learning and problem solving. Teachers at my school rarely re-create the wheel or make things up as they go along but build on the successes and failures of previous institutional work. Generalizability is not an impetus for the knowledge-making practices of invention.

In institutional contexts, then, rituals express values and interests, serve socializing functions, and embody knowledge practices. All of these roles are discernible in academic IT units, in large part because of the scope of the enterprise. In his discussion of rituals, North (1987) notes that the various roles of rituals help moderate the effects of dealing with a formidable institutional challenge in teaching and learning: "All of what is involved cannot be articulated, let alone codified. Thus, a great deal of what one knows must not only be held but passed on as ritual knowledge: Nobody could ever explain all that there is to know or do, so we simply do as those before us have done. It is the way" (30). The turn North makes here—situating rituals as historical elements that can help people manage the demands of knowledge and professional development—is unusual in discussions of rituals. As a conduit to tacit procedural knowledge, rituals guide behaviors in ways that are not readily available for introspection.

Examples of rituals in academic IT units can be readily found for all the categories supplied by Trice and Beyer (1984). I will discuss two examples that illuminate historical forces and involve the enduring questions of teachers. My first example is strategic planning, a ritual of renewal but also one of integration when it includes opportunities for everyone to participate. I have participated in two cycles of strategic planning for academic IT at Penn State. Both of them used an outside consulting firm to guide planning and took more than a year to complete. Strategic planning is ritualized at my school in that it occurs as a matter of course, in time periods ranging from three to five years; it reflects university mission statements, aligning institutional values and interests; it distributes roles and responsibilities according to rank, reinforcing existing institutional hierarchies; and it relies on institutional memory for how things have been done in the past, eliciting tacit procedural knowledge to understand and make sense of histories and their relationships to the present. Historical aspects are also conspicuous in the data collected to support strategic planning, such as user surveys and system performance reports. As for the enduring historical questions of teachers, strategic planning can encompass issues of obsolescence and previous user experiences. A major goal of strategic planning is to assess the effectiveness and sustainability of current approaches and systems and to make adjustments based on changing needs and conditions in institutions, literacies, and technologies. This goal can only be satisfied by understanding how today is different than it was before, and certainly since the last round of strategic planning.

My second example is a ritual of enhancement: publishing news about the activities and accomplishments of academic IT units. Publishing news is ritualized at Penn State in that it occurs as a matter of course, in time periods of one to three months; it indicates the forums for professional development that are valued by the institution; it communicates the types of pedagogical projects funded and supported by the institution; it enables the institution to distinguish what it considers to be noteworthy employee accomplishments, which are also understood to be institutional accomplishments; and it reaffirms the priority of established annual events. As for the enduring historical questions of teachers, publishing news can encompass the sociocultural roots of information technologies and rhetorical theories and practices. A major goal of publishing news is to communicate the value of academic IT units to the larger university community. This goal can only be satisfied by framing initiatives in terms that will be comprehensible and compelling to students and teachers. A strategy of the IT communications group is to interview teachers about their projects and initiatives, inviting them to explain what is significant about the work to colleagues and other interested groups. I used a video-based interview to explain how teachers of writing and communication have interpreted the institutional requirements for a Teaching with Technology certificate. Both teachers and academic IT specialists can undoubtedly learn a considerable amount about the historical dimensions of university commitments, worker roles, and work processes by paying attention to the ritualized activities of institutional planning and publishing.

CONCLUSION

Christina Haas (1996) reminds teachers that "as individuals, we may be tempted to think that technologies are given to us (or, more accurately, purchased by us) fully formed, but technologies have complex and vital histories—histories that are part and parcel of the impact that developing technologies will have on our intellectual and material lives" (222). I doubt that many teachers today would reduce technologies to well-wrought objects or subscribe to decontextualized accounts of development and use. However, the heuristic elements discussed in this chapter are not typically represented in field models of the rhetorical situation, despite the fact that writing and communication activities cannot escape the effects of their own institutional histories. Although circumstances and conditions will always vary from institution to institution, the histories of academic IT units inevitably involve standards, legacies, conventions, and rituals, all of which are consequential to writing and communication instruction and practice. The next chapter shifts from considerations of histories to spaces and explores the dynamics and implications of spatial institutional dimensions.

3

SPATIALIZING ACADEMIC IT

Spaces are not simply the setting for historical action but are a significant product and determinant of change. They are not passive settings but the medium for the development of culture. DAVID J. BODENHAMER (2010)

In December 2010, New York City mayor Michael Bloomberg announced a competition inviting academic institutions to propose plans for building a new graduate school in engineering and applied sciences on Roosevelt Island, a narrow strip of land in the East River. According to Google Maps, Roosevelt Island is about two miles long and eight hundred feet wide, resting between the boroughs of Manhattan and Queens. The new graduate school will replace an underutilized specialty care hospital on the north end of the island. As an economic development initiative meant to create jobs and revenues, attract innovative workers, and position the area as a hub for academic-industrial partnerships, New York City plans to invest one hundred million dollars in the sociotechnical infrastructure of the campus. In addition, it expects the university that won the competition, Cornell Tech, to invest an even greater sum in the new facilities, win research grants, and lure considerable investments to the metro region (Office of the Mayor of New York City 2011). Save for several abstract murals from the 1940s, the hospital was demolished, clearing the way for redevelopment of the land.

Cornell Tech is an institutional partnership between Cornell University in Ithaca, New York, and the Technion–Israel Institute of Technology in Haifa. Both schools are known for their research in information science and for alliances with information-rich industries and entrepreneurial initiatives. According to technical descriptions on the Cornell Tech website, the scope of the campus plan is ambitious and goal oriented: the first phase of facilities opened in the fall of 2017, and the last will open in 2037. Before the campus opened, students and faculty were housed at the offices of Google New York, where they piloted academic IT systems. In the end, the campus is expected to accommodate 2,500 students and 280 faculty members in over two million square feet of space. The people working at Cornell Tech will cluster into communities of practice focusing on three overlapping research lines: connective media, health care, and sustainability. A thread that will tie everything together is an attention to the communicative aspects of users' experiences with information technologies. In fact, a major goal for Cornell Tech is to apply principles from user experience design to the creation of institutional spaces. This goal is made all the more intriguing by the unusual opportunity to imagine a campus from the ground up, to build, from scratch, institutional spaces for teaching and learning with academic IT.

Avi Wolfman-Arent (2014) reports on the design thinking of administrators at Cornell Tech and their sense of what is at stake in space development projects. He starts with big-picture questions, which are linked to both strategic planning and the possibilities for pedagogies: "How do you create a new institution in an age where everything—office design, intelligent infrastructure, cloud computing, classroom technology—presents some opportunity to break with the past? What do you build? What do you wire? What kinds of interactions do you encourage?" Wolfman-Arent goes on to explain the answer from administrators: "Some institutions might create committees to try to anticipate specific changes. Cornell Tech is determined to do the opposite. Those responsible for building the campus of the future won't pretend to know what the future holds. They only hope they're building something malleable enough to handle it." Malleability, openness, and iteration—these are the principles from user experience design that are driving decisions about how space ought to be structured and managed for education. For example, the buildings at Cornell Tech will have loosely configured work areas that people can disassemble and reassemble at will to support the evolving needs of interdisciplinary research groups. The administrative systems will be built using open software standards to ensure interoperability and data sharing. And solutions to problems about space will be understood as tentative and contingent to encourage stakeholders to constantly evolve space solutions and revisit problems as circumstances change. Perhaps most strikingly, Cornell Tech has decided to skip building a data center on campus, a centralized facility for storing, managing, and disseminating mission-critical institutional data, including administrative, instructional, and research data. Instead, they will rely on a third-party hosting solution, outsourcing their data center to a cloud service provider. This decision is unusual and highlights the extent of the changes in possibilities for academic IT units.

Wolfman-Arent published his article in the *Chronicle of Higher Education,* and the comments generated by readers raise several concerns about the design plans. Commenters wonder about privacy issues and FERPA regulations: Could the open architecture impede students and teachers from having private conversations? Discourage teachers from working on assessment activities during high-use periods? Keep students from taking risks? Commenters are also uncertain about the relationship between open architecture and learning: Could the openness of the space create more distractions than insights? Favor certain kinds of intellectual work over and above others? More than a few commenters mention failures of the short-lived open classroom movement of the 1960s, which popularized the idea of schools without walls, and speculate that Cornell Tech is tempting the same fate, failing to learn from an instructive moment in the history of US schooling. Another concern has to do with the level of faculty involvement: Is the architectural vision for Cornell Tech coming from administrators, or are the people who will actually use the spaces being consulted about their needs? Accurately or not, quotes from the vice provost for Cornell Tech create the impression that the architectural vision is the product of a top-down approach. A final concern raised by commenters is about risk and reward: Could the considerable resources being used to finance the creation of this futuristic campus be more wisely invested in the tried-and-true spaces of higher education? Some commenters express the sentiment that in tough economic times, universities should invest their limited resources in established directions.

Although the absence of campus legacy systems makes the case of Cornell Tech somewhat atypical in certain respects, it does begin to illuminate substantive issues for institutional spaces involving academic IT. Institutional spaces are productive spaces in that they help produce the nature of social relationships and knowledge: one aim of the coworking areas at Cornell Tech is to reconfigure the geography of academic disciplines and their sociotechnical practices so that people who are normally walled off from one another by segmentalist structures can interact in new and different ways. The assumption is that physical proximity and accessibility will facilitate interdisciplinary collaboration and experimentation with innovative project approaches. Institutional spaces, moreover, are an influential element in teaching and learning activities. The decision to forgo building a campus data center and to instead adopt a cloud-based solution for data storage and management has everyday implications for students and teachers, who will need to develop institutional workflows that leverage the cloud as both a tool and a strategy for knowledge making in educational endeavors. Here is another matter illuminated by the case of Cornell Tech: the design of pedagogical spaces is an ongoing process with contested and changing interpretations, not an institutional project with beginning and end points. Cornell Tech does indeed have an overall time line of two decades or so, but administrators anticipate that people will appropriate institutional spaces to suit open-ended purposes and activities. The assumption is that the meanings of institutional spaces evolve and change in the tensions and functions through which they exist. Institutional spaces, in other words, are not static or inert but dynamic and full of potential transformation. I will continue to discuss institutional perspectives on space in subsequent sections.

I begin this chapter with an overview of how academic IT units tend to address spatial issues. Their perspectives are informed by a particular set of concepts from educational theory, environmental psychology, and managerial philosophy, which I evaluate for the purpose of characterizing the general nature of the conversation in academic IT units. I then offer my own view of how space ought to be thought about and treated in institutions. The next part of the chapter reviews enduring spatial questions in the field that make my heuristic relevant within and across institutions. The final section discusses the spatial elements of my heuristic: hierarchies, processes, methods, and bodies. The examples show that teachers of writing and communication can and should contribute in positive ways to institutional formulations of the spatial.

SPATIAL PERSPECTIVES ON ACADEMIC IT

The treatment of spatial practices represents a persistent and vibrant topic for analysis on university campuses. A 1972 publication by Jacques La France provides an example of an early instance in which the design and use of institutional spaces began to become a domain issue for academic IT units. In "Comments on the Administrative/Academic Interface," La France reports on why and how Wheaton College decoupled its administrative and academic computing systems and the institutional changes that followed. As was common in the 1960s, computer users at Wheaton shared a central machine—in this case, an IBM 1620. Because the 1620 was not a time-sharing machine, it was necessarily used in a serial (versus parallel) fashion by administrators and students, with each group taking turns in the role of users. But by 1969, as La France (1972) recalls, "the use of the 1620 by both groups had become so heavy that at certain time periods there weren't enough hours to go around, and each group tended to need to have the computer when the other one was supposed to have it. Students would need it to get class assignments done and the administration needed it to get out some reports" (48). This progressively routine conflict and the ever-growing demand for computing resources encouraged the academic IT specialists to purchase an additional machine, an IBM 1130, which they dedicated to education; administrators continued to use the 1620 for business purposes. The solution, on one level, was simply a techno-economic solution to the practical problem of physical access.

On another level, however, the solution involved spatial issues that entangle institutions, literacies, and technologies. According to La France, the decision to devote a computing machine to education was accompanied by a spatial reorganization of governance structures. As opposed to charging a single IT unit with the compounded task of supporting both administrative and academic initiatives, a second computer center was created to cater to the needs of students and teachers. The director of the second center (La France himself) would report not to administrative leaders or business managers but to the academic dean of the faculty. As a result, this new institutional geography increased physical machine access for students and teachers, allowed the center director to concentrate his energy on pedagogical undertakings, and aligned the mission of academic computing with academic priorities. As this example illustrates, spatial arrangements have long been important to teaching and learning in academic IT contexts, including the larger structuring patterns in universities. The influence of such arrangements is apparent in even the earliest publications from academic IT units.

If spatial practices have long been important to teaching and learning in academic IT contexts, the perspectives informing the conversation revolve in very particular ways around certain ideas from educational theory, environmental psychology, and managerial philosophy. I will introduce the terrain of these ideas and indicate their value (or lack thereof) for illuminating issues of spatiality in institutions. My goal is not to provide an all-encompassing review of the literature but to offer a general characterization of how spatial practices tend to be imagined in academic IT units. Constructivism is an educational theory that resonates in a range of pedagogical settings. As with any theory, it has been appropriated in various ways by its proponents. Not surprisingly, academic IT specialists gravitate toward views of constructivism that are prized in their own educational contexts. I discussed educational contexts in chapter 1, noting that many IT workers pursue degree programs in education, instructional design, or computer science or engineering. I will characterize the views of constructivism that are favored in such programs by enumerating key principles about learning that have become internalized in academic IT units.

To begin, constructivism is distinguished as a response to outdated understandings of the nature of learning (and thus also of teaching), understandings that are alive and well in courses that treat students as passive spectators in the process of knowledge development. The flipped classroom movement, which has been championed if not popularized by academic IT units, is a conspicuous response to transmission models of education. This movement encourages teachers who lecture to repurpose classroom time so that students and teachers can use their time together more judiciously by exploring questions, working collaboratively, and engaging in problem solving. Constructivism is considered to be an antidote to the limitations of pedagogical approaches that cast students into roles as receivers who are supposed to acquire knowledge for later use.

The constructivist learning principles that are popular in academic IT units have cognitive and social dimensions. Students, first of all, should assume responsibility for their own learning by owning educational processes to the extent that they can, which involves being proactive and self-directed. The underlying concepts are that personal motivation is an important factor in learning and that the ideas and interests of students should be admitted to and leveraged in learning situations. Students are not tourists but citizens of the classroom, with rights and responsibilities as members of learning communities. In addition, learning itself is an active process of meaning making that relies on experiences and interactions in the world. The underlying concepts are that constructing knowledge is a more powerful intellectual activity than reproducing knowledge and that knowledge is constructed in social contexts in response to situations comprising the need for students to explain, negotiate, and interpret the instructional landscapes for courses. Active learners engage in higher-order thinking skills and co-create meaning in effortful encounters with others.

Another popular principle in academic IT units is that reflection and assessment should be an integral component of classroom practices. The underlying concepts are that metacognition is a window into learning and that students should aspire to "learn how to learn" so that they can become more capable and confident learners. Teachers, therefore, should help students learn to evaluate their own learning approaches and equip students to become lifelong learners. Finally, it takes time to learn, for learning is not an immediate process or one free from errors or missteps. The underlying concepts are that learning is a dynamic and adaptive enterprise and that mistakes can be productive. Students need the space and freedom to explore and test their ideas about the world and themselves. To reiterate, these principles are not the only principles of constructivism in the domain of educational theory, and in fact there are critical strains of constructivism that are sensitive to issues of power and social justice, issues of schooling and democratic citizenship, and other critical pedagogical issues. My selection of principles is meant to depict the broad tenor of the conversation in academic IT units.

How does constructivism shape the priorities and actions of academic IT units as they imagine, develop, and manage campus spaces—material and virtual—for teaching and learning? Academic IT units invest significant resources in efforts to open up transmission pedagogies to student participation, to close the gap between students and teachers (and students and students) who are physically close in geographic space but intellectually distant or detached, at least in interactional terms. Examples of efforts in this sphere include classroom response systems such as clickers, smartphone polling apps, and back-channel forums, which enable students to ask questions, provide answers, register feedback, and more. Lecture capture systems are also an area of emphasis. For teachers who value transmission approaches to teaching and learning, these systems record lectures and permit students to review complex ideas and reencounter instructional materials according to their own needs. In addition, academic IT units invest significant resources to support collaboration and group work, to situate students as active participants with meaningful roles in learning situations. Examples of efforts in this sphere include file-sharing, tagging, note-sharing, and annotating systems and collaborative writing environments. Of course, spatial locations have a notable bearing on student workflows and meaning making: colocated and distributed approaches to collaboration and group work exhibit differing affordances and constraints. Although less obvious, a third instance of an investment-intensive area shaped by constructivist thinking is learning analytics. I am referring to applications that provide teachers with student demographic and performance data, following the assumption that having insights into such data can help teachers customize their courses for a given set of students. Demographic and performance data are historical but also spatial in that they relate directly to the ordering patterns of educational and personal experiences.

Environmental psychology is also a focus in degree programs in education, instructional design, and computer science and engineering, and a collection of principles from this interdisciplinary field is routinely employed by academic IT specialists. The field of environmental psychology is interested in the relationship between humans and their surroundings, taking people-environment interactions as the unit of analysis for research and teaching investigations. This broad agenda has resulted in an array of perspectives on how surroundings ought to be thought about and treated in institutions. The viewpoint aligning most closely with the interests of academic IT units posits that "all environments are patterns of information" and that "people are fundamentally information-processing organisms" (De Young 2013, 19) striving to make sense of the spaces they inhabit and how these spaces affect working and living. For everyone in universities, navigating institutional structures is an unavoidable mode of spatial problem solving.

The principles from environmental psychology that are discernible in academic IT units are associated with the always unfinished business of designing formal, informal, and hybrid learning spaces. Before anything else, institutional learning spaces are officially sanctioned spaces governed by federal, state, and local laws and by university policies, all of which initiate the need for an enforcement apparatus that helps define what is considered to be appropriate conduct in pedagogical settings. Although necessary and important, this apparatus can set the stage for tensions between teachers and policy makers, particularly if teachers feel constrained by institutional approaches to implementing technologies. At the same time, laws and policies alone do not constitute full institutionalization, nor do they determine solutions to teaching and learning problems. Consequently, academic IT specialists hew to the principle that how people experience their surroundings is a function of more than just the surroundings themselves. Support for this principle is based on the realization that mismatches can occur between the designs of institutional spaces and the learning styles of students and that students with disabilities can be affected differently by the spatial attributes of institutions. Another operating principle is that the boundaries of institutional spaces are not fixed but dynamic, evolving over time in response to changes in both technologies and pedagogies. The boundaries of institutions are negotiable (on some level) and stabilized (for periods of time) as everyday practices become routinized and regulated by teachers and administrators. Let me add one more principle from environmental psychology to my characterization of spatial perspectives in academic IT units: people may not notice or pay attention to the physical and social makeup of their surroundings, taking for granted the ways institutions influence learning spaces. This possibility is hardly surprising given the subtle manner in which institutional influence can be exercised in educational contexts.

Applications of environmental psychology principles are on ready display in academic IT settings. Academic IT specialists take great care in thinking about the ties among space, architecture, and learning and aim to deploy architectural elements that contribute to positive classroom experiences. This thinking has resulted in design guidelines that attend to physical, psychological, social, and institutional aspects of learning spaces. Lori Gee (2006), for example, advises people to design learning spaces that are healthful, concentrating on ergonomic and lighting conditions; stimulating, concentrating on sensory cues, sight lines, and room geometries; balanced, providing areas for both individual and group work; and adaptable, allowing students and teachers to reconfigure room geometries and incorporate their own devices. Design guidelines such as these acknowledge a basic principle of environmental psychology: humans affect, and are affected by, institutional spaces.

Academic IT specialists also take great care in thinking about how the boundaries of institutional spaces are acted on by distance education initiatives, mobile technologies, and other things that accentuate and intensify location-centric activities as elements of schooling. For distance education settings, academic IT specialists advise teachers to both re-create the rich sociospatial interactions of face-to-face classrooms and explore what might be unique to online interactions. The prominent question of how to create a social presence that can support distance education is, at bottom, an institutional question about how to organize spatial interactions across the increasingly distributed boundaries of learning activities. And for mobile technologies, academic IT specialists are creating smartphone apps that engage incoming students before they even arrive on campus, easing the transition to higher education by integrating data and information from home and school places and initiating the process of institutional socialization. There are also numerous other applications of environmental psychology principles in academic IT settings, including projects that illuminate student usage patterns in learning spaces and elucidate the thinking of those who design learning spaces.

The managerial philosophy that informs spatial perspectives in academic IT units reflects canonical concerns over risks and rewards, innovation and assessment, and institutional sustainability. These concerns derive not so much from an identifiable camp of managerial philosophy but from strategic considerations. As for risks and rewards, academic IT units are well aware of the symbolic character of learning spaces on university campuses, which can function metonymically to depict the more general status of academic institutions, signifying their directional commitments and well-being through specific points of material and virtual development. Learning spaces instantiate encounters with institutions and can even come to stand in for institutions themselves. Fairly or not, successes or failures in learning spaces can be considered successes or failures for entire institutions, especially if the situations employ high-profile academic IT initiatives.

The managerial philosophy for academic IT units also encompasses the linked domains of innovation and assessment in institutional learning spaces. Academic IT units are committed to the idea of innovating and assessing new approaches to teaching and learning—so much so that it is not unusual to find a line item for innovation in budgets or funds earmarked for pedagogical projects. This fundamental commitment follows from the commonsense belief that innovation is a fuel for growth in universities. The issues, of course, are what counts as innovation and what are meaningful methods for measuring innovation. In teaching and learning contexts, academic IT projects that are deemed to be innovative have spatial dimensions of one sort or another, exploring interactional relationships—physical, cognitive, and social—between individuals and their instructional surroundings. Finally, although academic IT units are capable of valuing spatial explorations for their own sake, the always-looming impulse toward institutionalization invariably begs questions about sustainability: Can innovations be operationalized and supported by academic IT units? Adopted and incorporated into the curriculum by teachers? Funded over the long term by administrators? Questions about sustainability are a component part of any institutional approach to managing technologies for learning spaces.

A good example of managerial philosophy in action comes from an EDUCAUSE initiative aimed at helping academic IT units assess the efficacy of their learning spaces. Despite the fact that learning spaces are expensive to create and require ongoing attention, institutions often fail to account for the full spectrum of design considerations when implementing or renovating building projects. The Learning Space Rating System is a rubric for scoring learning space designs and sharing design approaches with colleagues at other schools (Felix and Brown 2011). The rubric instantiates many of the principles I discussed under learning theory and environmental psychology. For example, sections of the rubric ask if the designs of learning spaces support active learning, provide good sight lines and reconfigurable furnishings, and optimize access for users. The rubric also outlines institutional criteria derived from managerial philosophy, emphasizing risks and rewards, innovation and assessment, sustainability, and more. For example, a section on campus contexts asks if the designs of learning spaces align with campus academic strategies, learning space master plans, IT strategic plans, and campus assessment plans. Furthermore, the section asks if learning spaces are associated with commitments to innovation. These criteria nest academic IT spaces within larger contexts that concern institutional priorities, educational standards, cost savings, and human capacities. The representation resulting from using the Learning Space Rating System provides an overall institutional snapshot of the spatial integration of academic IT. The score sheet is a spreadsheet that yields numerical, visual, and discursive comparisons across the six sections of criteria for learning space evaluation.

My characterization of the working spatial viewpoints in academic IT units acknowledges perspectives on teaching and learning that many teachers would endorse: for instance, students should be free to explore their interests in interactional contexts, and teachers should aim to help students learn how to learn. These viewpoints represent common ground between academic IT specialists and teachers, enabling the potential for fruitful collaborations. This common ground, however, is only a starting point for institutional cooperation. The argument I want to make about spaces and technologies critiques the apolitical strain of constructivism in academic IT units, emphasizes the in situ treatment of literacies and technologies, and proposes micropolitical action as an addendum to managerial philosophies for learning spaces. I am not advocating a one-sided view from the perspective of writing and communication teachers but attempting to broaden the common ground for more productive institutional relationships.

The apolitical strain of constructivism in academic IT units is effective to an extent, foregrounding the social construction of knowledge and situating meaning in context. But its political blind spot is a barrier to demystifying processes of institutionalization. By political, I mean something specific and spatial: institutional structures and relationships that regulate interaction patterns and define conventional behaviors, creating social order and stability. I am not suggesting that institutions determine a social order or that their regulating ability is always a negative force but rather that institutional structures and relationships instill patterns of authority and influence that have consequences for education. Consider the PassNote program at Purdue University, which provides software teachers can use to send students feedback about their work (Croton, Willis, and Fish 2014). I am sympathetic to the evidence-based reasoning for this academic IT project: students can benefit from receiving instructor feedback throughout the semester, but it must be timely, concrete, interpretable, and actionable, as the project indicates. PassNote enacts this reasoning in its messaging guidelines and features. The guidelines stress that messages should be short and to the point, use invitational words to underscore that students and teachers are collaborators, offer concrete steps for problem solving, and strike a positive tone. Although not comprehensive, these are good suggestions for providing feedback.

The software constructs a workflow for generating feedback messages. Teachers first select a performance level—low-performing, average-performing, or high-performing student—and then a topic: Blackboard Interaction, Attendance, Assessments, Resources, Work Ethic, and Encouragement. This three-by-six database grid is populated with a series of premade messages that teachers can add to a virtual notepad. If a teacher selects "Low-Performing Student" and "Assessments," for example, there are twelve messages to choose from, such as "Make sure to address any missing assignments as soon as possible" or "I am available to you during my office hours [insert office hours] at [insert office address], where we can go over available resources so you can be successful." Once messages are added to the notepad, teachers can copy them to an email or other communication program, edit the messages, and then send them to students. The workflow for PassNote is easy to understand but also too definitive and inflexible in structuring institutional relationships. Teachers cannot add message categories to PassNote or contribute to the database of premade messages. In addition, the premade messages are nearly always phrased as imperatives or directives, situating command structures as the predominant institutional grammar for educational feedback. The relational hierarchies promoted by PassNote are not conducive to either adoption of the software or productive student-teacher interactions. Teachers should be able to originate message themes and messages for their students. Moreover, they should be able to draw on a full range of locutionary acts for structuring feedback, as Sam Dragga (1991) might put it, offering directives but also compliments, criticisms, suggestions, questions, explanations, and observations (206–7). In PassNote, academic IT specialists exert a disproportionate amount of influence over the nature of feedback.

My second argument about spaces and technologies is an intensification and complication of the recognition in academic IT units that institutional spaces affect, and are affected by, learning activities and users. This principle focuses on a dyadic relationship between people and infrastructure in which the elements exist in dialectical tension with one another, with each influencing the other and both helping determine educational experiences. To a point, I find this formulation to be a profitable one for academic IT specialists and teachers, for it prioritizes the notion of human agency in institutions, assumes that spaces are mutable, and conceives of interactions as processes capable of shaping experiences. Such presuppositions are vital to understanding institutional spaces as nonneutral.

The people-infrastructure dyad, however, also advances a conception of space that neglects its performative properties. In one way of thinking, spaces are not the institutional areas—physical or virtual—that surround and house people and infrastructures but are constructed in and through their interactions and their interpretations of those interactions. Spaces are demarcated with boundaries and invested with meaning as students and teachers perform and defy institutional roles. Consider an ongoing conversation I have with the instructional designers at Penn State who oversee distance education courses. Their attention is absorbed by concerns over the design of content and the course-management system. When it comes to content, the instructional designers concentrate on establishing and measuring learning objectives, scaffolding lessons, and creating coherence and consistency. And when it comes to the course-management system, they concentrate on mapping software features to pedagogical practices and building navigation and reporting systems. These areas are worthy of attention and warrant considerable development work; I certainly spend a fair share of my own time concentrating on such matters. But in an important way of thinking, the course-management system and its content do not define or constitute learning spaces for distance education, which are created one interaction at a time—over and over again—as students engage with systems and materials, talk with one another and their teachers, and participate in problem-solving activities. Learning spaces for distance education are as ephemeral and fleeting as any pedagogical context, mirroring particular moments and patterns of interaction in dynamic situations.

Or reconsider the Learning Space Rating System as an example of managerial philosophy in action. Using the following evaluation categories, this rating system enables people to score the effectiveness of institutional learning spaces: Integration with Campus Context, Planning Process, Support and Operations, Environmental Quality, Layout and Furnishings, and Technology and Tools. But people cannot fully assess the adequacy of institutional learning spaces by considering the formal characteristics of classrooms or the planning processes of institutions. Learning spaces must also be assessed in situ through observations of actual classroom practices. In actual classroom practices, many aspects of spaces become articulated through meanings that have little reference to the evaluation categories of the Learning Space Rating System. I am thinking of the meanings produced through student-to-student interactions, teacher-to-student interactions, and teacher-to-teacher interactions.

My third argument about spaces and technologies has to do with the nature of agency and change. The bureaucracy and glacial pace of academia stand in stark contrast to the dynamic enterprise and rapid pace of technology development and use. For better and worse, institutions create structures that stabilize academic IT and enable it to function for users with varying needs. These structures, however, can feel like barriers to change, particularly for people focusing their efforts in unconventional or new directions. Teachers and academic IT specialists should commit themselves to working for sustainable change, advocating for sociotechnical arrangements that are congruent with the priorities of both institutions and academic disciplines. But they should also consider the possibilities for micropolitical actions, being opportunistic about interventions that can take place in the interstices of formalized institutional structures. Although contingent and short-lived, micropolitical actions can have direct and positive effects on students, teachers, and institutions.

There is already something of a hacker ethic in academic IT units. As I illustrated in the case of Cornell Tech, institutions design learning spaces to be refashioned by students and teachers. At Penn State, there is an experimental classroom that teachers can design to their own specifications in order to investigate new pedagogical approaches or approaches not supported by the current learning spaces. In addition, "hackathons" are part of the culture of academic IT units. Lasting anywhere from one day to a week, hackathons are intensive development events in which people suspend institutional routines and investigate ideas of their own choosing, breaking patterns of normality and exploring possibilities without the pressure of expectations. Although the products of hackathons can be appropriated by institutions, nothing about this practice is inherently repressive.

The hacker ethic in academic IT units begins to hint at the point I am making, but I want to emphasize the interpretive flexibility that accompanies processes of institutionalization. Let me provide an example from the digital badging movement. Digital badging is an emergent form of recognition that validates intellectual skills developed across and apart from formal curricular experiences. Proponents of the movement express dissatisfaction with grades and transcripts as sole indicators of knowledge development and learning and with institutional structures that separate rather than integrate learning experiences. Fundamentally, then, the digital badging movement is a response to the spatiotemporal orientation of education. Proponents aspire to introduce an alternative credentialing system that targets skills at the micro level, unbundling course components and decomposing them into modular units that can be validated by evidence and examples. In the Penn State badging system, students can earn badges for recognizing bias in research, being self-aware leaders, delivering dynamic presentations, knowing how to write accessible HTML code, and managing teamwork. Evangelists in the digital badging movement endorse badges as a replacement for grades and transcripts, which they consider to be antiquated and one-dimensional mechanisms for signaling educational accomplishments. Many academic IT specialists regard badges as a potentially useful supplement to grades and transcripts, offering a different mode of representation for documenting learning and showing expertise.

My issue is with systems that include badges for higher-order capabilities that are too complex to validate in checklists for completed skills. Higher-order capabilities such as writing, critical thinking, and problem solving are not achieved once and for all but must continue to be practiced and advanced throughout the course of academic and professional lives. Nonetheless, in my senior seminar, I ask students to work micropolitically with badging systems because the workflows challenge students to make and support arguments about what they can do and how well they can do it, marshaling evidence and examples and organizing arguments for audiences. Once students have invented their arguments in the badging system, they can import their materials into our WordPress installation, which does not really include support for invention activities, and then create an e-portfolio, the capstone project for the course. My approach remixes the institutional spaces for different software environments, using pedagogical encounters as a platform for micropolitical actions. The result is a solution to very real classroom needs that I have not been able to meet otherwise.

Academic IT specialists have major responsibilities when it comes to designing and maintaining learning spaces. Their spatial perspectives are informed by constructivist educational theories that advocate active learning; environmental psychology principles that address institutional design problems at the nexus of space, architecture, and learning; and managerial philosophies that address institutional priorities and sustainability. The spatial perspectives in academic IT units are also embraced by many teachers who attend to learning spaces. My contention is not that these perspectives are valueless or unimportant but rather that they are incomplete. In addition, they should also demystify processes of institutionalization that instill patterns of authority and influence in learning settings, account for the performative aspects of spatial practices, and promote micropolitical actions as productive responses to institutional configurations and their consequences. I am calling for an expansion in thinking that is more sensitive to the complexities of negotiating institutional spaces, which is a common challenge for everyone in universities.

ENDURING SPATIAL QUESTIONS

Teachers have elaborated the social turn in the discipline with investigations into the spatial nature of discourse production and consumption in institutions. This elaboration is a logical outgrowth of growing interests in the social situatedness of writing and the rhetorical specificities of texts and interpretive practices. In the contexts for literacies and technologies, teachers have generated at least four spatially oriented questions that have captured the ongoing attention of the field: What is spatial about using information technologies for writing and communication processes? What are the implications of information technologies for the "where" of writing and communication? How should instruction about information technologies be organized for students who are learning to write and communicate? And how is power exercised in the spatial contexts for information technologies? These questions are consequential for teachers working in any type of institution.

What Is Spatial about Using Information Technologies for Writing and Communication Processes?

The notion that writing and communication have spatial dimensions is hardly a new idea. As Jay David Bolter (1991) explains, "Writing is always spatial, and each technology in the history of writing (e.g. the clay tablet, the papyrus roll, the codex, the printed book) has presented writers and readers with different spaces to exploit" (105). Bolter is referring to the particularities and affordances of media systems and the varying and sometimes overlapping literate practices that people develop while learning to use those systems. In fact, for Bolter and other early theorists of hypertext, spatial characteristics are defining features that distinguish hypertext writing and reading from print-based writing and reading, suggesting diverging understandings of the relationships between writers and readers, readers and texts, and students and teachers. In basic terms, if the two-dimensional physical space of printed books encourages people to exploit the affordances of linearity and authorial control in read-only environments, the three-dimensional virtual space of hypertext encourages people to exploit the affordances of associativity and user control in write-read environments. Although writing has always been spatial, space is more dimensional and manipulable in digital technologies.

The evolution from text to hypertext expanded the spatial perspectives of teachers, who up to that point primarily concentrated on writing and editing with word processing programs and designing and publishing with desktop publishing programs. The pioneering work on word processing does not invoke deep arguments about spatiality and writing practices, but it does begin to illustrate why spatial questions have persisted in the field. Consider an early volume edited by William Wresch (1984), which includes sections on prewriting approaches, editing and grammar programs, word processing research and applications, and programs for the writing process. Chapters in all of these sections implicate space as an element of writing with technologies. In the section on prewriting approaches, for example, Dawn Rodrigues and Raymond Rodrigues (1984) describe software for invention that "may be used as a two dimensional field when first taught to students and later is easily expanded to a three-dimensional field. Thus, we begin visually with what might be described as a two-dimensional square plane and then move to a three-dimensional cube" (43). The software asks students to brainstorm topics and subtopics for argumentative papers, juxtaposes the subtopics using various spatial techniques, prompts students to articulate the logical and rhetorical interrelationships that exist among and between the subtopics, and then encourages students to elaborate and revise their plans. This software is based on juxtaposition as a spatial approach to prewriting.

In the section on editing and grammar programs, Michael Cohen and Richard Lanham (1984) describe software students can use to analyze their written style. The software identifies four different types of words and provides students with two different types of maps for visualizing how frequently the word types are employed and how they are arranged in a piece of writing. The first map is a "verbal surface map" that uses left and right columns to call out and identify the word types (85). According to Cohen and Lanham, "A student may regard the map as something like a high-contrast aerial photograph of the text, where ordinary words appear as hyphens, prepositions as P's, forms of *to be* as T's, and so forth. The map lets student writers see where the various word types appear, how they cluster, and how they interact" (86). The second map provides a "less denatured view" by simply adding a line break where each of the four types of words occurs (86). "The second display tactic," as Cohen and Lanham point out, "lets writers see the word types in context and works especially well with prepositions, as text displayed this way helps emphasize how prepositional phrases affect a sentence's rhythm" (87). The software can also produce graphs of sentence lengths to help students evaluate the "larger rhythmic features" of their texts (87). The software by Cohen and Lanham both re-spatializes verbal texts for analytical purposes and provides metadata about verbal texts in spatial forms. Their project anticipates the focus in the digital humanities on textual analysis and style, especially work on visualizing verbal information.

The pioneering work on desktop publishing is more animated about the role of space in discourse practices: after all, the point of desktop publishing is to overcome the spatial limitations of word processing, allowing writers to treat texts as compilations of discrete elements that can be located nearly anywhere in the geography of a page. Although word processing programs now include desktop publishing features, word processing and desktop publishing programs were initially linked in successive steps in a production workflow: students created their texts in a word processing program, "poured" them into a desktop publishing program, and then designed the spatial aspects. This workflow helped initiate the shift from writer to writer-designer that the field continues to explore today. As writer-designers, students and teachers began to "take control of the page" (Sullivan 1991, 44) and to learn to attend to such elements of composition as unity, balance, proportion, emphasis, and typographic design and layout. Mapping the fixed space of the printed page is something of an issue in word processing, but page specifications for student papers tend to be dictated by teachers and style guides. Desktop publishing widened the spatial terrain of texts and challenged students and teachers to become more capable of theorizing and representing spatial relationships in two dimensions.

Screens on digital devices can be static and two-dimensional, mimicking the affordances of printed pages. But hypertext provides a third dimension—depth—which turns the spatialities of production and consumption on their heads, as it were, enabling linking, layering, personalizing, tagging, and other discourse features that people now expect to find on the internet and elsewhere. Stephen Bernhardt (1993) discusses affordances of digital texts that tend to distinguish them from printed texts. Digital texts, especially hypertexts, are often situationally embedded, interactive, functionally mapped, modular, navigable, hierarchically embedded, spacious, graphically rich, and customizable and publishable (151–52). Bernhardt does not foreground space as an overarching concept within which to examine literacies and technologies, but let me quickly do so for the first five affordances to illustrate just how thoroughly the spatial has come to permeate writing and communication processes. As their descriptors indicate, the remaining affordances also involve spatial dimensions.

First, digital text is situationally embedded when it is "bound up within the context of situation—the ongoing activities and events that make the text part of the action" (Bernhardt 1993, 151). Reading digital text is often a secondary aspect of writing and problem solving, which provide the contexts for reading practices. For example, digital writing and reading often occur in multilayered, parallel spaces, and digital reading also often occurs in spaces that are parasitic to the environments that support writing and problem solving.

Digital text is interactive when it "invites readers to actively engage with it—both mentally and physically—rather than passively absorb information" (152). Interacting with a digital text can be spatial all the way down, from accessing to using to managing activities: readers open files and websites, navigate structures and content, and organize notes and resources.

Digital text is functionally mapped when the text "displays itself in ways that cue readers as to what can be done with it" (Bernhardt 1993, 152). Printed materials also cue readers with page numbers, indexes, section breaks, and more, but functional maps in hypertext are usually operational. Links, for example, when designed and implemented well, both provide information about available texts and actions and enact navigational choices within the spatial confines of the system.

Digital text is modular when it is "composed and presented in self-contained chunks, fragments, blocks" (Bernhardt 1993, 152). The amount of space a text occupies, and how it is arranged and consumed, is shaped by the attributes of information technologies. Screens have the capacity to scroll endlessly, but the fundamental architecture for hypertext is a node-link mechanism that conceptualizes texts as scaled-down nodes in a networked structure of interdependent literacy activities.

Finally, digital text is navigable when it "supports reader movement across large pools of information in different directions for different readers and purposes" (Bernhardt 1993, 152). The networked structures for hypertext are assembled and reassembled by active readers in concrete situations of use. Navigating among and within nodes of text is a key performative practice through which individuals construct and understand complex information spaces. As these examples illustrate, many of the distinguishing features of digital texts are designed by writers as spatial mechanisms for engaging information technologies.

Bernhardt (1993) demonstrates that "the screen is full of things to do, not just things to read" (158), but in 1993 he could not anticipate the extent to which the "doing" component would come to influence how the field thinks about writing and communication processes. This thinking is more additive than substitutive: invention, information design, and linking are ongoing concerns for students and teachers. Text-centered and user-centered frameworks, however, are beginning to be integrated into environment-centered approaches that invest heavily in the idea that understanding the spatial contexts for doing is essential to articulating how writing and communication processes ought to be taught and practiced. A good example is the Experience Architecture program at Michigan State University. In this program, and in courses in experience architecture at other schools with technical writing programs, students and teachers focus on tracing the activities and experiences of users as they attempt to do things with technologies. These tracings then become the basis for making decisions about how to structure writing and communication processes. Both parts of the endeavor are decidedly spatial in character. For example, students draw on journey mapping, ecosystem mapping, and eye-tracking techniques to create spatial representations of user activities and experiences and then use those representations to produce storyboards, sitemaps, and taxonomies for texts and hypertexts. Since the era of word processors, writing and communication practices have become increasingly spatial in their orientation and focus.

What Are the Implications of Information Technologies for the Where of Writing and Communication?

The geographies of pages and screens and how people go about designing discourses are important facets of the "where" of writing and communication, but here I am interested in the locations of literacies and technologies, in the shifting networks of physical and virtual sites occupied by both students and digital environments. Teachers have a growing sense that locations matter to literacy activities, that where people write and read influences how they write and read, and to no small degree. This is a basic proposition in the field, in fact, and is extrapolatable from (if not explicit in) models of the rhetorical situation that have guided teaching practices for years. Institutional contexts, of course, are a primary preoccupation for teachers and a site of extensive investigation into the roles of locations in discourse production and consumption. A popular essay by David Bartholomae (1986) drives home the need to pay attention to such roles. Bartholomae considers the discourses of academic communities and the challenges students face in attempting to appropriate the language-use practices of specialists from across a curriculum. As students traverse a university landscape, its disciplinary locations enable and constrain responses to writing problems, regulating what can be said and how in learning situations. The where of writing is partially constitutive of writing itself.

The classroom is a real world with future consequences, but a motivation underlying the social turn is the realization that writing is a form of social action and that it has the power to effect change in many arenas of culture. Nedra Reynolds (2007) identifies two notions of space operating in writing and communication situations. One is "the sense of place and space that readers and writers bring with them to [the] intellectual work of writing, to navigating, arranging, remembering, and composing," and the other is "the places where writing occurs" (176). The places the field has attended to include workplaces, community literacy programs, rural locations, religious locations, citizenship contexts, and homes. As sites of discursive practice, encountering such places provides an opportunity to experience the rootedness of literacy activities, discovering how local circumstances bear on the production and consumption of writing in nonacademic locations with significant consequences for education, work, and life. Place-based pedagogies forward the proposition that exposing students to nonacademic locations gives them "new ways of learning" and "different ways of seeing things that have been taught in our classes" (Heilker 1997, 72–73). Changes in the where of writing challenge students to accommodate the varying specificities of rhetorical situations and apply and adjust rhetorical frameworks to solve problems in the worlds beyond the borders of universities.

The physical locations for writing and communication have been fragmented and multiplied by the capabilities of mobile devices, which can turn any space into a location for the study and practice of literacies. In academic institutions with one-to-one laptop programs, traditional classrooms can become computer classrooms if there are Wi-Fi connections in buildings and power sources for recharging devices. One obvious benefit for students and teachers is ready access to low-tech solutions that can play a serviceable role in the enactment of digital pedagogies. And in both academic and nonacademic settings, the capabilities of mobile devices can collapse the distance between writing and research spaces, especially when the research involves fieldwork, allowing people to "research, write, and (ideally) publish on location" in seamless ways, in the places where rhetorical activities themselves take place (Bjork and Schwartz 2009, 224). The distinctions between writing spaces and other spaces are becoming increasingly blurred by mobile devices.

On the virtual front, writing and reading routinely happen in academic IT environments connected to wide-area networks. Wide-area networks have been a transformational development in the history of literacy technologies, and there is a vibrant discussion in the field about their implications for teaching and learning. Jeff Rice (2006) has gone so far as to argue that it would be profitable to turn to the network as a primary disciplinary metaphor because it emphasizes "the role connectivity plays in content management, information organization, and information production" and helps "information, people, places, and other items to establish a variety of relationships that previous spaces or ideologies of space (print being the dominant model) did not allow" (128). I agree that a focus on networked relationships provides a valuable lens through which to interrogate the domain of the field, recasting taken-for-granted practices and many assumptions about how writing and communication work and why. In classroom contexts, networks have enabled access to research materials that would otherwise be difficult if not impossible to use, interactions between students and authors that provide firsthand reflections on publication projects, collaborations between groups of students from different institutions, additional channels for communication in face-to-face environments, new options for civic engagement and public voice, workflows that reimagine the uses of instructional spaces and time, publishing venues for student work, and many other activities. The effects of networks touch on numerous relationships in learning situations.

One of the more immediate and consequential relationships affected by wide-area networks is between humans and machines. Teachers often think of machines as either separate from or extensions of student-users, but networks can make it difficult to determine where human activities end and where machine activities begin. As a form of spatial organization, networks do more than simply automate the circulation of data and information or connect people to people in a digital medium. Instead, as Shoshana Zuboff (1985) explains, networks also "informate" activities by creating new information about them or by contributing to their development. There are many examples of such human-machine collaborations in the discourse on posthumanism. Casey Boyle (2015) considers how the content and configuration of a software interface can be "the result of interactions that occur between the past uses of that interface, the device, and even geographical location" (18). Many of the algorithms that run the internet respond to the historical and spatial dimensions of writing and reading, including browsing and searching behaviors, and attempt to anticipate and cooperate with users as they engage in a range of intellectual transactions. And Jordan Frith (2015) dives deeply into the structures and dynamics of location-aware applications, which allow people to annotate digital media associated with physical spaces. As Frith details, the physical spatial experiences of people who use locative media can be very different from those who do not, for locative media continuously overlay existing representations of places with new and additional information. The where of writing, then, can involve human and nonhuman agents interacting in both physical and virtual spaces, with everything affecting everything else and the overall effect being more complex than it would at first appear.

How Should Instruction about Information Technologies Be Organized for Students Who Are Learning to Write and Communicate?

A long-standing concern in the field is how to integrate instruction about information technologies into writing and communication courses. Underlying this concern is a basic question about the boundaries of literacies and technologies. If I show my students how to use advanced features in a word processing program, am I still working in a valid instructional direction? Or should I ask them to take a course on the mechanics of word processing from an academic IT unit? If I assign a website project, should I require my students to code their projects in HTML, or can I allow them to use a visual web editor? If I ask them to write code, how should students learn how to do it? Can I teach coding as an element of the writing process? Ask students to complete tutorials? Allow them to cut and paste code from coding libraries? And if I outsource coding instruction, do I still need to supplement it in some way or another? For teachers of writing and communication, the boundaries between literacies and technologies have only become more and more porous and exploratory.

I suspect few teachers today would divorce the structures and processes of literacies and technologies, but the field has identified good reasons why teachers often proceed with approaches that subordinate technologies to literacies, ignoring or deferring the task of considering the recursive quality of their relationship. First and foremost, new teachers can be overwhelmed by the burdens of teaching as they attempt to learn about and prioritize work activities. One strategy for simplifying the curricular integration of technologies is to employ the instructional design strategy of first articulating pedagogical goals and then mapping out how technologies can support those goals. Such a strategy foregrounds disciplinary values and provides a measure of comfort for new teachers. Another reason teachers subordinate technologies to literacies is to help alleviate the demands of an overcrowded curriculum, which can stretch teachers to the limit and beyond. The curriculum in writing and communication programs seems to expand endlessly and in all directions, with new or newly invigorated areas continuously adding to teachers' repertoire. "Time," however, as Jenny Edbauer Rice (2008) reminds us, "is a serious issue where training and knowledge is concerned," and that means "learning new technology can be just one more thing to squeeze into an overcrowded day" (380). Staying current with academic IT can become a casualty of ever-widening agendas in the field. Lastly, in chapter 1, I discussed how tenure and promotion contexts value recognizable forms of engagement, thereby encouraging teachers to subordinate technologies to literacies. Tenure and promotion contexts tend to reinforce the status quo, not transform it. Projects involving technologies are no exception to this rule.

Despite certain challenges and risks, teachers have integrated instruction about technologies into writing and communication programs, identifying issues with spatial aspects and imagining effective and professionally responsible approaches. More than two decades ago, I studied the national scene to determine why and how teachers integrate computers into technical writing courses (Selber 1994). As far as I can tell, this study was the first to describe and organize such work as a whole. I categorized over one hundred computer-related courses from thirty-nine institutions into three broad categories to make some sense of the curricular geography at the time. The course categories reflect primary instructional goals of teachers: production courses, which introduce students to the skills and processes involved in using computers to support day-to-day activities; computer literacy courses, which broaden student understandings of computers as they relate to theories of reading, writing, and textuality; and courses that situate computers in historical, political, and social contexts, which help students examine the ideological nature of implementing and using computers (370–71). Although in 1994 I was surveying the use of desktop and laptop computers in labs and classrooms, the instructional goals I identified continue to resonate in the field.

Indeed, teachers remain preoccupied with thinking through how to address the functional aspects of technologies. For example, Stanley Dicks (2009) provides an approach to technological literacy that expands its scope and appeal, resituating functional skills in social terms and articulating new literacies for a knowledge society. Teachers also remain interested in the complex relationship between literacies and technologies and its influence on writing and communication. For example, Claire Lauer (2015) examines the affordances and constraints of visual design software for students who are creating multimodal documents. And teachers continue to consider how to situate technologies in cultural terms. For example, Leigh Gruwell (2015) offers a feminist intervention that raises critical awareness of the gendered dimensions of technological contexts, Adam Banks (2011) outlines a rhetoric for multimedia production grounded in the histories and vernacular practices of African American cultures, and Jonathan Alexander and William Banks (2004) consider how cultural notions of sexuality are instantiated in online pedagogical spaces. These areas are sometimes treated individually and sometimes bundled into integrated pedagogies.

One of the more pressing spatial issues has to do with scaffolding instruction. In a previous book, I provide a heuristic teachers can use for conceptualizing how to integrate technologies into writing and communication programs (Selber 2004). The heuristic includes technical, pedagogical, curricular, departmental, and institutional requirements for change (here I define *institutional requirements* as those existing beyond the purview of a single department). I distinguish three overlapping subject positions for students—users, questioners, and producers of technologies—and map out several curricular geographies that can support the development of multiliterate students, students who can employ functional, critical, and rhetorical literacies to solve consequential problems (210–24). The curricular geographies in my scheme represent different spatial options for integrating functional, critical, and rhetorical literacies into courses for teachers with varying institutional approaches and resources: programs can offer at least one course in each of the three areas, and teachers can integrate the literacies into a single course or assignment. In sum, I encourage teachers to conceptualize the framework of functional, critical, and rhetorical literacies as a fractal that can be applied in ever-smaller scales to the curricular components of programs—that is, to curricula as a whole, to specific courses, and to individual assignments. These different spatial options represent points of pedagogical extensibility in instructional contexts for technologies.

I should also elaborate on the spatial option of outsourcing instruction about technologies to academic IT units. Academic IT units are an official institutional location of support for teachers who are integrating technologies into classrooms and for students who are using them for projects, but this agenda is fraught with a challenge that reflects the diverse needs of university audiences: the support provided by academic IT units is necessarily generic and incomplete and must be restricted to rather general discussions. For example, students and teachers at Penn State can take short courses on how to use the software in computer classrooms. Teachers who would like a staff member from the Training Services group to come to their classroom and provide the instruction for everyone in a class can schedule these courses. I often invite a Penn State trainer to my classroom to introduce our WordPress publishing system, which students use to create e-portfolios. This session covers numerous topics, including how to create a site, select a theme, change a header image, manage page content, reorder pages, use widgets, and publish pages. Although trainers ask teachers to send them a course syllabus in advance, trainers cannot possibly tailor their training for everyone: it would be unrealistic to expect trainers to have domain knowledge in academic fields, which is crucial to customizing training for individual courses. Academic IT units therefore turn to a one-dimensional approach that succeeds by separating functional and conceptual knowledge, focusing on how to do things with academic IT rather than on why and how to do things in specific contexts.

So in my course, for example, the trainer shows students the menu commands for making linking structures but does not—and cannot, really—situate those commands in a larger pedagogical discussion about what constitutes useful linking structures and why in a writing portfolio. One of my roles, then, is to recontextualize the functional knowledge displayed by the trainer with conceptual knowledge from the field, providing elaborations—in real time and in subsequent class sessions—that address the recursive relationship between functional and conceptual knowledge and fill in other gaps in institutional approaches to training. My intervention bridges the unavoidable pedagogical spaces between academic departments and academic IT units.

How Is Power Exercised in the Spatial Contexts for Information Technologies?

The exercise of power continues to be at the center of field discussions of the spatial contexts for information technologies. Even discussions that attend to other matters often encompass issues of power and control. Consider my earlier treatment of desktop publishing. Although teachers focus on spatial design options, what is happening below the surface is a shift in power that enables writers to assume more control over publication processes. Or consider my earlier treatment of software created by teachers. Although teachers focus on the affordances for student writers, homegrown software is often inspired by a dissatisfaction with the prevailing choices in a marketplace. Power is an institutional phenomenon that helps determine what is possible in specific situations.

The possibilities are not dictated by academic institutions in a top-down fashion but emerge from the relationships in sociotechnical articulations, which are constantly regrouping. If I wanted to add a new course to the distance education portfolio in my department, I would need to consider the status and condition of a whole host of things: the policies and procedures of the World Campus, English department, and writing program; the resources provided by the TLT unit; the affordances and constraints of the course-management system; the content and design of existing courses in the portfolio; the e-book market for textbooks; the abilities of students and teachers; and the resources available for course maintenance. Although certain elements in this sociotechnical articulation could become more influential than others, no one element would dictate the outcome of the process: power emanates from a variety of sources and is enacted in institutions as people work to realize what is possible and why at particular times and places. All at once, power both enables and constrains pedagogical activities.

The enduring field interest in the exercise of power is distinguishable in all the primary areas organizing this book: institutions, literacies, and technologies. I will begin with some of the ways the field has thought about power in technological and pedagogical contexts and end with a concern I have about how the field ascribes agency to institutional formations. An obvious starting place is the digital divide, a spatial formulation that groups people into two distinct categories: the haves and have-nots. This formulation is an artifact of a one-dimensional understanding of access that gained prominence in the 1990s and is still discernible in educational initiatives. In 1995, newly elected Speaker of the House Newt Gingrich famously gave voice to issues of access by proposing an entitlement program that would provide tax credits to the poor for purchasing laptops, a proposal Gingrich later disavowed because of its price tag (forty billion dollars) and because the poor pay very little taxes anyway. But the sentiment underlying the proposal echoes a persistent perspective in Western culture: technology alone will make the difference between success and failure in solving complex societal problems.

A prominent example is the One Laptop per Child (OLPC) program (http://one.laptop.org). I very much admire this program, which has distributed over three million laptops to children and teachers in inner-city US schools and in more than fifty countries. The program supplies network-enabled laptops that are inexpensive and durable, require a small amount of energy, and provide useful applications. Access to hardware and software is essential to students and teachers, but implementation cases from the program illustrate problems with a technicist approach. In Rwanda, for instance, some government donors believe the money for laptops and networks would be better spent on teacher training programs, which are struggling to keep pace with the rapid expansion of educational opportunities throughout the country (Beaumont 2010). The OLPC program defines the gap in the digital divide as a technological one and bridges it with hardware and software initiatives. Their approach reduces a complex problem to a simple unit of analysis and measurement and views technology as the only solution to the crisis.

But there is more than just a technological gap between the haves and have-nots, for access is a multifaceted problem with many dimensions. This realization has been a motivating force in the field, which has responded to one-dimensional understandings of access with rhetorical interventions that account for a variety of determining factors in institutions. Adam Banks (2006) incorporates much of this work into a spatial scheme (a table) that avoids reducing the digital divide to a binary state of affairs based on a single factor or criterion. "Meaningful access," Banks notes, "requires users, individually and collectively, to be able to use, critique, resist, design, and change technologies in ways that are relevant to their lives and needs, rather than those of the corporations that hope to sell them" (41). The grid of his table thus organizes crucial questions of access around the parameters of critique, use, and design, constructing access as a dynamic sociotechnical process that is activist in nature. The ability to critique, use, and design technologies for specific purposes depends on infrastructure that encourages functional access, which promotes the capacity to use technologies effectively (41); experiential access, which produces the capacity to make technologies relevant in concrete situations of use (42); critical access, which produces the capacity to assess both benefits and problems (42); and transformative access, which cultivates the capacity to help transform the institutions in which technologies are embedded and constructed (45). Bridging the gap in the digital divide requires progress on several institutional fronts; students can have physical access to academic IT and still be techno-poor.

In addition, teachers have also done an effective job of critiquing the value systems embodied in the interfaces that mediate writing and communication. This critique is essential to any and all pedagogical programs and reminds teachers that interfaces function as structuring elements in teaching and learning situations, making suggestions about how literacy ought to operate in the university and beyond. A frequently cited essay on the spatial exercise of power is by Cynthia Selfe and Richard Selfe (1994). Selfe and Selfe imagine computer interfaces as borderland maps that "enact—among other things—the gestures and deeds of colonialism, continuously and with a great deal of success" (482). Although they note that interfaces can also support democratic aims, the point of the essay is to illuminate how interfaces reify dominant cultural values, especially the values associated with capitalism and class privilege, discursive privilege, and rationalism and logocentric privilege. Examples of the interface design practices critiqued by Selfe and Selfe include the use of the desktop metaphor, which is "constituted by and for white middle- and upper-class users to replicate a world that they know and feel comfortable in" (486), and the use of standard English as the default language for menu commands, which reinforces "the tendency to ignore, or even erase, the cultures of non-English language background speakers in this country" (488). Such practices are indeed exclusionary, promoting the perspectives of specific groups at the expense of others, and teachers need to respond to the practices by which interfaces come to be constructed according to a narrow sense of user needs.

Interfaces themselves, however, do not preordain power relationships or user activities. I am certain Selfe and Selfe would agree with this point, for they emphasize the cultural forces that shore up privileged positions in technological contexts. But the spatial boundaries for their analyses, as

Patricia Sullivan and James Porter (1997) argue, could be more inclusive of "the situated uses of the interface by practicing writers, the interaction between users and the physical/visual components of the computer" (135). The point Sullivan and Porter are making is that "it's hard to make judgments about the hegemony of the technology itself (as formalized, abstracted system) without examining the situated interactions between technology and users" (135)—that is, without expanding the spatial boundaries of interfaces to encompass the activity spheres of writers and writing situations. In practice, interfaces spread out across multiple elements and become imbued with meaning in the context of sociotechnical articulations.

If teachers have complicated commonsense notions of access and interfaces and the possibilities these areas signify for action and change, they have also been alert to the role technologies play in helping create and maintain power relations. In spatial terms, a main thrust of this attention has been on investigating strategies for decentering the role of teachers and opening up the canon of genre activities that teachers assign in courses. The idea of decentering the role of teachers acknowledges that teachers themselves are implicated in relations of power and must therefore take some responsibility for the nature of existing institutional conditions. An example of an ongoing effort is the use of networks to amplify multiple voices and points of view in classrooms. The initial wave of work was motivated by the proposition that information technologies have nonhierarchical features and that such features can be exploited for liberatory purposes, to multiply and diversify the available channels for participation and learning and to foreground student perspectives as valid forms of knowledge (Sproull and Kiesler 1992). Although this proposition continues to be explored and tested as technologies develop and change, the field has come to realize that networks are not inherently liberating or empowering and that a variety of elements in sociotechnical articulations can impede learning. For instance, disciplinary discourse is itself a locus of power that can regulate the boundaries of what is considered acceptable and unacceptable behavior in conversational exchanges on the internet (Johnson-Eilola and Selber 1996).

The idea of opening up the canon of genre activities acknowledges that teachers must be willing to become learners in their own classrooms. Genres instantiate power and authority in that they enable and constrain the possibilities for communicative action—pedagogical action included—in specific situations: power and authority are not distributed across institutions in a uniform fashion but experienced and enacted in space and time. Genres aid writers by providing inventional and organizational frameworks and constrain them by limiting form, content, and style; in part, the constraints are productive because they help writers create and meet audience expectations. But disciplinary investments in genres can also constrain teachers from considering nontraditional approaches and building instructional capabilities with technologies, especially in classrooms where teachers determine in advance the genres and media for assignments. Jody Shipka (2011) admonishes teachers to step outside of their comfort zones and to structure assignments in which choices of genre and media follow student decisions about the "purposes, potentials, and contexts of their work" (88). Her approach challenges teachers to try new things and learn from compositional processes that require a critical openness to all modes of meaning making. Such openness is a source of vulnerability but also power because it can serve to expand the field of possibilities in writing and communication courses.

I want to end this section with a concern I have about how the field ascribes agency in institutions. Although the field has developed a rich theoretical understanding of the workings of power in institutions, in everyday practice, teachers are capable of expressing an "us-versus-them" mentality, which pits teachers against institutions and creates false dichotomies between power and powerlessness or liberation and oppression. In this traditional perspective, power is tied to a hierarchy of authority in which institutions hold power over teachers and teachers, as institutional agents, hold power over students. The only way to achieve change is for institutions to redistribute power to the oppressed. However, as I have already discussed, institutional power operates in more complex and subtle ways, as spatial practices and relationships open and close potential avenues for action.

In discussing the prevalence of an "us-versus-them" mentality in the humanities, Cathy Davidson (2000) observes that "power always looks monolithic from below" (105) and that it is too convenient for humanities colleagues who are feeling beleaguered by institutions to portray administrators as an "all-powerful 'they' who will not like us or understand us or have our best interests at heart" (98). She encourages such colleagues to imagine institutions "less as binaric and hegemonic structures of power than as conglomerations of power, with elaborate checks and balances, advisory capabilities, democratic glimmerings, and complex levels of reporting and responsibility in which the individual—however minor a figure one cuts or feels like one cuts—has some shaping power" (104–5). I cite Davidson because she reminds teachers of their active role in power relations but also because she wants to clarify the "them" in the "us-versus-them" formulation: Who, exactly, is the *them* here? What are their priorities and constraints? And what is within their realm of possibilities? Institutional agents, including academic IT specialists and upper-level administrators, can certainly act as barriers to change, but barriers cannot be addressed effectively without a concrete sense of who the institutional agents are and what they are actually capable of doing.

The enduring spatial questions involving academic IT encompass writing processes, the locations of writing activities, methods for organizing technology instruction, and power dynamics in institutions. Writing processes are inherently spatial and have only become more so since the advent of digital technologies, which emphasize linking, layering, tagging, and other spatialized discourse features. These features, in addition, emphasize doing as well as reading, creating an imperative for writers to understand the spatial contexts for doing, which are beginning to influence how teachers think about workflows and pedagogies. The locations of writing, physical and virtual, shape how people write and read, and to great effect. But the "where" of discourse production and reception has also taken on added complexity as people leverage the capabilities of mobile devices and as internet algorithms leverage the spatial and historical dimensions of human activities. Methods for organizing instruction about technologies are a crucial spatial aspect of curricular development, one that requires teachers to scaffold some combination of functional, critical, and rhetorical literacies into writing courses and to contextualize the training academic IT units provide. Finally, power dynamics in institutions are determined by the nature of the relationships in sociotechnical articulations, which open and close possibilities for conceptualizing digital divides, representing and interpreting mediating interfaces, and structuring student-to-student and student-to-teacher interactions. In ongoing ways, spatial attributes are a domain of institutional life for teachers of writing and communication everywhere.

SPATIAL ELEMENTS OF THE HEURISTIC

This part of my heuristic covers a variety of different types of spatial elements, for the spatiality of institutions permeates academic IT contexts in thoroughgoing ways. The elements examined here are not so easily separated in practice or theory, but I will treat them independently for explanatory purposes (table 3.1). Hierarchies organize institutional practices in central ways, for better and worse. I will consider the hierarchies that

TABLE 3.1   Spatial elements of the heuristic

Dimension elements	Spatial elaborations
Hierarchies	Academic IT units reside in hierarchies that institutionalize actions and activities and organize sociotechnical relationships. Hierarchies provide a framework for designating responsibilities but also accommodate different types of hierarchies and other forms of spatial organization.
Processes	Academic IT units employ systematic work processes at macro and micro levels. Process-driven approaches provide a holistic view of institutional practices and a sense of spatial continuity in project and product development.
Methods	Academic IT units use research methods to produce knowledge and understanding about teaching and learning activities. Institutional needs, which can be understood in spatial terms as either internal or external, are key factors in determining methodological choices and setting expectations for the quality and rigor of the research.
Bodies	Academic IT units embrace perspectives on bodies that assign different roles and capacities to information technologies. The embodied spatial practices of students and teachers are themselves (at least in part) institutionally constructed aspects of teaching and learning contexts.

organize academic IT units and the types of interactions they encourage and support. Processes are a core asset in academic IT units, organizing their approaches to institutional work in a systematic fashion. Methods, particularly research methods, are used to produce institutional knowledge in academic IT units. I will discuss popular methods and the challenges they present for studying teaching and learning contexts. Finally, bodies are involved in all the human-machine interactions that academic IT units support. I will present prevailing perspectives on the embodied practices of students and teachers and discuss the variety of ends these perspectives can serve. As a whole, hierarchies, processes, methods, and bodies constitute a rich conceptual framework for imagining spatial dimensions of institutions.

Hierarchies

Hierarchies are a (if not the) primary organizing structure in academic institutions. According to historian Frederick Rudolph (1990), in the late nineteenth century, universities turned to hierarchical structures to help them manage growth on more than one front: "An academic hierarchy was a response to the expansion of the institutions themselves and to the growth of knowledge itself, and it was a conscious and clearly necessary effort to deal efficiently and effectively with problems that could not be met without order and organization" (398). The problems Rudolph refers to were precipitated by the ascendancy of American universities as research institutions and centers of science and scholarship, a phenomenon that involved the disaggregation of knowledge into knowledge domains, the formation of disciplinary specialties, the creation of academic departments to house and support those specialties, and the development of measuring techniques for awarding institutional status and resources. In the hierarchically infused world of universities, competition became a yardstick for measuring progress, and research publications became a keystone of the academic economy. It follows from this spatial logic that faculty would be ranked according to their ability to produce publishable work. The heightened focus on research relegated teaching to an inferior hierarchical position, initiating an asymmetrical institutional relationship that has been a long time in the making.

Teachers have been critics of many of the justifications for hierarchical structures in universities, including arguments for using technologies to make education a more efficient process. Michael Bérubé (1998) confronts the cultural view that universities are no different from corporate organizations and that they should therefore be run like a business enterprise—that is, in a top-down fashion and with an eye toward maximizing productivity and profits. Although universities must be entrepreneurial and sensitive to costs, especially rising tuition rates, Bérubé comments on two contradictory realities. First, despite what critics of academia might think or demand, in many respects universities already function like businesses, using reward structures to reinforce institutional values: "The more contact you have with undergraduate writing," Bérubé explains, "the lower your salary" (B5). Second, those very institutional values work against the concurrent desire of critics to treat students as individuals and provide them with the support they need to achieve their potential. The contradiction is between standardization and personalization, two potential outcomes in academic IT initiatives that could coexist or complement one another but oftentimes collide. In the case of measures that aim to cut costs by rationalizing and dehumanizing instruction (such as automating essay grading or increasing class sizes without addressing quality issues), Bérubé admonishes that "a better university for students in the liberal arts is, above all, an inefficient university. It is a university where student writing is copious and carefully read, and where students themselves are names, faces, and advisees, not modular production units" (B5). Teachers have attempted to resist institutional hierarchies and the associated labor practices that devalue the work of the field and diminish learning.

Of course, as spatial forms of organization, hierarchical structures both solve and create problems: they are not always or necessarily negative in their impact. In academic IT units, hierarchies offer advantages for certain aspects of work. As I will discuss in the next section, there are any number of decision-making processes in academic IT units, but all of them have at least one thing in common: specifying points of accountability in institutional practices. At the end of the day, there needs to be clarity about who is responsible for what and who has the authority for decision-making, especially when there are differences of opinion about how to do things. The managerial control hierarchy creates a chain of command that extends from the top of an institution to the bottom. This chain of command is meant to ensure that academic IT units meet deadlines and budgets and accomplish their work in a coordinated fashion. It is also helpful in emergencies, such as when a course-management system goes down, or in situations where the problems are worse: all institutions have disaster recovery plans that provide a road map for restoring damaged systems. These plans assign responsibilities to individuals.

The advantages of hierarchies also have to do with centralizing facets of authority. There is a formal communication channel in academic IT units in which messages flow downward from individuals in higher levels of the hierarchy to those in lower levels. Downward channels create a clear line of communication for broadcasting vision and mission statements, explaining policies and procedures, assigning and delegating tasks, and appraising work performance. It is hard to imagine how academic IT units would be able to function without clear lines of communication or responsibility.

At the same time, hierarchies are not monolithic spatial structures but can be unpacked to reveal various managerial styles and institutional tensions and relationships. To use a binary formulation prominent in discussions of institutional management, managerial styles range from hard to soft approaches, and attributes of both styles are often discernible (in different ratios) in a single workplace setting. Leaders with a managerial style on the hard end of the spectrum think about workers as institutional resources that need to be supervised at the highest practical level to achieve efficiency and performance targets and maximize collective utility. A hard management style exercises tight control over worker activities. In contrast, leaders with a management style on the soft end of the spectrum think about workers as individuals that should be empowered to make certain types of decisions and contribute their own unique talents. A soft management style embraces the notion that workers are most productive and satisfied when their jobs provide room to maneuver and grow and when their perspectives are listened to and valued.

Leaders in academic IT units tend to appreciate soft managerial approaches, in part because IT units share a belief in collegiality with the broader academic community and in part because soft managerial approaches recognize that people are different from other types of resources and thus should not be treated like cogs in a machine. In reflecting on his own development as an academic IT leader, Timothy Chester (2015) notes that "as individuals begin their careers, leadership tends to look, from a distance, a lot like making decisions, allocating resources, and sitting atop a hierarchy. But as perspectives mature and careers advance, we come to the realization that leadership is about something else entirely" (38). What leadership is really about, according to Chester, is having the insight to see the chain of command as a series of trusting and respectful relationships that results in honest and frank conversations and thoughtful collaborations. A misconception about such relationships is that they produce a cacophony of worker voices that can stifle institutional efforts. But with soft managerial approaches, Sherri Parker (2014) of Harrison College clarifies, "there is still hierarchy in the organizational chart, and we certainly have vision coming from the top; however, there is also a collaborative approach to rollout, with freedom to discuss, collaborate, challenge, and tweak as necessary." Furthermore, Parker adds, "when things are not going as they should and problems crop up, we are expected to bring these issues forward with solutions to address them." Soft managerial approaches prize feedback loops that involve people from all areas of an institution, including teaching.

In addition to feedback loops, institutions also include different kinds of hierarchies that can reorder the spatial positioning of workers in specific situations. It is commonplace to assume that the hierarchical status of workers is fixed and stable, that the organizational chart displays a static authority structure that is relevant in all instances. In academic IT units, the spatial arrangement of the organizational chart represents a direct reporting line from ranked managerial positions to hourly workers. Ranking workers according to their level of institutional authority for decision-making appears to be self-evident and unambiguous. But there are other kinds of hierarchies in which the authority status of individuals is not connected to their formal responsibilities for exercising control. I am thinking of hierarchies of access, experience, and expertise. An example of access hierarchies can be seen when it comes to histories. Workers with long-term institutional memories provide vital insights into how and why projects and processes were initiated and implemented, helping academic IT units avoid repeating past mistakes or reinventing the wheel. Hierarchies of access—to data and information, historical or otherwise, but also to other types of resources and to people—can redraw lines of authority in particular instances and affect the status of workers.

Internship programs provide an example of experience hierarchies. Student interns, who most often have the least amount of authority on an organizational chart, inevitably seem to show their supervisors something valuable about how to use academic IT. In one of my more memorable meetings, a student intern showed her supervisor how to link his social media accounts in order to better manage the flow of content creation and publishing. For social media projects at least, the experience of the intern changed her authority status from a novice to a more advanced position. And an example of expertise hierarchies can be seen when it comes to the knowledge domains that are salient to the development of academic IT projects. The knowledge domains involved in projects are numerous and overlapping, but organizational charts often indicate specialty areas for institutional workers, such as software programming, server administration, and instructional design. As I noted in chapter 1, the vast majority of academic IT specialists have never taught a college course, yet they would agree wholeheartedly that pedagogical expertise is an essential knowledge domain for most projects. In projects in which pedagogical expertise is germane to the issues at hand, teachers move up the hierarchies of authority and responsibility within academic IT units, encouraging academic IT units to align themselves with teachers who can function effectively as active members of collaborative teams. Where teachers are located in those hierarchies will vary from situation to situation, depending on the specifics of individual projects.

If institutions contain different kinds of hierarchies, they also include other forms of spatial organization. In academic IT units, the most prevalent additional spatial form for organizing work is the network. Although networks exist within hierarchies and hierarchies within networks, they are frequently viewed as opposing paradigms for running institutions: hierarchies are vertical structures that centralize power and decision-making authority at the top of institutions; networks are horizontal structures that disperse power and control across the functional boundaries of organizational charts. From my experiences, I am not inclined to see hierarchies and networks as dueling institutional structures, particularly if one is considered superior to the other in any and all contexts. Instead, it may be more profitable to think of them as not only intertwined in the fabric of institutional life but also good for different things.

John Kotter (2011) contends that "the successful organization of the future will have two organizational structures: a Hierarchy, and a more teaming, egalitarian, and adaptive Network." He goes on to note that "both are designed and purposive. While the Hierarchy is as important as it has always been for optimizing work, the Network is where big change happens. It allows a company to more easily spot big opportunities and then change itself to grab them." One reason networked configurations can encourage change is because they remap communication and interaction patterns, giving rise to opportunities to think outside the box of normal institutional arrangements. For example, the TLT unit uses "hot teams" to investigate the potential of new technologies. These teams, which are based on interest and expertise, are composed of four to six people from different institutional areas who are networked together to assess the applications and prepare reports. The people can include managers, technologists, instructional designers, multimedia developers, librarians, teachers, and students. In the past, hot teams have explored the potential of Google applications, paperless grading tools, online video editors, mobile technologies, and digital pens. Hot teams are constituted for each specific inquiry and then disperse when the job is done, usually in a month or so. In productive collaborations that result in useful reports, team members believe in the value of shared leadership and trust each other enough to let down their guards and express divergent viewpoints. What is more, effective teams have clearly defined tasks and genres. If a summary report suggests that a pilot program is warranted and if the pilot program concludes that the new application should be developed for students and teachers, then the application and its support structure are operationalized and scaled via the managing routines of institutional hierarchies. In this example, networks as aids to invention are embedded in larger spatial forms for organizing work.

Hierarchies provide a coherent system for institutionalizing actions and decision-making. Teachers have identified problems with hierarchies, especially in critiques that consider the enduring field question of how power is exercised in the spatial contexts for information technologies. Hierarchies, however, are not totalizing structures for academic IT workers, for hierarchies always exist in the midst of institutional tensions and contradictions that open up fields of possibilities for interaction and communication. Hierarchies provide a transparent framework for designating responsibilities and directing communication in a downward fashion, but they also include different kinds of hierarchies that reposition the authority status of workers in specific situations and accommodate networks that flatten hierarchical structures and enable horizontal interactions. These shifting spatial patterns are an institutional resource teachers can use to involve themselves with academic IT units.

Processes

Ad hoc approaches can be adequate in certain situations, but much of the work of academic IT units is process driven and iterative by design. By process driven, I mean the work is decomposed into phased tasks that lead to the implementation of products or services for university communities. Process-driven approaches are also used to generate data and information about university business practices, including assessments and reflections. By iterative, I mean the work is evaluated incrementally with other academic IT specialists, administrators, and users as phases unfold or end. I distinguish two process categories—macrolevel and microlevel—in order to illustrate touchpoints at different spatial levels where teachers and students can contribute to academic IT enterprises. Macrolevel processes are characterized by a strong coupling between academic IT units and broader institutional structures. The main example I will consider is academic IT governance, which involves nearly all the domains of institutional organization. Microlevel processes, in contrast, are more insulated from broader institutional structures, targeting tasks at the unit level. The main example I will consider here is product management. Both process categories contain meaningful possibilities for institutional interventions.

Discussions of process-driven operations are often located in business books that introduce Six Sigma, lean management, and other approaches to helping organizations transition from organizational models based on functions or specializations to those based on work processes and cross-disciplinary teams. For my purposes, I want to note three traits of process-driven approaches that are compatible with the goal of expanding engagement with academic IT units. First, process-driven approaches provide a holistic view of institutional practices, allowing people to contextualize and troubleshoot the tasks for which they are responsible. Consider the task of designing the desktop configuration for a computer classroom, a task usually given to a systems administrator. Although multiple designs are valid for the classroom, the most effective one can only be determined by understanding the purposes and users of the space, the instructional methods that will be enacted in the space, and how the space relates to other classrooms. Such an understanding requires the systems administrator to be enmeshed in the full end-to-end process of computer classroom design, from planning to implementation with actual students and teachers.

Second, process-driven approaches provide a sense of spatial continuity that is independent of individuals. In chapter 2, I argued that institutions want to sustain continuity between past and present actions but also that continuity is both perpetuated and disrupted by routine institutional practices, which associate elements or events (in seemingly continuous sequences) through recursive linkages that point backward and forward in time. Process-driven approaches aid the desire to sustain continuity by defining how work is accomplished in spatial relationships and establishing a semblance of uniformity in project execution. For example, if an academic IT unit hires additional instructional designers to support a growing distance education portfolio, those designers will be introduced to an approach that defines the phases—planning, prototyping, assessing, and so on—and the actors, as in programmers, artists, editors, teachers, and students. The process recruits cross-functionally and at various levels within the institution, and continuity is preserved (as much as possible) as particular individuals in specific job positions come and go. For teachers, what is decisive in the first place is being defined in academic IT processes as relevant institutional actors.

Third, process-driven approaches heighten sensitivity to fundamental rhetorical considerations. A key distinction of process-driven approaches is that all the tasks share the objective of meeting the needs of audiences (versus satisfying the functional targets of organizational units). In fact, each task in a process, no matter its scope or spatial location, is informed by institutional answers to the same sorts of rhetorical questions: Who are our audiences? What do they need from our products or services? How do our processes help meet their needs? Workers in all areas, at least in theory, understand how what they do advances an overall strategy for creating value for audiences and helping deliver that value above everything else.

As I mentioned earlier, macrolevel processes are characterized by a strong coupling between academic IT units and broader institutional structures. Broader institutional structures, such as strategic-planning cycles, faculty and student consultation workflows, and approval requirements, provide some of the more inclusive processes for determining the shape of academic IT enterprises. At most if not all schools, establishing new systems for a majority of the university population requires robust planning and implementation processes and various approval stages. Even boards of trustees can become involved: at Penn State, an expenditure exceeding five million dollars must be approved by our board, which asks more than a few questions about the nature of the project. Although this amount may sound high or only applicable to large schools, start-up and ongoing costs for enterprise-wide initiatives add up quickly. But even endeavors on a modest financial scale can employ processes that incorporate broader institutional structures, for cost is only one dimension of institutionalization. An example is the adoption of academic IT standards for accessible design. At a minimum, accessible design standards should be adopted and adapted in consultation with legal, policy, and disability offices and with students and teachers with disabilities (for a process-driven approach to accessibility, see Horton and Sloan 2014).

When it comes to macrolevel processes, academic IT governance is a good example because it is a routine practice that involves multiple institutional structures. Spatially, the concerns of academic IT governance rank over and above those of development, implementation, and management in the planning hierarchy for universities, addressing broad issues of ambition, alignment, performance, assessment, and risk. By making explicit and public the goals for academic IT endeavors, the ways those endeavors align with institutional priorities, the expectations for performance and returns on investments, the methods for measuring outcomes, and the procedures for mitigating risks, institutions aim to be transparent about how academic IT is organized and managed. Governance processes also attempt to broaden university involvement in all aspects of decision-making and articulate an overall direction that can lead to more integrated approaches in cross-institutional work.

As with many approaches to governance, the framework at the University of Minnesota emphasizes consultation and deliberation (https:// it.umn.edu). The framework itself is conceptualized as an annual process with four phases: input (spring), decision (summer), funding (fall), and execution (winter). During the input phase, users are invited to fill out a survey asking them about their role at the university, satisfaction level with the current systems, and academic IT priorities. Users can also request a face-to-face meeting with an associate CIO to share ideas or express concerns in a more personal forum. During the decision phase, people synthesize the gathered information and finalize priorities: associate CIOs collaborate with university constituencies to identify themes and issues in the survey data and to review information from individual meetings; the CIO shares the themes and issues with chancellors, vice presidents, and deans, who provide feedback; and then a final list of recommendations is presented to the Operational Excellence Committee, a presidential-level committee charged with improving how the university functions as a whole. During the funding phase, the finalized recommendations are shared with the university community, and budgeting and preliminary planning processes begin. Budgeting for academic IT expenditures coincides with the general budgeting process. Global priorities for the university system can be funded more or less immediately while local priorities enter the compact planning process, which involves generating written agreements between university leadership teams and academic IT units that specify goals, action plans, and accountability measures. These written agreements are available to the public.

During the execution phase, leaders from academic IT units are assigned to projects as project sponsors, and the first task for sponsors is to draft and review charge statements. Project sponsors then constitute formal communities of practice (including students and teachers) to implement the recommendations. As this example illustrates, macrolevel processes for academic IT governance enact institutional commitments to openness and inclusion that span many spatial scales, and academic IT specialists take these commitments seriously. As James Penrod (2003) stresses in his guidelines for designing effective governance programs, "It is imperative for the IT governance structure to be representative and for the decision-making processes to be reasonably deliberate, enabling a wide range of IT clients to have some meaningful voice in how their services are provided" (19). Teachers should embrace such opportunities for participation and deliberate knowledgeably as university citizens.

The execution phase of IT governance at the University of Minnesota highlights an institutional moment of demarcation between macrolevel and microlevel processes. As initiatives transition from proposal to project stages, academic IT units introduce microlevel processes that bring order and coherence to complex situations of practice. Although the two types of processes are connected—macrolevel processes define strategies and parameters that affect microlevel processes—academic IT units still exercise a fair degree of control over their own approaches to solving institutional problems. The approaches at their disposal are not idiosyncratic or expressive of particular personalities but part of the skilled repertoire of professionals in the field. There are even established processes for managing processes. For instance, many academic IT units use the Information Technology Infrastructure Library (ITIL) as an overarching framework for unifying the various process-based endeavors at their schools. As with macrolevel processes, microlevel processes afford regular occasions for users to engage the scenes of practice for academic IT units (user involvement is a cornerstone principle of the ITIL method). Because all academic IT units spend a considerable amount of time managing products, product management is an area in which microlevel processes are constantly mobilized and refined.

The focus of product management is on sustaining existing systems for academic IT users. Sustaining a system involves both technical and social components, but the social components provide some of the most meaningful insights for teaching and learning. Product managers prioritize the tasks of reaching out to users and learning about their concrete experiences. "There is no substitute for going out on campus and visiting directly with end users, distributed IT staff, business managers, and others," says a product manager at the University of Notre Dame. "Even better," he continues, "watch users interact with your products, and you will open your eyes to how people *actually* use them" (Grundy 2015). To realize the hands-on philosophy of product management, managers apply a variety of microlevel processes to assess and improve the ongoing experiences of users, including those for structuring training sessions, usability evaluations, focus groups, and help desks. Training sessions, for example, can span from informal peer-to-peer mentoring sessions in offices to formal workshops in labs, and usability tests can be text centered, user centered, or environment centered, with testers investigating locations for increasingly social and spatial user actions. Microlevel processes are layered across the end-user life cycles of academic IT products and their use contexts, integrating occasions in which product managers can and should advocate for teachers and students and in which teachers and students can and should advocate for themselves.

Understanding how things work is a first step toward institutional change. In academic IT units, systematic processes at the macro and micro levels routinely define how things work. These processes, by definition and design, provide a holistic view of institutional practices and a sense of spatial continuity in systems development. They also accentuate the importance of user advocacy and participation and delineate areas in which students and teachers can contribute in meaningful ways to the endeavors of institutions. Teachers should be sympathetic to process-oriented environments, immersed as they are in their own processes for writing and the teaching of writing. But there is also a natural alignment with the enduring spatial questions in the field. For example, academic IT processes for supporting networks have an impact on where and how writing is practiced by students, academic IT processes for structuring software training have an impact on how teachers approach teaching about technologies, and academic IT processes for prioritizing the features of mediating interfaces have an impact on what is possible in classrooms and on institutional power dynamics. The enduring spatial questions in the field are of a piece with the process-driven approaches of academic IT units.

Methods

My discussion of processes focused on spatial patterns that organize work in academic IT units. Here I consider research methods used to produce knowledge about teaching and learning with information technologies. Teachers of writing and communication are trained to select their methods after establishing research questions, matching methods to the purposes of studies, the questions and contexts, and the available resources. This approach also makes sense for academic IT specialists, especially when writing for publication, but their overriding consideration is a spatial one: Does the research fulfill an internal or external need? Although institutions are able to support a panoply of research projects, there is a hierarchy that positions internal over external research, to support planning, recruiting, and branding efforts and to support complying with certification standards and regulatory requirements. If external research is a second-place priority, however, it is a close one: academic IT units are committed to contributing to pedagogical knowledge bases, including publishing about internal research when it makes sense to do so. In addition to the distinction between internal and external research, there is also a subdistinction between secondary and primary methods, resulting in four categories of research: internal secondary research, internal primary research, external secondary research, and external primary research. For each spatial category, I will discuss a popular method and some of its challenges for institutional meaning making.

Internal secondary research attempts to gain insights from data and information that institutions have already collected. Universities capture details about all manner of transactions and activities, storing data and information in databases that can be mined as research archives. Gordon Wishon and John Rome (2012) describe their efforts at Arizona State University to create an enterprise-level system that provides access to an enormous amount of institutional data and information about student activities, teaching activities, research contributions, recruiting programs, human resources, facilities uses, and more. Their emphasis is on making the system usable to nontechnical users, on creating an intuitive interface dashboard that also collects analytics about who is accessing the data and information and how. Although databases can be used for any number of reasons, they are crucial to institutional benchmarking, a popular method of internal secondary research.

In varying degrees of formality and explicitness, universities benchmark their practices against those of comparable schools to investigate how they measure up to peers and how they might improve their practices. When I began directing the writing program at Penn State, I asked directors at other Big Ten schools for information about class sizes, teaching loads, online courses, and practicum requirements. This was a quick-and-dirty project, but I learned invaluable facts that helped me make evidence-based arguments to upper-level administrators. For instance, with a cap of twenty-four students per section, the size of our writing classes is on the large end of the conference spectrum. Leah Lang (2015) outlines methodological steps that are common to benchmarking efforts: identify goals, identify audiences, identify data sources, evaluate data quality, develop a plan for reporting, consider possible outcomes, and improve practices (42). In chapter 2, I discussed an EDUCAUSE database that institutions use to share and access data and information about numerous academic IT topics. My concern there was to point out the shaping power of conventions on future-facing practices, but the database is also a good example of an apparatus that structures internal secondary research.

In addition to using databases sponsored by professional organizations, academic IT units also originate their own benchmarking programs geared toward specific goals. The Massachusetts Institute of Technology (MIT) and Stanford University designed a collaborative framework to address their shared needs for performance and cost data, concentrating on help desk services as a starting point (Dougherty, Clebsch, and Anderson 2004). One of the advantages of originating a benchmarking program is that the participating institutions can determine the targets and parameters. By clearly defining comparative measures, such as help desk cases per full-time equivalent employee or cost expenditures per case, MIT and Stanford did what they could to ensure that their internal secondary research yields meaningful comparisons.

Apples-to-apples comparisons can be difficult to realize without an originating framework. Penn State learned this lesson when it benchmarked its academic IT programs against those at the University of California, Los Angeles; the University of Illinois; the University of Texas; the

University of Michigan; and the University of Wisconsin (Office of Computer and Information Systems, the Pennsylvania State University 1995). The Penn State researchers discovered that numerical data were actually the least useful product of their research, in large part because of the differences that exist among even comparable institutions. In fact, save for the most basic of measures, the researchers noted, "We were sometimes not just comparing apples and oranges, but apples and orangutans. For example, where some institutions include capital expenses in the information technology budget, others do not; comparisons would be irrelevant, at best" (20). But these comparison problems did not prevent the benchmarking project from yielding useful results. The researchers were able to work inductively with the data and information to produce four broad principles that can guide productive institutional change: exemplary institutions "use policy, budget, and strategy measures to maximize the benefits of information technology" (21); "encourage early implementation of information technology infrastructure and standards" (25); "emphasize customer service in order to integrate technology into the institutional culture" (25); and "use the elements of standards, security, and architectural planning to create a supportive environment for change" (26). These quality indicators derive from a synthesis of resembling experiences and are as valuable to academic IT units as input and output measures. They also indicate potential areas for building alliances across the spatial divides of peer groups: interinstitutional collaborations are often a byproduct of benchmarking projects.

Internal primary research attempts to gain new institutional insights from original investigations. In this case, academic IT specialists are researchers themselves with varying levels of experience. It is not uncommon for new researchers or researchers undertaking complex investigations to partner with another in-house unit, such as an institutional center for assessment or data and statistics, in order to assemble a team with the right mix of competencies. Methods for internal primary research include surveys, questionnaires, interviews, case studies, observations, focus groups, and document analyses. The available methods are the same as those for external primary research, although the results only need to be sufficiently useful for institutional purposes. Internal primary research can be conducted to support specific initiatives or can be imagined as stand-alone studies. I want to elaborate on survey approaches because they are widely used.

Institutions survey users to learn about their experiences, expectations, and requirements. Institutions are understandably cautious about the number of surveys they ask users to complete, so an extensive survey is often conducted annually that integrates both descriptive and exploratory components. The descriptive components employ predefined answer sets for a random sample of users, yielding quantitative empirical data that are projected to a larger university population; these data can also be compared longitudinally if the questions are constant. The exploratory components employ open-ended questions that invite insights, opinions, and personal reflections, yielding qualitative empirical data that round out the research picture, making it richer and more complex. Carl Berger (2002) offers a synopsis of how and why academic IT units should use surveys to produce internal primary research, drawing on examples from the University of Michigan, Rio Salado College, and Penn State. He covers key aspects of survey design and administration and also discusses how to analyze survey data and present the information to university audiences. This portion of the article is invaluable for the way it contextualizes the basics of survey methods for new researchers studying academic IT settings. Perhaps even more invaluable is the application section, which illustrates how institutions bring the results of surveys to bear on decision-making: at the University of Michigan, survey results have been used to justify the reallocation of resources toward priority areas identified by users; survey results have been used at Rio Salado College to determine the technical specifications for online courses; and at Penn State, survey results have been used to reshape faculty development programs. As Berger shows, the results of user surveys can guide institutional actions in consequential ways.

I have learned a great deal from reading the annual Penn State surveys. I have learned about configurations (technical and social) for learning spaces, patterns of device ownership and usage, preferences for reading and accessing online course materials, preferences for collaborating on course projects, preferences for hardware and software platforms, attitudes toward personal device use in classrooms, attitudes toward support services, practices for managing digital assets, and more. The survey reports are extensive, ranging from thirty to fifty pages, and contain a vast amount of data for readers to consider and apply to their own situations. Applying the data, however, can be a challenge for both academic IT specialists and teachers, for survey reports from academic IT units describe results but often do not try to explain them. I am not condemning studies with descriptive purposes for failing to do something they were not designed to do but pointing out that people may need to take the additional step of making sense of the data for themselves. At times, this task is a straightforward one: if fewer than half of student respondents are aware of Lynda.com, an online training site with software tutorials, then I should make time in class to introduce this resource. Likewise, academic IT units should initiate a campus campaign to raise awareness of the resource.

At other times, and I would argue oftentimes, the task of making sense from surveys is not so easy or obvious. For example, what does it mean if a survey shows that the most frequently used devices on a campus are laptops (79 percent), smartphones (65 percent), and desktop computers (51 percent)? That 20 percent of respondents have two or more email accounts and that Gmail is the most popular one? That the reference software most used by students is Endnote (26 percent)? That most teachers rate their expertise with academic IT as either advanced (29 percent) or intermediate (53 percent)? Or that 75 percent of respondents use a social media platform? All these data are potentially useful, but making sense of the data requires people to construct institutional narratives with them, to use them to answer the "So what?" and "Now what?" questions critical to any research project: Why is the data important? What can be done with it? Constructing institutional narratives from survey data is what gives the results meaning and significance. In other words, the narratives, not the data, are the contributions to institutional knowledge. There is limited value in simply posting survey results in the hope that people will find them useful. Ultimately, the results should be used to make institutional arguments that can move the conversation forward by contextualizing the data with classroom practices and clarifying what they mean for teaching and learning. Teachers of writing and communication are necessary partners in the orchestration of this interpretive dialogue for institutions.

The spatial shift from internal to external research indicates a desire on the part of academic IT specialists to share with and learn from their counterparts at other schools. External research still derives from internal needs—universities do not invest in institutional research without strategic goals—but the more public aim of consuming and contributing to field knowledge raises the methodological bar for researchers and can require them to receive approval from an institutional review board (IRB). The publicness of external research can also challenge researchers to articulate the sociotechnical character of their institutions, both for themselves and for readers of research, which is an invaluable exercise in and of itself: institutional assumptions and dynamics often remain unrecognized until a conscious effort is made to articulate them.

Academic IT specialists engaged in external secondary research use search engines, databases, and other systems to locate reports and publications that can help shed light on problems they are trying to solve. These texts, as external sources of secondary research, serve several concrete functions, providing background information for proposals or projects, explaining what disciplines know about their subjects, helping researchers refine their directions and questions, helping researchers validate or compare the findings of primary research, and identifying research areas that need to be addressed. Although academic IT specialists publish external secondary research in various formal venues, there is also a culture of blogging and self-publishing that is impatient with long publication delays, instead valuing the quick dissemination of research over the peer-review process. It is therefore important for academic IT specialists to be able to evaluate the reliability of external secondary research.

Literature reviews are a prevalent source of external secondary research. Their purpose is to summarize and synthesize the published material in a field area so that readers can learn about what has already been done and what remains to be studied. Literature reviews are often used to articulate the exigence for external primary research but can also function as stand-alone articles. They can be comprehensive in nature, covering the full publication history in a domain, or be time-bounded, space-bounded, or otherwise more selective in scope: there is room in the genre for varying degrees of emphasis and expansiveness. Although literature reviews are often considered a less demanding form of research, they can be difficult to produce and interpret. If well written, literature reviews center on themes and issues and synthesize sources into an argument about the current state of the art and future considerations; the argument is an original contribution that advances understanding and further research activity. If not so well written, literature reviews have the linguistic markers of annotated bibliographies, foregrounding sources and their authors and stringing together quotes and summaries without adequate analytical commentary. On the interpretive side, productive readings of literature reviews bear in mind the contexts for the research and situate the findings for local institutional practices. Read uncritically, literature reviews are treated as best-practice documents that apply to institutions as a whole.

An example by Trevor Murphy (2004) illustrates some of the characteristics of literature reviews and the complexities of producing and interpreting them as sources of external secondary research. His review aspires to educate academic IT specialists about techniques for designing instructional materials in PowerPoint. Academic IT specialists can use what they learn to create more effective instructional materials or to show teachers how to do the same. For his review, Murphy draws on thirteen sources of information, including personal blogs, instructional design books, and articles published in the proceedings of academic IT conferences and education journals. Teachers of writing and communication will certainly recognize a number of these sources, and some of them are cited frequently by the field.

The sources shape the organization of the literature review, which discusses how to select and design media for instructional purposes and avoid common pitfalls. After reading the literature review, academic IT specialists will be informed by tested advice for designing screens, coordinating color schemes, working with graphics, choosing typefaces, editing audio and video clips, chunking texts, and sequencing animations. However, they will also have to contend with an imperative grammatical mood that expresses the advice in unconditional terms, as commands to be followed without question: "Use a dark text color on a neutral unsaturated background" (Murphy 2004, 372); "keep video to 3 to 5 minutes" (374); and "limit audio to what is relevant and use the active voice" (373). There will be times in which this advice works, but the decontextualized nature of the discussion precludes rhetorical considerations. Active voice, for example, should be the preferred voice when it is important to locate agency in the subject position of a sentence. It could also be the case that students are motivated to watch instructional videos that exceed five minutes or that light text on a dark background is a more effective color combination (in large classrooms, light backgrounds can be too bright and tiring on the eyes). Writing or interpreting guidelines as absolute conclusions risks missing the situated nature of teaching and learning and assumes that instructional materials can be transplanted from one spatial context to another without altering designs or meanings. External secondary research must always be evaluated for its potential to inform the development of pedagogical elements in specific situations.

As with internal primary research, external primary research aims to achieve new institutional insights from original investigations, but the investigations are meant to create value beyond reporting and decision-making. Primary research helps institutions satisfy external needs by contributing to their reputations and prestige, creating partnerships that leverage resources and expertise, and transferring knowledge and technology to support instructional and economic development. External primary research can begin with grants or cooperative agreements and result in presentations, publications, patents, and commercial and noncommercial products. It can involve more than one institution or multiple sites within an institution and draw on the full spectrum of empirical methods prized by academic IT units.

The academic IT units at Penn State employ workers who are hired to direct external primary research. The people with whom I work are classified as research project managers; they are required to have a doctoral degree in education or a related field. Their job responsibilities are divided into four tasks: building and managing relationships, which includes identifying faculty with relevant interests and recommending projects that support faculty needs; collaborating on research projects, which includes managing IRB applications, designing research protocols, and establishing objectives, time lines, and metrics of success; assessing academic IT systems, which includes implementing research studies that help the institution evaluate the effectiveness of its initiatives; and developing professional competencies, which includes staying abreast of the latest technologies and approaches for analyzing, visualizing, and managing research data and information. These tasks build institutional bridges between academic IT units and faculty members, formalizing research partnerships that are mutually beneficial and reinforcing for both sides.

I was a usability tester for an intra-institutional research team investigating the creation of a noncommercial software platform for generating open-source textbooks and other types of instructional materials (see Liang et al. 2015). The software is called BBook, which stands for Bionic Book, to indicate that the textbooks produced with the software are a product of human-machine collaborations. The research team is interested in exploring solutions to problems with textbooks, particularly their high cost and tendency to become outdated due to rapid technological changes. Furthermore, as users of open educational resources themselves, the researchers want to contribute something to open innovation movements. The heart of the platform is an artificial intelligence engine that queries a repository of open-access textbooks and Wikipedia pages to help teachers remix a new book (or other text) for classroom use. The front end has a web-based interface that ranks results according to their relevance to search terms. Users work through a recursive process of defining book chapters and headings and searching and refining search results until they are satisfied with the content and organization; they can then export the content to HTML for editing and publication. I am glossing over the algorithmic features of the platform, but this is a basic description of how things work.

For my usability test, I was asked to use BBook to draft an open-source textbook for our technical writing service course. The test lasted an hour, and I was observed by one of the principal researchers from an academic IT unit. I began by generating search terms that reflect key activities in the course, such as analyzing audiences, planning projects, and writing reports. I then created a new file in BBook and began the recursive process of defining chapters and headings and searching, refining, and organizing search results. By the end of the test, I had become comfortable with the software, collecting numerous candidate texts for possible inclusion in the book and producing an initial draft of a chapter on audience. The drag-and-drop interface was easy to use, and the software performed as advertised. But what about the product? Could a finished version of the book become a viable option for our course? At this point, I am inclined to say no—a conclusion that has as much to do with the status of open educational resources in the field and institutional constraints as with the design of the software itself. The principal researcher observed that usability is not a property of academic IT systems but a spatial experience that extends from a human-machine interface to encompass the rhetorical situation, which in this case includes novice teachers, teachers with heavy teaching loads, general education pedagogies, and writing program policies. I am not confident that novice or busy teachers could use BBook to create open-source textbooks that would serve the needs of everyone involved.

The first issue is the status of the open-source repository. Although I was able to find resources, almost all of them would need to be edited to fit our purposes and to work collectively, which is time consuming and might not even be permissible in the first place (open educational resources can still retain copyright restrictions). In addition, there were gaps in content coverage. For instance, I could find plenty of readings on ethics from philosophy and business, but none had been prepared for writing and communication students studying workplace contexts. This problem is a real one for our program because it requires teachers to use a book that takes a rhetorical approach. Novice teachers would also struggle with the challenge of scaffolding the disparate sources into a coherent whole, for these teachers themselves are still in the process of learning about both the field and how to teach it: two corresponding undertakings aided by the same textbook we assign to students. Such problems become visible only when BBook is used in actual situations with teachers who can gauge its viability as a noncommercial product of external primary research.

Academic IT units employ a variety of methods to make sense of their professional contexts. Institutional needs, which can be understood in spatial terms as either internal or external, are key factors in determining methodological choices and setting expectations for research. The secondary and primary research conducted for internal purposes is critical to adhering to certification standards and regulatory requirements. It is also central to planning, recruiting, and branding efforts. The secondary and primary research that is conducted for external purposes enables institutions to grow their reputations, leverage resources, and transfer innovations to other settings. As my examples illustrate, teachers of writing and communication are necessary allies in the research process, helping academic IT specialists conduct investigations and also situate them in concrete terms and interpret findings. The role of research ally is a natural one for teachers because the enduring spatial questions in the field entangle institutions. In my experiences, research projects are enriched by the exchange of ideas across institutional boundaries and between people from different relevant fields.

Bodies

The human actors I have been discussing—students, teachers, administrators, managers, programmers, designers, and others—are themselves (at least in part) an institutionally constructed element of academic IT contexts. The next chapter considers the role of institutional subjectivities, but here I want to address embodied spatial practices and their features and relationships. Teachers of writing and communication have expressed at least two senses of embodiment in their work on academic IT. I have already mentioned one of them in several places: technologies instantiate human preferences. This concept of embodiment emphasizes the nonneutrality of technologies, and the research employing it investigates the ways technologies come to be imbued with meaning in development activities. The focus of such investigations is both functional and critical in scope, considering everything from the cognitive assumptions that influence interface designs to the cultural biases that shape high-tech settings. The sense of embodiment I want to discuss here has to do instead with the embodied spatial practices of students and teachers. I am especially interested in how academic IT specialists represent those practices for themselves and others.

By embodied spatial practices, I mean the institutional practices— material and virtual—that constitute human-machine interactions in teaching and learning settings. Embodied spatial practices are concrete and situated (rather than abstract and absolute) and the product of everyday habits and routines. They are often deeply entrenched and internalized and thus can be resistant to change. Embodied spatial practices, in addition, are fundamental to acting in institutions and to institutional knowledge making.

T. Kenny Fountain (2014) makes the basic point that all human practices are embodied practices, for "there are no practices without bodies" (13), to put it simply and directly. He goes on to explain that "we only know the world because we are embodied in the world, and that world comes to us through the bodily phenomenon of perception. The body, then, is more than just the material inscribed by discourses; it is our means of making sense of such discourse and our capacity for action" (13). For Fountain, this second sense of embodiment, which posits human bodies as interfaces to the world, is a necessary predicate to rhetorical modes of doing and making, to acting and learning to act professionally in settings of consequence. Although Fountain does not emphasize the spatial in his analysis of how students are trained in labs and classrooms, he demonstrates how embodied spatial practices—such as viewing, touching, moving, using, and communicating—are central to educating students and developing expertise in sociotechnical domains. He shows that as bodies and technologies entwine in the pedagogical practices in learning spaces, it becomes impossible to conceive of one without the other or to imagine them as discrete entities existing in isolation prior to or somehow outside of processes of institutionalization.

Academic IT specialists have embraced at least four perspectives on the embodied spatial practices in human-machine interactions. Each perspective addresses bodies differently and also assigns different roles and capacities to technologies. The perspectives are not always incompatible or even separable but present alternative visions for the same problem context. In the first perspective, academic IT systems are understood to automate the embodied spatial practices of students and teachers. Automation efforts replace manual tasks (digital and nondigital) carried out by people with machine-based solutions for accomplishing work. Proponents celebrate the efficiencies, controls, and cost savings that automated practices can realize for institutions. Critics express concerns over human impact, particularly outcomes that deskill and deprofessionalize workers and reduce the complexity of problems so that machines can solve them. As with most things technological, automation presents a mixed bag of considerations, a reality I noted in my previous discussion of machine grading and MOOCs, which explains how evaluation is impoverished to a series of rules that machines can process, in the service of eliminating inefficient bodies from the educational feedback system. The example I take up now incorporates the embodied spatial practices of students and teachers and also illustrates instances in which automation can be more productive.

Penn State has developed a digital video production system called the

One Button Studio. It is available in certain campus labs and in the Penn State Digital English Studio, which is a production studio I manage. The thinking behind the One Button Studio is imaginative, responding to the institutional challenge of needing to help large numbers of students and teachers produce digital video projects. Although anyone with a smartphone can shoot video footage, the point of the One Button Studio is to provide access to a more professionally outfitted workspace that includes higher-end video cameras, microphones, lights, backdrops, sound panels, and more. The software application for the studio automates the workflow process. Users simply insert a USB thumb drive into the studio dock and then press the start/stop button: pressing the button turns the lights on and begins a recording session; pressing the button again ends the session and saves the file to the thumb drive. Users eject the thumb drive and take their file with them, either for editing or for use as is. The advantage of the One Button Studio is that students and teachers can quickly and easily make high-quality videos without needing to know anything much about the complexities of the recording process or equipment, eliminating access barriers to video production as a mode of writing and communication. Eliminating barriers has resulted in the creation of tens of thousands of digital video projects.

But the advantage of the One Button Studio could also be seen as something of a disadvantage, at least to teachers who deem it important to demystify digital literacies by making workflow processes visible to students, including by learning the embodied spatial practices of adjusting shooting angles, lighting intensities, sound levels, and foreground and background contrasts. Systems such as the One Button Studio enable access by automating a considerable amount of intellectual and material work, but teachers should make conscious decisions about when to accelerate projects with the help of machines and when to slow things down and ask students to develop their own functional and critical abilities. In either case, users will want to be clear about the advantages and disadvantages of employing systems that automate teaching and learning activities.

In the second perspective on human-machine interactions, academic IT environments are understood to mediate the embodied spatial practices of students and teachers. The notion of mediation I am using here refers to intermediary or go-between elements in rhetorical situations—human and nonhuman—that materialize the connections between thought and action. There are multiple layers of mediation in any institutional setting. As I will discuss in the next chapter, language is a medium that contributes to how academic IT specialists construct their relationships with students and teachers. Fountain (2014) posits bodies as mediating interfaces between learning and knowing how to do things in professional worlds, and some of his examples reveal how teachers serve as intermediaries between students and institutions, performing various socializing and authorizing roles in knowledge-making processes. Of course, academic IT environments are unmistakable mediating structures that can literally stand between students and teachers and organize their interactions. These multiple layers of mediation—discourses, bodies, institutional roles, technologies, and others—are all discernible (in varying degrees and intensities) in individual pedagogical moments and coexist as articulations of sociotechnical elements that shape the interpretations, experiences, and embodied spatial practices of students and teachers.

At issue for my discussion is the perceived nature of mediation in academic IT units. Let me provide a ubiquitous example that illustrates conventional thinking about bodies and technologies in this institutional location. Although institutions continue to question the wisdom of supporting computer classrooms that include one workstation per student, such spaces are nonetheless alive and well in universities. On my campus, there is ongoing demand for access to thirty-three general-purpose computer classrooms, and there are similar sorts of situations at numerous other schools. In creating and maintaining computer classrooms, academic IT specialists draw on design models that contain assumptions about the embodied spatial practices of students and teachers. A historically persistent set of assumptions specifies that computer classrooms will include desktop machines, keyboards will be the main input device for users, the type of interaction with the machine will be single-user interaction, and the primary sense modality will be a visual one. These assumptions create problems for people with disabilities, normalizing institutional understandings of bodies and their capabilities. They also prize certain approaches to teaching and learning, such as individual visual approaches. I would be the first to admit that no one model can account for all the different types of bodies in instructional settings, but a crucial mindset for teachers and academic IT specialists is being sensitive to the bodily assumptions informing the design of mediating structures. Knowing how or if mediating structures might accommodate or resist bodies is essential to negotiating institutional contexts.

In the third perspective on human-machine interactions, academic IT environments are understood to augment the embodied spatial practices of students and teachers. If the automating aspects of technologies replace the manual tasks carried out by people with machine-based solutions for accomplishing work, the augmenting aspects of technologies enhance or amplify the capacities of bodies, making them more effective in the world. The idea that technologies augment bodily powers and thus make possible new thought and action is an unambiguous sentiment in universities. People should debate the efficacy of augmenting environments and the extent to which they are responsible for change, but there is little doubt that technologies are routinely seen as extenders of embodied spatial practices. In fact, augmentation was an initial impetus for integrating networked computers into writing classrooms: teachers were interested in stretching the learning boundaries imposed by arbitrary institutional structures such as class schedules and locations.

Academic IT specialists who support systems that enhance or amplify user practices assert positions about bodies and their status and relationships in institutions. More specifically, augmentation environments remediate bodies that are considered to be defective and respatialize bodies into new pedagogical arrangements. Both of these processes involve teachers as much as anyone else. In the case of assigning status to human functioning and development, academic IT specialists are not alone in embracing normative views of embodied spatial practices and developing augmentation systems for people whose functioning fails to match normal cultural expectations for able-bodiedness. Jason Palmeri (2006) illustrates how teachers can promote "unconscious ableist biases" (57) that "marginalize the embodied knowledges of people with disabilities" (50). His analysis of mundane contexts in technical writing demonstrates how users with disabilities are represented as substandard people to be pitied and cured rather than as people to be valued for their own strengths and capacities. It also shows how people with disabilities are treated as special cases to be accommodated or managed rather than as members of complex audiences that necessarily consist of diverse abilities. Palmeri admonishes teachers to disrupt normalizing tendencies in institutions and enact approaches that construct disabilities as sources of insight for understanding how to improve technical writing as a whole. Similar examples of ableist biases are everywhere in academic IT environments, as suggested by my previous discussion of the naturalness of keyboards and visual modalities in computer classrooms.

Augmentation systems also respatialize bodies into new pedagogical arrangements, amplifying certain types of practices (while diminishing others) and supporting the evolution of different relationship patterns in sociotechnical contexts. This reality is apparent in academic IT environments that have always been central to writing and communication. I am referring to how computer conferencing systems eliminate the interruptions and body cues found in face-to-face conversations, which can shape student-to-student interactions; how distance learning systems shrink geographical distances and time zones and eliminate the need for students and teachers to be physically close to institutions for formalized instruction; and how hypertext systems confound distinctions between writers and readers, remixing their embodied spatial practices in ways that allow them to take on both roles simultaneously. Using crowdsourcing as an illustration, let me elaborate on the breakdown of institutional roles to show how augmentation systems can respatialize bodies into new pedagogical arrangements.

One of the benefits of enhancing or amplifying the capacities of bodies is distributed problem solving, an approach to work that uses networks to harness the collective intelligence of online communities. Although Alicia Peaker (2015) emphasizes that crowdsourcing is "well suited to simple, repeatable tasks" (90), such as transcribing texts into machine-readable documents and building and curating online collections, crowdsourcing is also an institutional approach that can serve instructional ends. For example, many academic IT units use crowdsourcing to help maintain the comprehensiveness of their documentation knowledge bases. Before crowdsourcing, academic IT specialists created self-contained instructions and uploaded them to servers. Users, in turn, downloaded the instructions and consumed them passively. This traditional publication model allowed academic IT specialists to control the presentation of instructions, but it also created the need to constantly update them for an ever-growing portfolio of systems. Another drawback was that the approach lacked a feedback loop for leveraging user experiences. Self-contained instructions are still a mainstay in knowledge bases, but the introduction of Web 2.0 features spawned new publication models, embedded and open, that augment bodily capacities with crowdsourcing techniques (Selber 2010).

The content of embedded instructions is delivered in an environment that collects user-generated metadata. Academic IT units now produce instructional screencasts—video-based demonstrations explaining how to perform tasks—that allow users to rate content and search by user ratings, recontextualize screencasts by embedding their code in another website, add notes to help others interpret the instructions and navigate screencasts, filter notes to see only those added by other users, and leave comments, suggest and add tags, and post responses. There has always been a need to have structured data about data, but Web 2.0 features elevate mechanisms for metadata to the level of the interface and integrate them directly into user experiences, augmenting those experiences with advice from numerous informed others. In another model, open instructions encourage users to become institutional authors and editors in their own right. Academic IT units now use wikis as a platform for hosting open instructions, which depend on the willingness of volunteers to contribute their expertise to a shared resource for problem solving. In open instructions, information is not developed through one-to-many communication patterns functioning in a hierarchical manner. Although experts can be useful to the enterprise, academic IT units instead assume that users at all levels can offer valuable insights. This many-to-many approach is an exercise in distributed usability, but open systems are also emblematic of a full process approach, for nothing in the system is ever really concluded: users can always submit feedback on entries, add new entries, and write and edit entries. These embodied spatial practices reposition students and teachers as academic IT specialists with institutional expertise.

In the fourth perspective on human-machine interactions, academic IT environments are understood to hybridize the embodied spatial practices of students and teachers. The first three perspectives—automation, mediation, and augmentation—all retain a separation between the boundaries of humans and machines: machines replace humans, machines function as interfaces for humans, and machines extend the capabilities of humans. In these perspectives, there are acknowledgments that the relationship between humans and machines is a complex one and that each influences the other in institutions. But in a hybridized view, the boundaries are blurred to a point where there are seemingly no boundaries at all. This is literally the case with cochlear implants, which stimulate the auditory nerves in the ear to help deaf people hear sounds. The boundaries between human and nonhuman elements also seem indistinguishable in the emerging research area of pharmacology and learning, which is interested in how neuroenhancing drugs might improve student performance. Physical, electrical, and chemical components merge bodies and technologies to create new and different conditions for teaching, learning, and living.

More commonplace scenarios involving hybridization use wearable technologies—head-mounted displays, glasses, headsets, hearables, watches, wristbands, and sensors in clothing—to contract and trivialize the spatial distance between bodies and technologies. In writing about full-on virtual environments, Meredith Bricken (1992) explains that ideally people are "inside an environment of pure information that [they] can see, hear, and touch. The technology itself is invisible, and carefully adapted to human activity so that [they] can behave naturally" (363). By invisible, Bricken does not mean that people can no longer see or sense wearable technologies but that they recede from consciousness to such an extent that their interfaces become transparent. In universities, applications of full-on virtual reality can be found in science and engineering labs and new media labs. They can also be found in training programs for surgeons, pilots, and other professionals who need to practice their skills in a low-stakes environment. In recent years, however, wearable technologies have become smaller and less cumbersome, faster and cheaper, wireless and networkable, and much simpler to use, so much so that hybridized spatial practices are insinuating themselves into the everyday landscape of teaching and learning.

One of my colleagues is partnering with academic IT specialists to study how the Apple Watch might be used to help students self-regulate their learning (Hughes 2015). Students wearing the watch receive prompts to assist them in structuring learning processes and tracking progress. The prompts include the types of cognitive, metacognitive, and motivational questions that successful self-regulating students ask themselves and their instructors: What am I working on? Why am I working on it? How motivated am I to complete the work? What is the best way to approach the work? How well is my approach succeeding? How am I reacting to assessments of my work? Teachers who adhere to the principles of self-regulated learning believe in interrupting the flow of learning in order to stimulate reflection and self-review; teachers then ask students to incorporate this feedback into their ongoing work. The students wearing Apple Watches have access to a dashboard view that visualizes their responses, aiding with the task of learning from reflection. Although the self-regulating prompts elicit qualitative information, this project is in keeping with the goals of the quantified self movement, which uses wearables to monitor embodied spatial practices and provide feedback that can aid decision-making.

In another example of hybridization, students at Georgia State University can use Google Cardboard to explore virtual museum exhibits (Sinclair and Gunhouse 2016). Google Cardboard deploys cardboard, plastic lenses, and other components to turn a smartphone into an inexpensive virtual reality (VR) system that can shrink spatial distances and provide deeply immersive experiences, and not just for museum exhibits: there are VR apps for telling stories, reading newspapers, viewing maps, watching videos, playing games, creating 360-degree photos, and taking expeditions (Google has created hundreds of guided tours for classroom use). Such embodied spatial practices are immersive in that students can lose track of the fact that they are staring at a smartphone and instead permit the environment to completely absorb their attention: the first-person point of view is achieved in spite of and because of the technologies that make it function.

The relatively seamless nature of hybridized systems challenges teachers to retain a commitment to orchestrating moments of unsuturing in which the conventional (not natural) character of the systems is foregrounded and considered.

Academic IT specialists model at least four different views of embodiment. Systems that automate embodied spatial practices substitute manual tasks carried out by people with machine-based solutions for accomplishing work. Although there can be benefits to automation, students and teachers need to be mindful about when to advance projects with the help of automation and when to develop their own capacities. Systems that mediate embodied spatial practices materialize connections between thought and action with structuring interfaces, which both accommodate and resist user actions. Understanding how interfaces mediate work is crucial to negotiating institutions. Systems that augment embodied spatial practices enhance human capabilities, remediating bodies that are considered deficient or respatializing them into new pedagogical arrangements. There is potential in the new pedagogical arrangements for students and teachers to be repositioned as academic IT specialists with institutional expertise. Finally, systems that hybridize embodied spatial practices confound the boundaries between humans and machines to such an extent that the boundaries seem to dissolve into a seamless, cohesive whole. Material and rhetorical emphases on the so-called natural behaviors of users mask the conventional character of hybridization. It is instructive for students and teachers to discuss the distinctions between what is conventional and natural and consider problems of disambiguation in human-machine interactions. These different views of embodiment—automation, mediation, augmentation, and hybridization—can coexist in the same academic IT environment and serve a variety of purposes. They are also significant to the enduring spatial questions in the field, for spaces and bodies are intra-actively produced in the ongoing making and remaking of institutions.

CONCLUSION

Jason Farman (2011) argues that "spatial relationships have always determined the way we understand ourselves, our place in the larger context, and the cultural meanings infused into gestures, objects, and sign systems" (17). In academic IT settings, hierarchies, processes, methods, and bodies help bring specificity and concreteness to this general theoretical claim, illuminating and illustrating the spatiality of institutionalization projects.

These spatial elements are fundamental to the experiences and practices of academic IT specialists and represent vital sites of engagement for students and teachers. The enduring spatial questions in the field serve as a bridge to such interventions by reflecting the unity of interests between teachers and academic IT specialists. The next chapter shifts from considerations of spaces to texts and explores the dynamics and implications of textual institutional dimensions.

4

TEXTUALIZING ACADEMIC IT

The institutions that form our modern lives—government, commerce, industry, the arts, sciences, and so on—are mediated by written marks in databases, laws, regulations, books, the Internet. DAVID R. RUSSELL (2015)

The Center for Online Innovation in Learning (COIL) at Penn State awards research grants for projects aimed at enhancing teaching and learning through online innovations. The center is sponsored by academic IT units, academic colleges, and the administrative unit that oversees distance education. The research grants provide seed money for projects that are considered strong candidates for external funding. COIL has awarded dozens of grants for projects in a range of academic IT areas, including research on designing MOOCs, leveraging learning analytics, creating interactive videos, gamifying courses, and teaching in virtual reality environments. Researchers who are interested in grants submit a proposal with the following sections: a cover page, abstract, statement of innovation, statement of impact on learning, statement of alignment with COIL priorities, narrative, references, biographies, budget, research dissemination plan, and supporting materials. Although researchers are encouraged to discuss their plans with COIL administrators, reviewers' decisions are based solely on the written proposals themselves, which is typical of grant processes. Researchers who win grants are rewarded for their ability to textualize academic IT—in particular, to make arguments that persuade reviewers of the value of the projects for students and teachers. Those who lose grants might have worthwhile ideas but fail to describe them to the satisfaction of reviewers, who are guided by institutional criteria for decision-making and assumptions about institutions, literacies, and technologies. The practices involved in submitting and evaluating COIL grants are decidedly textual practices.

I submitted a grant that proposed to create an academic IT system to improve the approach my department uses to deliver distance education courses. The proposal, which assembles a collaborative team of academic IT specialists and teachers, addresses the challenge of striking a balance between standardization and customization in distance education courses offered in multiple sections (cf. Dutkiewicz, Holder, and Sneath 2013). Academic institutions often respond to growth in distance education by adopting a standardized approach, creating prepackaged courses authored by master teachers, copying those courses into multiple sections, and then asking other teachers, typically adjunct faculty and graduate students, to administer the sections ("administer" here means responding to students and evaluating their work). The teachers assigned to the courses have not had any input into the content or approach, nor can they modify either one—a situation that inhibits teachers from investing in their own courses and teaching to their strengths. Despite certain institutional efficiencies for design and maintenance, prepackaged courses deprofessionalize teachers, harm morale, and construct overly generic experiences for students. This was the exigence for the proposal.

My department has taken a prepackaged approach to our distance education portfolio, which includes two high-impact courses. First-Year Composition is a required general education course in writing and communication taken by Penn State students during their first year. Writing in the Disciplines is the second required general education course in writing and communication, which Penn State students take during their junior or senior year. Three versions of Writing in the Disciplines are available in a distance format: Social Science Writing, Technical Writing, and Business Writing. Technical Writing and Business Writing fulfill accreditation requirements for degree programs in engineering and business. In a typical year, we offer about one hundred sections of First-Year Composition and Writing in the Disciplines as distance sections, enrolling more than 2,200 students; these sections are capped at 24. In terms of staffing, the department assigns around twenty-two teachers to thirty-five sections in the summer term, twenty teachers to twenty-five sections in the fall term, and thirty teachers to forty sections in the spring term. The department runs numerous sections of individual courses and employs over 100 adjunct faculty and graduate students, all of whom are eligible to teach distance courses. By nearly any measure, the operations of general education programs are substantial and complex.

I applied for a COIL grant to help us leverage the most productive aspects of standardization and customization in our general education program. The goal of this endeavor is to improve teaching, and thus learning, in the online offerings. One of our guiding assumptions is that engaged teachers create favorable conditions for student success. Although the research on distance education addresses methods for designing student-centered courses, the contexts and conditions for teachers are no less important to the experiences of online learning (Arend 2009). A second guiding assumption is that standardization and customization are not binary oppositions but rather interdependent modes of institutionalization (Simon 1980). It is not difficult for teachers to recognize the importance of standardizing certain pedagogical elements, especially in general education courses. Standardizing policies, learning objectives, and grading rubrics helps ensure that students are being treated fairly and consistently across sections and that the quality of courses meets institutional expectations. Standardization, however, should not bleed into decision-making that is best left to teachers, such as selecting course readings and designing assignments. As the CCCC position statement for online writing instruction emphasizes, teachers should be able to maintain "reasonable control" over their course content and approach (CCCC 2013).

The system described in the proposal has three components: a software interface for customizing online courses; a crowdsourced database of customized materials, such as assignment sheets, invention prompts, and peer-review questions, which would be annotated and tagged by both their creators and users, enabling teachers to see how the materials might be integrated into customized versions of online courses; and a teacher training program, which would socialize teachers to become active contributors to the database. The research questions focused on managing the relationship between standardizing and customizing activities and are relevant to all three components of the system: What elements of online courses should be standardized or customized? Does the ability to customize online courses improve the experiences of students and teachers? What sociotechnical infrastructures are needed to support customizable approaches? How should teachers annotate their customized materials? And how should teachers be trained to use the system? I proposed to study these questions by conducting interviews and focus groups with teachers and testing the usability of the system in actual situations of use. The expectation was that the system would be useful in other programs also delivering prepackaged online courses in multiple sections.

The proposal was not funded, but the grant process begins to illuminate the textual dimensions of academic IT. Requests for proposals are commonplace texts that call for explicit attempts at institutional argumentation, inviting people to submit formal written responses and to compete for funding resources in a zero-sum game of winners and losers. Proposals that win do not always reflect the most ambitious or interesting systems, but their arguments are compatible with prevailing notions of innovation, transformation, and change. Winning proposals, in addition, are successful at projecting an ethos of institutional cooperation and conveying the ability to deliver on seemingly feasible commitments.

My proposal received strong scores for assembling a capable interinstitutional team, describing the system's potential impact, estimating the cost-effectiveness of developing and using the system, and identifying suitable outlets for publications and external grants. In these areas, I was able to make the case that the project should be funded by using a variety of appeals to align the arguments in the proposal with the requirements in the call for proposals. Among other things, I appealed to the funding priorities for projects that address aspects of personalization, demonstrate considerable promise for enhancing teaching and learning, and include collaborative partnerships with people from different campus units. The arguments were about wide-scale pedagogical problems in a general education program, and reviewers acknowledged the relevance and cogency of the arguments.

Although I could have done a more thorough job of discussing the research evaluation plan—proposal authors always have choices to make about emphasis and elaboration in narrative sections—the main issue was in misreading how the reviewers understood the concept of innovation. My assumption was that reviewers would see innovative projects as those that realize meaningful institutional change in online settings of consequence for students and teachers. Following this assumption, I proposed to disrupt the reigning approach to instructional design by creating a new sociotechnical system for a high-impact program that would decentralize control over pedagogical processes while maintaining institutional expectations for consistency and quality. Reviewers, in contrast, emphasized the abstract status of the technical components, noting that tool sets already exist for customizing online course materials and contending that my team was simply proposing to reinvent the wheel. In this view of innovation, the key measure of consideration is technical novelty, but in a generic, not specific or locally rooted, sense. Reviewers pointed out that course-management systems such as Blackboard and ELMS already allow teachers to customize course content, but those systems do not include the annotating and archiving features I would like to see in a crowdsourced database of online teaching materials. In addition, adopting and adapting either one of those products would require the writing program to abandon our institutionally supported course-management system and secure ongoing resources for maintaining an alternative platform.

What I am getting at here is the distinction between what is possible in theory given the technical state of the art and what is possible in concrete institutional situations where technology is but one element in sociotechnical articulations that helps determine the pedagogical prospects for transformation and change. The discursive construction of innovation as a process by which wholly new products are invented in moments of inspiration distorts the complexities of institutionalization—that is, the continuous making and remaking of institutions; distorts the complexities of invention and design, especially the role of histories in development activities; and impedes progress in individual locations, for innovation is not distributed evenly within and across settings but is a relative and contextual condition. As this example illustrates, textual dimensions are significant to the institutional treatment of academic IT.

My inquiry into textual dimensions begins with a discussion of how academic IT units tend to think about texts. I argue that they adopt pedagogical perspectives to create sympathetic contexts and adopt managerial perspectives to establish authorial ethos. I then turn to my own view of how texts ought to be thought about in institutional contexts for teaching and learning with technologies. Next, the chapter considers the enduring textual questions that unite writing and communication teachers, highlighting shared problems in the field. The final section of the chapter presents the textual elements of my heuristic: metaphors, subjectivities, genres, and stories. I define these elements and provide examples that incorporate the priorities of teachers.

TEXTUAL PERSPECTIVES ON ACADEMIC IT

The third dimension of my heuristic, texts, rounds out my analysis of influential frames of reference that shape how academic IT units think about processes and products. By texts, I mean written institutional artifacts such as proposals and reports, and by textual perspectives, I mean how academic IT specialists view the role of institutional texts. In addition to encompassing written artifacts, my heuristic also admits textual elements such as metaphors, which influence how people envision institutional relationships, and subjectivities, which are products of institutional discourses, at least in part. Although my discussion foregrounds the textual nature of knowledge and practice in academic IT units, it does not assume that their problem contexts are discursive constructs, acquiring meaning within narrative structures alone. As I have argued already, there are real material bases for institutional actions and systems.

Let me begin my analysis with three boxes of archival materials from the Eberly Family Special Collections Library at Penn State. These boxes contain university records from 1984 to 2000 from the Office of the Vice President for Information Technology. (If a record is deemed appropriate for the public, it is released twenty years after the creation date, thus my time frame.) Penn State Policy AD35 defines what counts as a university record and stipulates how the institution must handle materials that fit the definition. According to the policy, university records include "information that documents a transaction or regularly conducted activity of the University and that is created, received, or retained pursuant to law, University policy, or in connection with a transaction, business, or activity of the University." The policy goes on to explain that records can include "documents, papers, letters, books, drawings, maps, plans, photographs, tapes, film or sound recordings, microforms, digital or analog files, information stored or maintained electronically, and data- or image-processed documents." University records are maintained in accordance with policies that cover a broad set of circumstances.

It is important to note that there are different types of university records and that they tend to be sorted into categories based on access privileges. As the name denotes, confidential records, such as documents from legal investigations and minutes from closed administrative meetings, are only available to a very limited number of people at Penn State. Restricted records also carry a high degree of confidentiality but are available to a larger subset of employees who need to use the records to perform job duties. Examples include personnel files used by department heads and student records used by academic advisors. Official records, which constitute the majority of university records and include governance documents and policies and procedures manuals, are available to faculty and staff members within institutional units but not always to the general public. And vital records, such as deeds, contracts, and conferment lists, are crucial to the continuation or survival of an institution if disaster strikes, as in the case of fire or floods. Vital records are also important to protecting the legal and financial interests of an institution and its employees. Examples include consent forms, payroll records, and patent and trademark documents.

Although universities have different methods for categorizing records, all have records management programs. Furthermore, all records are themselves texts that have been constructed for a range of audiences, purposes, and occasions and shaped as much by institutional circumstances as by anything else. Records as texts tell stories that must be interpreted within their own institutional contexts.

Running a records management program is a significant undertaking that involves offices of institutional actors, classification schemes, policies and workflows, archiving platforms, and initiatives aimed at promoting a culture of record keeping and building employee trust in record-keeping systems. Fundamental to the operation are the definitions institutions establish for university records, which effectively constitute an official perspective on textual dimensions. In Penn State's definition, university records are understood as informational texts that document processes of institutionalization, specifically transactions and routine activities with a legal or policy basis or business purpose. Records management assistants within units help determine which records belong in which categories and which records should be archived or destroyed. Records that are destroyed are deemed to have no permanent value, such as those relating to minor administrative functions. What is relevant for my purposes is that the definition assigns an instrumental function to permanent official records, treating their semiotic systems as transparent and self-contained systems that record and convey data and information about institutions. In this view of texts and textual production, academic IT specialists simply write up the results of their problem-solving activities for administrators, users, and other audiences. Language is a neutral conduit for documenting and transmitting institutional knowledge.

On occasion, an instrumental perspective on language can be a useful (if reductive) perspective for academic IT specialists to adopt, for it stabilizes and registers—for a period of time, at least—collective understandings of the nature of institutional affairs, aiding planning and decision-making. The official records in the library boxes that most reflect an instrumental perspective are annual reports. The directors and managers who write annual reports are aware of the benefits of showing a return on investments, but the charge is to document activities and accomplishments in ways that substantiate institutional claims about progress and change and that allow for historical comparisons. This charge organizes reporting efforts and the reports themselves, precluding other ways of textualizing academic IT.

Consider the sections of annual reports dedicated to the Training Services group, which provides software training for students and teachers.

The academic IT specialists in this group are most interested in knowing if their systems and services enhance institutional practices. They want to know, for instance, if the workshops for WordPress improve pedagogical websites or if the tutorials for Adobe Connect improve virtual meetings. It is possible to learn about the influence of software training, but as teachers know, instructional impact is not always immediately apparent or even quantifiable. In addition, impact is not so easily traced in sociotechnical articulations, where causality is a complex and multivariate phenomenon. The Training Services group therefore relies on approaches to textualizing academic IT that can be captured by institutional tools and techniques and reported as documented actions. These approaches provide descriptive summaries of countable transactions and relationships—among them, how many people attended live training sessions and completed asynchronous online training sessions; how many people visited help pages on websites and which ones; how many tutorials were created and revised and which ones; how many and what types of promotional materials were distributed to users; and how many trainers participated in professional development activities and which ones. To illustrate, here are some typical sentences from an annual report: "A total of 300 seminar sections on more than 80 unique topics were offered in 19 computing and technology areas; 5,000 registrations were received and 2,500 seats filled. Attendees were from 23 campuses. Attendance averaged 9 people per seminar and 60 percent of attendees were teachers." The report is also replete with tables of comparative numbers from previous years and rank-ordered lists that indicate user preferences for training formats and materials. Such sentences do not tell people in the Training Services group what they really want to know about their operation, but the data do provide certain repeatable, reliable, and accurate measurements of institutional performance, which can contribute to generative dialogue about how resources are invested and valued. However incomplete or one-dimensional, documenting transactions and relationships is a basic discursive practice that brings order and coherence to representations of academic IT initiatives.

Although all the materials in the library boxes are classified as official records that document institutional histories, many of them do in fact confound a purely instrumental perspective on language use by reflecting multiple purposes and contexts and acknowledging more explicitly the persuasive functions of discourse. If an instrumental perspective is discernible in the annual reports, the how-to texts and strategic plans express pedagogical and managerial perspectives that encompass explanatory gestures and gestures that aim to establish authorial ethos by asserting status, building identification with readers, and controlling information. The how-to texts in the library boxes include computer manuals and bulletins. The manuals were written for users and contain instructions for operating software. The bulletins, also written for users, contain news items, updates, and lists of resources. There are two types of manuals in the library boxes. The first type are generic manuals provided by third-party vendors. A good example is the debut manual for PC DOS, which IBM bundled with the operating system. This manual is generic in that it was prepared for all work settings. Informed by an instrumental perspective, its instances of language — human and machine — are considered universal and therefore context-free: the objective for users was to learn the command syntax, which is fixed and unambiguous, and apply it correctly at the right times and places. This is still an objective in human-computer interactions today.

The second type of manual attempts to accommodate the specificities of particular work settings. A good example here is a manual titled "PSU Guide to INTERACT" (INTERACT was an early institutional time-sharing system with word processing, messaging, and other text-based features). As the opening page notes, the manual was "intended to introduce the INTERACT system by showing examples of its use, and also to describe certain features which are unique to Penn State." This manual, which was customized to address the needs of people on a particular campus, was complemented by a second, even more situated manual written to address the needs of people in a particular academic area: "An Introduction to the Use of Script" shows liberal arts faculty how to use the formatting program in INTERACT to design academic and administrative texts. The bulletins — published quarterly, beginning in 1966 — review software updates that have occurred since the manuals were written, describe new training opportunities, update contact information for support personnel, and more. Even early academic IT systems were marked by instability and continuous change.

The pedagogical imperative of the customized manuals and the bulletins reflects a textual perspective that begins to acknowledge the persuasive nature of language in institutions. Explanations are not neutral elaborations of procedures but rhetorical techniques for constructing sympathetic contexts for academic IT. By this I mean that the customized manuals and bulletins address inevitable gaps between the literacy practices of users and the development practices of academic IT specialists, with the goal of influencing user attitudes and experiences. Jack Carroll and Mary Beth Rosson (1992) contend that "a self-instruction manual can be seen as embodying a range of assertions about what learners know, what they do, what they experience, about the nature of the learning tasks and the contexts within which these tasks are carried out, etc." (183). For example, the manual for SCRIPT, a text processor, makes assertions about writing activities in the liberal arts (e.g., writers produce single-authored books; use accent marks and other special characters, such as circumflexes and cedillas; and create copious footnotes and endnotes), about the features in SCRIPT that can support these activities (e.g., the procedures for maintaining separate chapter files, overstriking one character with another, and automatically numbering footnotes and endnotes), and about the access users have to other help resources (e.g., a separate manual provides general reference information). These assertions are necessarily bound up with how users feel about SCRIPT, projecting a situation in which users encounter institutional assumptions as they approach and solve concrete problems.

Users have options when confronting assertions in the manuals and bulletins: they can accept, reject, hack, or work around them. Users can also deploy a combination of these options, even within a single work session. Generally speaking, the closer the match between the assertions and the literacy practices of users, the more likely it is that users will accept and use academic IT environments, while real mismatches often lead to their rejection. Beyond the binary opposition of acceptance and rejection, there are also "satisficing" or making-do practices that are sufficiently satisfactory to users, allowing them to achieve good-enough results in their task domains (Simon 1972). The customized manuals and the bulletins aim to construct sympathetic contexts by situating academic IT environments in local settings and helping users become familiar with the institutional lay of the land, as it were, in an attempt to support their specific needs, however imperfectly. There is a desire here to display university commitments and encourage users to accept or make do with complex environments that require patience and a willingness to work collaboratively with academic IT specialists as sociotechnical circumstances evolve.

Strategic plans are vision documents that advance institutional agendas. I mentioned strategic plans in previous chapters and discussed their planning processes as formalized approaches for including students and teachers in university decision-making. The strategic plans in the library boxes range in time and scope from annual plans for the work of subunits to multiyear plans for the entire academic IT enterprise. Although strategic-planning processes tend to be inclusive of multiple perspectives, the written plans domesticate institutional complexity in order to render it understandable, representable, and actionable. In other words, the plans impose a dominant view meant to focus the efforts of institutions in strengthening or changing directions. This dominant view is performed by academic IT directors and managers who are responsible for helping to turn the plans into concrete realities. According to Margaret Ann Baker and Carol David (1994), management writing often achieves its objectives by "projecting leadership, assuming commonality, and controlling information" (166). Projecting leadership involves owning institutional processes and establishing goals and outcomes, assuming commonality involves building identification with readers in ways that emphasize shared needs and values, and controlling information involves decisions about how much and what information to communicate to readers. These "ethos-creating strategies" (169) reflect hierarchical dynamics in institutional contexts.

Baker and David (1994) describe some of the tactics employed in management writing to enact ethos-creating strategies—for projecting leadership by using a direct style and positive tone; for assuming commonality by using first-person plural pronouns, jargon, and enthymemes that link plans and goals to accepted norms; and for controlling information by determining levels of elaboration. A strategic plan for the entire academic IT enterprise at Penn State provides good examples of these tactics in action. The plan comes from the executive director of computer and information systems and details processes, accomplishments, challenges, goals, and next steps. In discussing processes, the plan projects leadership by rehearsing the extensive consultative structures for deriving the plan and listing committee members who provided input and advice, including teachers. In considering accomplishments, the plan assumes commonality by discussing institutional goals as shared goals that have meaning and value for everyone and by articulating accomplishments using first-person plural pronouns, as in the following sentence: "Over the past decade, Penn State has made significant investments in the information technologies that have enabled us to remain competitive." In reviewing challenges, the plan controls for information by listing critical problems but then emphasizing budgetary approaches that inhibit institutional solutions to these problems. In discussing goals, the plan assumes commonality by linking a new professional development program for minority graduate students who are interested in academic IT careers with the accepted institutional norm of valuing a diverse workforce. And in outlining next steps, the plan projects leadership by using the imperative mood to direct institutional actions, as in the following sentence: "Provide a permanent funding base for the Professional Development Program and other outreach programs like it." There are many additional examples that illuminate the writing tactics described by Baker and David.

The official university records in the library boxes illustrate at least three operative textual perspectives in academic IT units. An instrumental perspective is discernible in the annual reports, which document processes of institutionalization by recording transactions and relationships. Although this sort of instrumentalism is arhetorical and counterproductive in many cases, it does yield performance data for academic IT units, adding a piece to the larger puzzle of representing institutional histories. A pedagogical perspective can be seen in the customized manuals and the bulletins, which construct sympathetic contexts for academic IT by localizing how-to texts. And the strategic plans, which advance institutional agendas by asserting status, building identification with readers, and controlling information, provide a managerial perspective. These operative textual perspectives are neither inherently helpful nor harmful in institutions but an aspect of academic IT environments that should be consciously adopted. I can see both upsides and downsides in applications of the perspectives at particular times and in particular situations.

In addition to the persuasive qualities that can be identified in pedagogical and managerial perspectives, there are also constitutive dimensions to language use that give meaning to institutional experiences. Understanding such dimensions is also an important part of being able to conceptualize institutional dynamics and engage academic IT units. Textual practices enable people to communicate membership roles and responsibilities in institutions, to articulate what they do to contribute to the greater good of a community, and to explain why and how they do it. Academic IT specialists are makers and remixers: they spend a considerable amount of time building, modifying, and maintaining software applications, integrating applications into larger systems, and developing services and resources to support applications and systems. Applications, systems, services, and resources are the mainstay of academic IT specialists and the units of analysis by which they are understood and evaluated. Although end-user products are a visible aspect of institutions and a usual target for praise or criticism, the work routines of academic IT specialists are mysterious to students and teachers and sometimes even to colleagues and administrators. Texts can demystify work routines by communicating actions that are hidden from everyday view.

Job descriptions provide some sense of the official activities of institutional workers, but they can be vague or outdated and ignore decision-making aspects of a job. In addition, job descriptions are also one-dimensional in that they fail to reflect how workers think through problems and solutions. A more insightful textual practice is blogging, particularly long-form blogging on platforms hosted by universities, which provide an institutionally supported (and regulated) environment for publishing. The bloggers most frequently acknowledged in universities are students and teachers: both academic IT specialists and teachers have debated the merits and limitations of blogs for classes and the risks for teachers who blog regularly about work (Bouwma-Gearhart and Bess 2012). Although less apparent to university communities, academic IT specialists also maintain blogs as a facet of their jobs, and these blogs can elaborate the workings of institutions and communicate membership roles and responsibilities.

Consider the blog of Cole Camplese, the CIO at Northeastern University and a onetime senior director of Penn State's Teaching and Learning with Technology unit (https://www.colecamplese.com). Camplese has been running a blog since 2004, and he uses it to share leadership perspectives that would otherwise be unavailable to students and teachers. For example, his entry titled "Organizational Frameworks" provides a behind-the-scenes look at how subareas within the TLT unit fit together to form a coherent institutional structure in which academic IT specialists from across the unit collaborate in the end-to-end process of investigating emerging technologies, implementing them in pedagogical settings, driving adoptions, and communicating affordances (Camplese 2011). Students and teachers tend to see the subareas as separate vertical organizations—one contacts the Classroom and Lab Computing group for help with classroom projectors, for instance, or the Training Services group for help with software programs—but the blog post explains how the subareas constitute a "value chain of sorts" that organizes institutional activities at a macro level. This big-picture view provides access to an overarching vision informing the entire operation.

The blog post also describes a new composing process for producing annual reports. It used to be the case that directors of subunits were asked to write individual reports for their areas, which were then compiled into an overall document. But this divide-and-conquer strategy created various coherence problems, including clashing stylistic registers and conflicting data for overlapping projects that could not be easily reconciled. The new process began by taking the most recent annual report and breaking its headline initiatives into separate blog entries so that people could discuss them and vote on the most important initiatives. According to Camplese, "The blog gave us a multipage digital representation of a static document." The process, however, also involved putting the headline initiatives on sticky notes and then color coding them to assign institutional ownership in order to designate who is responsible for which aspects of initiatives.

This spatial vantage point enables writers to more easily identify and group themes and consolidate and prioritize projects. The new approach takes a document designed around hidden institutional structures and turns it into thematic representations of the TLT unit; directors then collaborate on wiki pages to develop the themes. Lastly, the senior director uses the wiki pages to edit and produce the annual report. Although the annual report itself documents processes and products of institutionalization, the blog functions as a mechanism through which information about actions is circulated and comes to influence the actions of others. It makes the invisible visible and thus more available for inspection and engagement.

Textual practices not only enable workers to communicate roles and responsibilities but also help produce and maintain institutional relationships. The maintenance function is conspicuous enough in the operative textual perspectives in academic IT units: managerial writing for strategic plans advances institutional agendas, as I have already noted. It is also self-evident in policies and procedures documents and in the downward communication channels discussed in chapter 3. But what about the production function of textual practices? How does it help create institutional relationships? In one way of thinking, relationships are predetermined by organizational charts and job categories and roles, which differentiate workers according to their responsibilities to each other and the institution. I offered an example in chapter 1 of four job roles—conceptualizers, developers, modifiers or extenders, and supporters or tenders—correlated with educational degrees. These are instances of relevant distinctions that play a part in shaping the activities in academic IT units. Institutional relationships, however, are constantly being reconstructed by textual practices in situated contexts. They are always, it is safe to say, contingent and in flux, reflecting underlying values and assumptions that evolve and shift with changing circumstances.

For example, a Penn State website for the College of the Liberal Arts constructs several different institutional relationships between academic IT specialists and faculty members (https://it.la.psu.edu). The website explains that the college IT unit is divided into four subunits: the Web and Creative Services subunit designs websites and documents for "stakeholders" in the college, the Application and Data Services subunit develops software programs and data services for "clients" in the college, the Customer Experience and User Engagement subunit provides technical support for "customers" in the college, and the Infrastructure Services subunit administers servers and networks for "users" in the college. Although each of these signifiers—stakeholders, clients, customers, and users—has a plurality of changing meanings in institutions, the meanings in the college IT unit construct differential levels of access to development processes.

On one end of the spectrum, the stakeholder discourse of the Web and Creative Services subunit is the most invitational and inclusive, encouraging faculty members to become co-designers of academic IT systems, including pedagogical websites. On the other end of the spectrum, the user discourse of the Infrastructure Services subunit limits faculty collaborations to troubleshooting phases. I can understand why the Infrastructure Services subunit might adopt an insular stance: it is responsible for maintaining data security and integrity and administering back-end systems, which are opposed to the front-end systems developed by the other subunits for and with faculty members. But the distinctions between front-end and back-end systems are more technical than anything else and do not diminish the need for inclusive approaches: design decisions on the back end have ramifications far beyond the technical sphere. The user discourse of the Infrastructure Services subunit reinforces an unnecessary dichotomy between institutional protection and faculty invention, prioritizing the former and reducing the latter to diagnostic activities. Although I am being critical of user discourse, the point is that the college IT website textualizes relationships that govern access to development processes. Teachers should be alert to this potent aspect of institutionalization.

There is at least one more relevant perspective on the constitutive dimensions of language that is hard to sense in academic IT units: textual practices and institutional knowledge are inseparable and indivisible. Institutional knowledge making receives considerable attention throughout universities, and academic IT units have a good track record of creating systems for capturing, curating, storing, and distributing consequential texts. A conspicuous example is knowledge bases, which I mentioned in my discussion of augmentation systems in chapter 3. Part of the rationale for knowledge bases is that they help institutions retain memory content. Memory degrades in institutions when workers change roles or jobs, groups are reorganized or disbanded, or agendas shift from one focus to another. Knowledge bases provide a strategy and a workflow for collecting and representing what institutions know and for making it available to workers and other interested audiences.

The University of Wisconsin hosts an extensive knowledge base that incorporates thousands of texts from over one hundred on-campus partners, including academic departments (https://kb.wisc.edu). Other schools can also adopt the platform. Users can access a wide range of texts, such as instruction sets, policies and procedures, pedagogical materials, and administrative reports, and they can suggest new texts, comment on texts, suggest search terms, and grade texts as helpful or not. It is important to note that knowledge bases are not always stand-alone platforms but can be a component of larger knowledge systems. Knowledge systems incorporate institutional texts, repository technologies, and communities of practice to forge environments for both individual and group problem solving (Norris, Lefrere, and Mason 2006). The inclusion of communities of practice presupposes that knowledge acquisition is a social enterprise involving more than just searching for and downloading institutional texts. Knowledge bases and systems can also acknowledge the distributed nature of expertise by allowing users to edit texts.

In the perspective I want to foreground, textual practices have a robust capacity to condition how institutions produce and stabilize knowledge. Institutional knowledge exists not in texts themselves but in how they are used to coordinate and accomplish action. I know how to employ a course-management system because I know how to integrate numerous elements in sociotechnical articulations: computer classrooms, e-books, writing program policies, pedagogical theories, and university resources, to name a few of the more obvious ones. My teaching outcomes and accomplishments are measures of my knowledge, not the ability to read and consume information: institutional knowledge is not about things but about actions in situated contexts. But the distinction between things (symbolic and material) and actions breaks down in practice because texts can be said to perform actions in institutions. By this I mean that texts help people make institutional meaning and that this meaning engenders concrete practices and experiences. Such a performative view is attuned to how texts inscribe representations about practices and activities into institutional memory and how those representations span time and space in constitutive and transformative ways. In everyday scenarios, institutions act through the texts they produce.

An illustrative example is meeting minutes. Academic IT units conduct a great deal of business in face-to-face and online meetings. There are many different reasons for holding meetings, but a universal challenge is representing what happened and who was involved and how. Joanna Wolfe (2006) describes three types of meeting minutes and their relationships to knowledge making: transcript style, parliamentary style, and action-oriented style. Transcript-style minutes textualize by providing the full transcript of a meeting, capturing the "entire conversation in the order in which it occurred" (355). Although Wolfe notes that transcript-style minutes "have no clear rhetorical purpose" (355), they span time and space in useful ways by making the conversation available to people who could not attend the meeting. In addition, the transcripts can be reviewed as institutional artifacts to answer questions about past decision-making. Wolfe also refers to transcript-style minutes as information dumps, but I am inclined to see them as data dumps because the transcripts have not been processed by humans or machines to make them helpful to institutionalization efforts. I borrow this distinction between data and information from Liza Potts (2013), who asserts that data become information when they are contextualized and interpreted in actual situations of use (24). In a subsequent phase discussed by Potts, information then becomes knowledge when it is shared in social spaces and acted on by groups of people. In the other two types of meeting minutes, parliamentary style and action-oriented style, writers construct partial textual depictions of actions that in turn are used to help make and remake institutions. In fact, in a certain sense, one could say that meetings exist only to produce minutes, for meetings themselves are ephemeral and easily forgotten. Minutes are the only tangible residue and distributable aspect of the work.

Parliamentary-style minutes textualize meetings by characterizing what was discussed and agreed on by the attendees. Wolfe (2006) explains that parliamentary-style minutes are appropriate for self-governing bodies, especially large ones, and that they "foreground motions, votes, and individual positions on issues" (356). My department follows Robert's Rules of Order, so our meeting minutes reflect its structuring schemes, characterizing who said what about agenda items and noting votes on motions and amendments. Minutes come to stand in for meetings as a whole, and actions are predicated on their selective content. We approve draft minutes in order to authorize how they textualize interactions and events—to institutionalize sanctioned interpretations, recognizing that there are future stakes in how minutes represent meetings. For instance, my department maintains a list of presses and journals that are considered top-tier venues for tenure-line faculty. Any revisions to the list are discussed and voted on in department meetings, but the characterizations in the minutes can affect how the list is treated in knowledge-making activities. If the list is presented as the mechanism by which we judge ourselves, then faculty members will be inclined to publish their work with the presses and journals on the list, crafting their knowledge-making activities for those reviewers and audiences. If the list is presented as a (not the) mechanism by which we judge ourselves—one used for benchmarking purposes but not definitive in tenure and promotion cases—then faculty members will feel freer to publish their work with the presses and journals that make the most sense for their methods and arguments. Both contracted and expanded characterizations of our list have appeared in meeting minutes, and people have approached publishing projects differently based on those various characterizations.

Supervisors hierarchically manage academic IT units, and so they do not follow Robert's Rules of Order. But meeting minutes in this context, which are action oriented, still construct partial textual depictions that are used to help make and remake institutions. If the goal of parliamentary-style minutes is to characterize what was discussed and agreed on by meeting attendees in order to represent histories, the goal of action-oriented minutes is to advance workflows for solving institutional problems. In action-oriented minutes, "the rhetorical focus is on regulating future actions" (Wolfe 2006, 355). The distinguishing feature of this type of minutes is a list of action items: a to-do list that configures work by solidifying consensus views, and thus defining boundaries and descriptions of work, and assigning and tracking responsibilities. The Office of Information Technology at North Carolina State University uses Portfolio Project Management (PPM) as a framework for developing academic IT projects, and this framework supplies a template for creating action-oriented minutes. The top table in the template has rows for listing attendees and agenda topics and recording decisions. The bottom table has columns for listing action items, the people responsible for those items, initiation and completion dates, and comments. The template can be said to perform action by prompting committees to agree on what they know and want to do and represent their plans as procedures for guiding institutional activities. It defines and legitimates certain approaches to thinking and doing and allows them to be transmitted across time and space and incorporated into other deliberations and actions, constructing rational and unified views of future aspects of projects.

Academic IT specialists adopt pedagogical perspectives on language use to create sympathetic contexts and managerial perspectives on language use to establish authorial ethos. In these ways (and others), they mobilize persuasive dimensions of texts. Academic IT specialists also recognize the role of texts in preserving and sharing institutional knowledge, as evidenced by their ongoing attention to platforms for capturing and circulating expertise. In addition, I would argue that texts and textual practices function in a more constitutive fashion, making the invisible visible and thus actionable, defining and shaping relationships between academic IT specialists and teachers, and conditioning what is considered to be knowledge. All academic IT units participate in and are influenced by how institutions textualize actions and activities. Textualization is a process and a performance that produces real and lasting effects.

ENDURING TEXTUAL QUESTIONS

Teachers of writing and communication often begin investigations into institutional life by considering textual practices and contexts. From a rhetorical perspective, textual practices and contexts are a vibrant force in the sociotechnical articulations that lend meaning to teaching and learning, helping produce and naturalize ways of thinking and problem solving in the classroom and beyond. The enduring textual questions in the field address both representational and action-oriented aspects of the academic IT enterprise: How are information technologies like texts? What are the assumptions in textual depictions of information technologies? What are the textual depictions involved in developing information technologies? And how should information technologies be documented for users? These questions are pertinent to any and all teachers and to their prospects for engagement with academic IT units.

How Are Information Technologies like Texts?

Since the mid-1980s, cultural studies approaches have asked teachers to see cultures and their artifacts as texts that can be read and interpreted on a number of levels. Seeing cultures and cultural artifacts as texts is an activist vision of literacy and literacy instruction, one that aspires to "increase democratic participation in public life, to give voice to the needs and experience of those who have been silenced and marginalized, to articulate political desires" (Trimbur 1988, 13). These goals are focused not so much on dismantling other approaches but on historicizing writing and communication practices, on admitting and validating the everyday lived experiences of students as sites for invention and production, including the previous technological experiences that I wrote about in chapter 2. There are many reasons why the cultural studies agenda gained so much traction in the field. John Trimbur associates its adoption with four possible factors: a rejuvenated political interest among faculty whose formative years were during the turbulent and socially momentous times of the 1960s, an improved professional climate in universities that emboldened teachers to expand the boundaries of the discipline, the opening up of the literary canon to be more inclusive of the population, and a rise in critical theory that is interested in action as well as critique (6–8). The conceptualization of everyday cultural forms as texts is a rhetorical move that is discernible in all of these developments.

In discussing cultural studies and popular culture courses and their shared ground of ordinary things, Diana George and Diane Shoos (1993) stress that cultural studies "is about critiquing institutions, especially as those institutions embody power relations. We would even argue that a course that attempts to use cultural studies without acknowledging its domain as an interrogator of institutions is simply a course in pop culture" (201). In their essay, they are interested in questions of resistance, in how to admit everyday experiences and artifacts into writing and communication courses, critique popular culture without necessarily rejecting all of its institutional influences, and avoid falling back on traditional power dynamics between students and teachers. For George and Shoos, a key to achieving a productive cultural studies classroom is employing texts that offer "a kind of cultural and interpretive richness, one in which meaning is unstable for instructors as well as students" (207). Although the meaning of texts is always already unstable, I take this suggestion to imply that teachers should assign cultural artifacts with which they themselves have a complex and ambiguous institutional relationship, one that leaves room for various aspects of the context of discovery, including conclusions. Uncertainty is a classroom resource for extending the field of possibilities for teaching and learning.

George and Shoos (1993) examine television shows, but teachers have considered a wide range of cultural artifacts as texts that can be interpreted in institutional contexts, from T-shirts and ballet shoes (Shipka 2011) to 3D-printed objects (Sheridan 2010). A semiotic approach has had purchase for teachers because it provides a ready framework for conceptualizing and critiquing technologies as well as integrating them into classrooms. Conceptual frameworks are analytical tools that enable people to organize their thinking about complex problems. In imagining technologies as texts, teachers apply concepts and methods for writing and reading in order to understand capabilities and implications. In a subsequent section, I will discuss metaphors as a textual element of my heuristic. Here I am picturing something more encompassing and closer to what Kenneth Burke (1989) calls a "terministic screen," a disciplinary filter for seeing (and not seeing) that channels and deflects the attention of students and teachers. Let me provide an example from computer programming.

Annette Vee (2013) traces historical and contemporary parallels between programming and writing and reading by using literacy studies as a conceptual framework for explaining the cultures and practices of programming and their relevance to students and teachers. More specifically, she asserts that literacy studies can "help us understand the material affordances of code and computers as well as the ways that programming's social values, contexts, and communities shape practices of computational literacy and the identities associated with those practices" (55). Vee outlines tenets from literacy studies and then illustrates how programming practices are social practices, how conventions and standards help programmers coordinate work activities, how computer programs have multiple audiences and functions, and how programming approaches are involved in the construction of identities, socializing people into particular kinds of institutional roles. The tenets serve as generative guides for imagining programming as a mode of production.

In addition to modeling a conceptual framework, the technology-as-text formulation has also provided teachers with approaches to critique. One prevalent approach is from Richard Lanham (1995), who aims to foreground the materialities of media with his bi-stable oscillation technique of looking both at and through technologies. Lanham is responding to the common tendency to treat media as transparent vehicles for communication: "We are accustomed to being told that the computer is a neutral tool; as far as text is concerned, and the humanistic education which rests upon it, nothing could be further from the truth" (150). His technique is a way of seeing that consists of toggling back and forth between looking through a text for meaning and looking at how a text itself is materialized and encountered. The goal of toggling is to break down habituated attention structures in literacy practices, bringing consciousness to the meaning-making capacities and biases of technologies. Many in the field have appropriated the notion of bi-stable oscillation as a component of critique. Heidi McKee (2005) uses it to help students reflect on sociotechnical dynamics in online discussions, Tharon Howard (1998) uses it to defamiliarize design features in multimedia projects, and Collin Brooke (2009) uses it to refashion the rhetorical canon, encouraging the field to adjust its site of study to encompass digital interfaces. In his essay on critical technological awareness, Aaron Toscano (2011) underscores that he hopes to "move students to consider not just computers but all technologies as texts for uncovering cultural values" (16). This objective continues to be a central aspect of critique.

In terms of classroom integration, I have already mentioned several field approaches for information technologies, such as scaffolding functional, critical, and rhetorical perspectives at the levels of programs, courses, and assignments. The technology-as-text formulation suggests a process for technologies that roughly mirrors how teachers integrate texts into classroom settings. There are a myriad of ways to use texts in writing courses, but many if not most of them involve selecting texts, situating them in a context, reading actively and with a purpose, interpreting possible meanings, and applying the texts to new contexts. George and Shoos (1993) select popular texts that pose epistemological challenges for themselves and students, situate those texts in institutional contexts that highlight power dynamics, foster dialogic discussions, value interpretations based on personal experiences, and ask students to apply the texts in writing about their own lives. Such discursive practices have been extended to technologies to aid the task of curricular integration. Teachers select technologies as both tools and subjects for courses; situate technologies in social, political, and economic contexts; prompt students to explore the dynamics and constraints of technologies in online forums; ask students to make sense of technologies using personal literacy narratives; and ask students to remix technologies to create new projects. The results are curricula that are congruent with the aims of a rhetorical education.

It is worth noting, too, that the inverse formulation resonates with academic IT specialists in ways that can be helpful to institutional cooperation. If technologies can be considered texts that are read and written by students and teachers, texts can function as technologies that are used to support complex problem solving. Jason Swarts (2004) demonstrates how "texts become tools when users adapt the way the texts structure and represent information for specific tasks" (67). His study examines the textual grounding practices of organizational workers who are conducting document reviews and shows how they variously mark texts and layer in other texts (for context) to accomplish situated actions, "actively creating tools out of their texts" (68). Texts as technologies, technologies as texts: this dialectic is generative because it allows ideas to come from either direction, complicating and enriching both directions. It invites teachers and academic IT specialists to entertain opposing ideas in the interest of shared institutional projects.

What Are the Assumptions in Textual Depictions of Information Technologies?

An ongoing preoccupation in the field is interrogating textual depictions of information technologies, especially assumptions about the status and process of innovation and change. I include visual as well as verbal artifacts in my examples because I am operating under the extended sense of text introduced in the previous section on cultural studies. Considered from the outside in, teachers have interrogated textual depictions of technologies in popular discourses, disciplinary discourses, and institutional discourses, analyzing trade magazines, advertisements, journals, bureaucratic documents, websites, databases, email exchanges, and other genres and forums.

The motive to analyze assumptions comes from both argument-based and critical approaches to rhetoric. In argument-based approaches, assumptions are often a formal element of an analytical scheme. A good example is the Toulmin model. Stephen Toulmin (1958) constructs a model for argumentative reasoning that includes six parts: (1) claims, or the assertions rhetors want to advance; (2) data, or the evidence rhetors reference to support their claims; (3) warrants, or the assumptions that bridge the data and the claims; (4) backing, or support for the warrants; (5) qualifiers, or limitations of the claims; and (6) rebuttals, or counterarguments. For Toulmin, one of the more vulnerable aspects of an argument is a weak warrant or assumption. Consider the claim that all students should receive a free laptop from their university. Referencing data on the significance of access to learning could prove to be compelling to administrators who assume that laptops (like networks) are infrastructural components of academic institutions. In contrast, referencing data on the rising costs of higher education might not prove to be so compelling to administrators who assume that laptops (like textbooks) are extrainstitutional components of an education. An argument collapses on itself when audiences fail to accept the underlying assumptions that bridge the data and the claims. Rhetors are therefore alert to how assumptions function in reasoning chains.

In critical approaches to rhetoric, assumptions are a window into the nature and expression of power relations, into what is imaginable and possible in sociotechnical articulations. A good example here is the notion of common sense found in the work of radical educators such as Henry Giroux (1997) and Michael Apple (1990). Giroux and Apple value the everyday understandings of students and teachers as valid sources of insight into the human condition. Everyday understandings represent a type of commonsense knowledge (or know-how) that can be useful in solving practical problems. Reasoning from personal spheres is both a meaningful starting point for invention and a valid source for argumentative evidence and commentary, as illustrated by the prevalence of literacy narrative assignments (see chapter 2), which ask students to interrogate their assumptions about institutions, literacies, and technologies. The issue is when assumptions become so much a part of our common sense that people take them for granted and do not think to imagine other possibilities, a situation that can impede reflection and reproduce structures of inequality. One assumption I often encounter is related to the consumerization movement: the consumer marketplace is setting the agenda and pace for academic IT units, which will become irrelevant if they fail to compete or partner with the likes of Google, Adobe, and Microsoft. This assumption is based on the general recognition that the consumer marketplace is modifying literacy practices faster than teachers are modifying educational approaches. The time lag between development and adoption is understood to be hurting universities and their ability to prepare students who are ready to join the twenty-first-century labor force. Although time lags can be useful to reflection and learning and to stabilizing and supporting academic IT systems, time lags are often taken for granted as problems that must be solved or eliminated through outsourcing engagements.

In popular discourses, the textual depictions of information technologies examined by the field shed light on assumptions about gender roles and subjectivities. Analyses by feminist scholars have interrogated assumptions that contribute to the reproduction of status quo power relations in cultures. Cynthia Selfe (1999) interprets a series of commercial ads for computers to show how they rely on "traditional narratives that tell the same old gender stories over and over again" (321), which depict women as sexualized objects, mothers, or subordinated helpers in business settings. Likewise, Patricia Webb (2003) interprets a series of covers, ads, and articles to show how "the old guard is ever in control of our engagement with, understanding of, and musings on information technologies" (163). The images in these materials associate women with irrational bodies or the senses and men with reason and the rational mind. Feminist scholars challenge the assumption that women and technology are naturally incompatible in certain fundamental respects.

Ads have also been a focus for critics who are interested in how ideology works to construct subject positions. Susan Stein (2002) analyzes the original Macintosh television ad from 1984 to surface its assumptions about the function of new technologies in the contemporary social world. Although the ad is rife with rhetorics of freedom and revolution, positioning computer users as hero-subjects who can single-handedly change the face of politics by defying authoritarian regimes of thinking, Stein concludes that the ad ultimately situates computer users as principal consumers who must make the right choice in a capitalist marketplace. The right choice, Macintosh, leads to freedom and independence of thought; the wrong choice, any competing option, leads to tyranny and groupthink. The assumption is that technology is autonomous enough to cause radical social change. The ad also presupposes that "the solution to the problems of technology is always a better technology" (Stein 2002, 189). Such assumptions have become articles of faith in Western cultures, escaping accountability in a variety of contexts, including education.

In disciplinary discourses, the textual depictions of information technologies examined by the field shed light on assumptions about academic borders and methodological appropriation. An enduring project for teachers of writing and communication is disambiguating and relating the intellectual ground shared with other disciplines. I myself am working to articulate the shared intellectual ground of academic IT so that teachers can play a more influential role in institutions. The broad intention of my project is not so unusual in a field that has a history of borrowing approaches from other academic areas. Thomas Skeen (2009) disambiguates and relates the fields of rhetoric and human-computer interaction (HCI) by tracing assumptions about designers and users that have influenced the shape of interfaces. His main argument is that "the rhetorical relationships of power in each field are complex, fluctuating on a continuum between users on one end and designers on the other, mediated through technology" (102). What Skeen is getting at here is that "an ideal of democratization and empowerment exists in both fields" (102), but expectations vary as to the most profitable level and type of user involvement in development activities. It is useful for teachers to be aware of the cultural turn (or third wave) in HCI and the shared assumption that democratization is a process that encompasses users, designers, and interfaces in some measurable ratio.

In terms of methodological appropriation, teachers have made a practice of evaluating assumptions about technologies in depictions of research approaches. Jay Dolmage (2009) is an exemplar here: he analyzes the discourses of usability to show how assumptions about normality and technology tend to prioritize an "average, majority user" (180), the depictions of which stifle progress when it comes to addressing disability issues. In recognizing the utility of usability methods for teachers, Dolmage proposes a new guiding assumption: "Disability should remake the spaces of writing" (184), not technologies or ableist visions of users. The point of proposing this alternative assumption is to reframe usability methods so that they align with the values and practices of the field.

I have already noted several assumptions about technologies in institutional discourses. Institutions, for example, often assume that technologies are levers for cost savings, productivity improvements, and instructional innovations. They also often assume that technology is itself strategic and part of the structure and governing logic of higher education. But what I want to emphasize here is that the assumptions of institutions are not always so different from those of teachers, especially early adopters and heavy users, who tend to be highly integrated into academic communities. I also want to emphasize that the effects of even paradoxical assumptions can serve the same end. In her survey of discourses in the discipline, Ellen Barton (1994) shows how both negative and positive assumptions actually merge in the dominant discourse, "in effect leaving the field with only one voice, which focuses on the assumed benefits of technology" (56). Barton admonishes teachers to be attentive to how even negative assumptions about technologies can reinforce the very educational problems they are working to solve.

What Are the Textual Practices Involved in Developing Information Technologies?

Teachers of writing and communication need to understand the work contexts for technical professionals so that they can design relevant courses for two groups of students. One group includes students in science, engineering, and other technical fields who are required to take a course in disciplinary writing. I am thinking of service courses in technical and professional writing. A second group includes English majors who aspire to become practicing communicators in scientific and technical contexts; some of these students earn degrees or minors in technical and professional writing. Although these groups have different needs, both of them are relevant to a second reason teachers have had a long-standing interest in the textual practices of technical professionals: the realization that the status of the field is bound up with how others view the function of writing in organizations.

One common approach to studying the textual practices of technical professionals begins by extending current field interests from classrooms to workplaces. Consider what teachers have done when it comes to composing. The composing processes of students have been a site of investigation since at least the 1960s, and teachers continue to evolve their understandings of why, how, where, and when students communicate and write. But starting in the 1980s, this ongoing interest in composing widened out in earnest to encompass workplace settings, as teachers continued to professionalize the field by strengthening its research enterprise. Jack Selzer

(1983), for example, reports on how a technical professional plans, drafts, and revises his work. Selzer notes that he is surprised by how this professional emphasizes the early phases of composing at the expense of revision and how the composing process is more linear than the characterizations typically offered by teachers. Jeanne Halpern (1986) reports on how technical professionals compose with the new media of the time, such as electronic mail and word processing. She doubles down on the rhetorical arts as they have been imagined in the field but reorients them around the specificities of media, arguing that teachers should reinvigorate notions of invention, arrangement, style, memory, and delivery by situating them as elements of new media composing. And Dorothy Winsor (1990) reports on how a technical professional produces knowledge while composing. For the person she studied, there is very little daylight between his understanding of a technical object and his talking and writing about it, substantiating the view that discourse and knowledge are closely intertwined and knotted. These studies stipulate pedagogical exigencies and the desire to use workplace research to inform programmatic initiatives, whether or not the results align with conventional wisdom from the classroom.

If one approach to studying the textual practices of technical professionals begins by extending current field interests from classrooms to workplaces, a second approach flows in the opposite direction, particularly for English majors who aspire to become practicing communicators in scientific and technical contexts. Teachers have long acknowledged that there are specificities in workplaces and that these are vital to the communication activities of professionals, differentiating them from students and also presenting challenges. Teachers have endeavored to learn what is particular about workplace writing so that they can prepare students to become productive, ethical professionals. Much of this work is discussed in managerial terms that address the dynamics of producing communication products within the complex structuring systems of organizations. Although teachers talk with students about managing time, resources, collaborative projects, and more, in workplace settings the conversations tend to revolve around issues and methods for publications management, content management, and knowledge management. These terms are closely related and often used interchangeably, but they can and do accentuate different things.

Publications management has the narrowest scope, involving the materials and methods writers use to plan, create, and publish workplace documents. Edward Gold (1989) advises writers who work with computer programmers to acquire domain knowledge about the applications and teach programmers about user contexts in order to plan accordingly and deliver the most effective communication products. Don Samson (1995) discusses how people in high-tech firms need to be able to write quickly, avoid pride of authorship, deal with overwork, and succeed with supervisors. Barbara Weber (1995) illustrates how workplace writers manage deadlines. And David Smith (1995) explains how to estimate costs. There are many other aspects to publications management to consider as well.

By content management, I mean how the content for workplace documents is organized, stored, and handled by organizations. A good example is single sourcing. It used to be the case that workplace professionals developed new content for each writing project, shaping it for the rhetorical situation at hand. They may have copied content from other documents, but that content was not organized and stored in ways that made it easily reusable. Today, writers use single-source databases to separate content (input) from format (output); they then assemble and edit documents for specific audiences, purposes, and occasions. This approach requires professionals to model information structures and write modularly and generically (Robidoux 2007).

And by knowledge management, I mean how organizations manage and leverage what they know about their domains of expertise and the processes and systems they use to operate and succeed. In the version of knowledge management appropriated by technical and professional writing, writing is considered a vehicle through which knowledge is produced, and knowledge is considered a strategic asset for generating value. In one important role in knowledge-management situations, workplace writers become stewards of writing activities, helping organizations coordinate their knowledge work and transform it into content that helps audiences solve problems (Hart-Davidson 2013). As stewards at a high level, workplace writers develop macrolevel frameworks that help entire groups of people work more effectively together.

The status of the field is an issue that cuts across the approaches teachers use to investigate textual practices in workplace settings. By definition, service courses in technical and professional writing are weakly positioned as institutional sites for improving status or influence: they are supporting courses and often seen as less important than courses in major programs. Still, by conducting research that demonstrates the nature of workplace writing and its value to the careers of technical professionals, the field has been able to grow its presence and even participate in accreditation procedures. Furthermore, the service course has been a reliable source of funding for assistantships that support graduate students.

But there has been a greater potential to improve the status of the field by considering the activities of workplace writers and communicators, especially in the development of information technologies. One reason for this potential has to do with the changing nature of the workplace. As my discussion of knowledge management indicates, information itself has become a commodity, confounding distinctions between technologies and the texts that support them. Teachers have followed this development with interest, seeing it as an unusually good opportunity to advance arguments about writers' contributions to the primary work of organizations. One vector of advancement shifts the focus of technical and professional writing from a service orientation to one of systems thinking. These postindustrial models reposition writers and communicators as symbolic analysts who function at a more abstract level, producing, collecting, analyzing, and synthesizing data and information; discovering knowledge gaps; and developing solutions that increase the value of products and services (Johnson-Eilola 1996).

A second vector of advancement asks the field to be more explicit and precise about how textual practices improve the bottom line in organizations, generating revenue, containing expenses, and aiding efforts to comply with regulatory standards. Lori Anschuetz and Stephanie Rosenbaum (2002) illustrate these vectors with six case histories of professional growth in the computer industry. The people they studied transitioned from more traditional writing and editing jobs to positions with greater responsibility, such as usability and interface design manager and business operations strategist. These individuals were able to transition and grow because the practices of technical and professional writing are becoming less and less distinguishable from those of software development, organizational management, and other higher-level jobs. As symbolic-analytic work, technical and professional writing disrupts classification boundaries that have defined, and at times limited, the field.

The textual practices involved in developing information technologies have been an enduring concern for teachers, who extend current field interests from classrooms to workplaces and investigate what is specific to workplaces. The reasons for this enduring concern include responsibilities for service courses in technical and professional writing and for major courses for students who aspire to become practicing communicators in scientific and technical contexts. In such contexts, many of the practices tend to revolve around managing publications, content, and knowledge. Knowledge management is an area where the field has more room to assert its value: from a knowledge-management perspective, information is a commodity and a medium of exchange. In response to the development of this viewpoint, teachers have shifted at least part of their focus from a service orientation to one of systems thinking, demonstrating how textual practices affect productivity and profitability in organizations. Maintaining relevance is a priority for teachers of writing and communication everywhere.

How Should Information Technologies Be Documented for Users?

The tasks for documenting information technologies have become hallmarks of the field. According to James Souther (1989), the path to hallmark status was initiated by cultural developments related to the communication needs of publics, including the consumer movement, which challenged companies and government agencies to create informational and instructional texts in plain language, and the advent of personal computing, which required documentation to be usable but also a facet of marketing and sales. Souther also mentions research studies from the 1980s, which began to provide empirical support for the theories and practices being taught in universities. Many of these studies produced guidelines for procedural writing. A focus on procedures was the first phase of emphasis for the field, and it remains an important focus for documentation writers. Since then, the field has passed through at least two additional phases, focusing next on human-computer interfaces and then on sociotechnical networks. These phases of emphasis—procedures, interfaces, and networks—did not so much replace each other but rather accumulated into an evolving collection of considerations for documenting technologies.

Procedures were a logical starting place because they lie at the heart of software documentation, a genre that links the field to information technologies in direct and visible ways. The purpose of software documentation is to help people perform tasks in application environments. As a task-oriented genre, software documentation makes certain assumptions about workers as readers of documents. It assumes, for example, that reading is secondary to problem solving: people read in order to do things, to accomplish primary work (Redish 1992). Administrators read documentation to help them balance budgets or write reports, not learn about software. Another assumption is that problem solvers are active, selective readers, skimming and skipping content to find solutions. Workers as readers do not read documentation from start to finish but dip in and out as needed to find information. There are also assumptions about use contexts that are worth noting—for example, they divide worker attention between sources or spaces of information, requiring people to switch back and forth between help and work. Assumptions about readers, use contexts, and other elements of rhetorical situations shape how writers design procedures. Procedures are designed to be accessed quickly and easily by using navigation aids, headings, and vertical lists; stand alone as coherent chunks of text by reflecting structured writing techniques; emphasize problem solving by employing recognizable mental models and mirroring user tasks at organizational and sentence levels; and enable user control by allowing people to have some say over how they access, navigate, and interact with content. Teachers have referenced procedural writing approaches in arguments about what makes technical and professional writing different from first-year composition (Britton 1978; Tebeaux 1988).

The transition in emphasis from procedures to human-computer interfaces became apparent when online documentation achieved a notable level of implementation in the 1990s. Few books before then discussed in detail how to design online documentation. Although documentation writers considered the design implications of delivering procedures online, they became more interested in the general affordances of online environments and in their potential to transform documentation systems. One of the factors driving this interest was the emergence of hypertext, which allows writers to link help texts according to concepts and associations and offers readers greater flexibility to follow their own problem-solving paths. A second factor was the contraction of space—physical and metaphorical—between documentation systems and information technologies, a development that allows writers to integrate help and work in new and different ways. Merging help and work into a single environment not only erodes distinctions between these historically distinct areas but also resituates the design of documentation as an interface design task, affiliating it with the development of information technologies. In a relatively quick fashion, documentation writers started to become members of product design teams, participating in many phases of development to help create marketable and usable applications. On product design teams, documentation writers as interface designers assume many different roles. Susan Dray (1994) outlines several of them: user advocates who help define software requirements; subject matter experts who can explain the work practices and contexts of users; communication facilitators who can help teams function effectively; usability specialists who can translate the results of usability tests into design recommendations; and software developers who can prototype and design interfaces. These roles either broke new ground for writers or expanded existing responsibilities.

The transition in emphasis from human-computer interfaces to socio-technical networks became apparent when online documentation started to encompass users as help resources. If the hypertext capabilities of interfaces associate texts to support problem solving, the distributed nature of networks associate users in pools of participants that leverage expertise. In prenetworked systems, there was a visible and obvious divide between writers and users: writers produced help texts for users to consume. The medium of print assisted this divide, and early instances of online help did very little to change things. Networked documentation systems were a radical departure in that they decentralize expertise, harnessing the wisdom of the crowd to help individuals solve problems. There are still plenty of occasions in which it still makes sense for procedures to be controlled in a top-down fashion, but in situations where problems are not well defined or self-contained, networked documentation systems situate help users as producers, which in turn creates additional roles for writers.

Jason Swarts (2015) considers online user forums as an emerging genre of networked technical writing. He begins by unpacking assumptions about users that have long informed the design of documentation, particularly the assumption that user tasks are "associated with well-defined goals one reaches through well-defined procedures, via well-defined steps, and by avoiding well-defined faulty paths" (164). "That is," he continues, "a prototypical task has an idealized end state, predictable intermediate states, and known error states" (164). For example, there is only one way for me to access the course-management system from a computer classroom on campus: log into the instructor station with my Penn State access ID and password, launch Canvas, select Penn State WebAccess, and double-authenticate with a trusted device. This task has a well-defined goal—logging into Canvas—and well-defined procedures, and the errors I could make are easy to identify. Once in Canvas, I can access instructions for creating assignments, discussions, conferences, and modules, all of which are essential to organizing course spaces. At this point, however, tasks can become more uncertain and complex: What is the best way to employ the available features, which have overlapping operations? In what combinations and to what extent? And how can I communicate my decisions to students through course design techniques? In Canvas forums, I can solicit the help of networked users by starting new discussion threads or joining existing ones. As Swarts notes, many of the responses will likely aim to clarify the problems and tasks, and many of the suggestions will likely be presented as possibilities to explore and test. In this way, networked users participate in group invention activities, with documentation writers serving as moderators who can guide discussion and curate content. These additional roles are pivotal to the usefulness of active user forums.

The enduring question of how to design documentation involves phases of emphasis that increasingly associate the field with information technologies and continuously affect writers' professional expectations. In response to plain language movements and the consumerization of computers, teachers first emphasized procedures and how people use software documentation. The result was a body of structured writing techniques that remains relevant and widely taught today. Teachers made the shift to emphasizing human-computer interfaces when online documentation became a reality for everyday users. Online documentation shrinks the distance between help and work and resituates the design of documentation as an interface design task. The result was that technical writers broke new professional ground and expanded existing responsibilities as members of product design teams. Teachers turned to sociotechnical networks when online documentation started to incorporate users as help resources. Networks leverage the expertise of distributed users, especially for problem solving involving uncertain or complex tasks. User forums are an emerging form of networked writing that incorporates users as help resources. In user forums, documentation writers not only provide procedural help but also moderate discussion and curate content. Teachers have regarded the evolution from procedures to interfaces to networks as a series of fruitful emphases that challenge conventional notions of literacies and technologies.

The enduring textual questions that unite teachers are significant to academic IT contexts. By imagining technologies as texts, teachers can draw on accessible frameworks for conceptual modeling and critique and for curriculum design. By examining assumptions in textual depictions of technologies, teachers can illuminate power relations and the institutional possibilities for change. By investigating the textual practices involved in developing technologies, teachers can provide relevant instruction for students and help institutions manage publications, content, and knowledge. And by investigating how technologies should be documented for users, teachers can emphasize product design teams and fading distinctions between texts and technologies, developers and writers, and writers and users. Teachers of writing and communication have multiple textual avenues for advancing the interests of the field.

TEXTUAL ELEMENTS OF THE HEURISTIC

The textual elements of my heuristic include metaphors, subjectivities, genres, and stories (table 4.1). Metaphors are everywhere in institutions, influencing how they make knowledge and meaning and how academic IT environments are understood by users and academic IT specialists. Subjectivities are institutional modes of thinking about and structuring what workers do and how they do it. I will examine common work configurations that structure subjectivities and consider their implications for teaching and learning. Genres are a discursive attempt to formalize interactions and relationships in institutions. I will appropriate a classification scheme from Carolyn Miller (2017) that helps explain the functions of genres in academic IT units. Finally, stories function as bridges between the general propositions of institutions and the concrete experiences of students and teachers. I will consider the role stories play in reinforcing institutional narratives that involve literacies and technologies. As a group, metaphors, subjectivities, genres, and stories illuminate the textual dimensions of academic IT in informative and instructive ways.

TABLE 4.1 Textual elements of the heuristic

Dimension elements	Textual elaborations
Metaphors	Academic IT units employ metaphorical constructions that filter and delimit their own experiences and those of users in concrete ways. These constructions, which associate seemingly disconnected ideas or things, have implications (positive and negative) for institutions, literacies, and technologies.
Subjectivities	Academic IT units include subject positions that are effects of institutional discourses. These subject positions, which are structured relationally in contexts that include job classifications, project teams, and collectives, instantiate institutional modes of thinking about and organizing what workers do and how they do it.
Genres	Academic IT units employ a wide range of genres that textualize and formalize institutional interactions and relationships. Genres are stable enough to serve coordinating functions in communication situations and unstable enough to serve invention functions in discourse communities.
Stories	Academic IT units construct and circulate stories that play a reinforcing role in the maintenance and advancement of institutional narratives. Stories reinforce institutional narratives by amplifying identities, contextualizing artifacts and practices, and substantiating claims.

Metaphors

Metaphors are an everyday feature of language use that stretches across boundaries of time and space to connect seemingly disconnected ideas or things. Metaphors have epistemic dimensions, meaning that they help construct institutional knowledge, in the main by filtering and delimiting experience. Max Black (1981) provides an account of how metaphors function as filtering devices. According to Black, metaphors contain two constituent halves: a principal and subsidiary subject. A subsidiary subject filters the experience of a principal subject by providing context that imposes an extension or change of meaning; this operation occurs when people attempt to connect or reconcile the realms of thought summoned by what metaphors juxtapose (73). For example, if an institution characterizes online teachers as coaches, then the activities and systems associated with the latter will organize the view of the former: elements of teaching that can be discussed in coaching-related language will gain prominence and influence, while those that cannot will fade into the background or simply fade out of practice. Institutions can easily find other subsidiary subjects with which to characterize online teachers, such as master artists, network administrators, concierges, or curators (Siemens 2008). Each subsidiary subject invokes a different "system of associated commonplaces" or set of cultural connections (Black 1981, 74). As Black notes, these connections might include "half-truths or downright mistakes (as when a whale is classified as a fish); but the important thing for the metaphor's effectiveness is not that the commonplaces be true, but that they should be readily and freely invoked" (74). This filtering process, then, relies on cultural myths as well as more accurate understandings of the relationships between the ideas or things juxtaposed in metaphorical constructions.

Because metaphors provide different filters through which people approach academic IT environments, the decision to select one over another has implications for institutions, literacies, and technologies. To illustrate this point for institutions, let me return to my previous example from the College of the Liberal Arts; their website variously characterizes faculty members as stakeholders, clients, customers, and users. This example is useful because it illustrates how institutional relationships shift with changing circumstances, even for an individual person. I do not have a single relationship with the academic IT unit in my college but multiple relationships, and these are constantly being redefined in particular situations. The discourse of the Customer Experience and User Engagement subunit, which provides hardware and software support, encourages interaction and knowledge sharing, but what does it mean for teachers to be customers of an academic IT unit? Is the teacher-as-customer metaphor a fruitful one? The answer varies and usually depends on multiple factors. Teachers tend to hold a negative view of the customer metaphor because it situates education as a product to be delivered and consumed. Maryellen Weimer (2002) expresses concerns that arise from the meaning system of the subsidiary subject: "When the product is education, the customer cannot always be right, there is no money-back guarantee, and tuition dollars do not 'buy' the desired grades" (xvi). Although classrooms and academic IT units are distinct contexts, many teachers are skeptical of the growth of corporate influence in higher education and view any use of the customer metaphor as contradictory to the basic purpose of schools.

Academic IT specialists, in contrast, use customer-centric models to guide systems development. A germinal book explicating the thinking here is by IT professionals at Hewlett-Packard (Kreta and Hyatt 2003). The authors offer a vision of how to design for the web as a shopping mall, which is the controlling metaphor for the book, and focus on such tasks as analyzing consumer habits, building customer relationships, and defining customer interface requirements. Teachers at Penn State can see the influence of customer-centric thinking in the infrastructure provided by the Customer Experience and User Engagement subunit. For example, there is a front-end self-service catalog that allows teachers to install, patch, and uninstall software. Most teachers do not have administrative privileges on their computers because the college operates under the principle of least privilege, restricting what users can do to what is considered (by others) to be essential to routine work, but the catalog is an area where users can help themselves to products and services, saving time and making choices about institutional technologies. The self-service catalog makes sense from a business standpoint: as opposed to installing a software program on all computers, the college only pays a licensing fee for people who download and use it.

But the customer metaphor breaks down around issues of purpose and responsibility. I would make three arguments about this breakdown: teachers who need support from academic IT units to attend to the fundamentals of their jobs should not be thought of as customers; teachers who do not know what they need from academic IT units should not be thought of as customers; and many academic IT specialists have institutional responsibilities that do not position them very well to be internal vendors, such as helping maximize a common technological good. I would encourage people to exploit the customer metaphor if it makes sense to do so, but on balance, it is not a particularly good metaphor for encouraging productive institutional relationships.

The decision to select one metaphor over another also has implications for literacies. John Carroll (1990) reports on difficulties users have had with certain aspects of the desktop metaphor, including actions associated with terms such as *clipboard, stationery pad, tear-off stationery, typing,* and *folders* (63). In fact, Carroll noted early on that "some of the metaphorical desktop operations seemed to add unnecessary complexity" to user tasks (63). In a more recent example, Beatriz de Almeida Pacheco, Ilana Souza-Concílio, and Eliani Maria Kfouri (2013) report on difficulties that teachers in Brazil have experienced with certain aspects of a Moodle learning-management system, including the actions associated with visual metaphorical representations for navigating platform areas and managing files. The difficulties in these examples are hard to avoid, for subsidiary subjects necessarily mask some elements of principal subjects. As George Lakoff and Mark Johnson (1980) explain, "The very systematicity that allows us to comprehend one aspect of a concept in terms of another will necessarily hide other aspects of the concept" (10). But even in cases where academic IT specialists can employ metaphors that seem to effectively represent a collection of teaching and learning tasks, individuals still bring different backgrounds and experiences to their work that complicate universal notions of what might constitute user-friendly design. As Thomas Duffy, James Palmer, and Brad Mehlenbacher (1992) explain, "Even if interfaces are simple and clear—which is always a goal—we may expect users with different knowledge bases to interpret the capabilities and perhaps even the procedures differently" (7). Interfaces are not so much intuited as decoded in active efforts to follow metaphorical abstractions and discern instructive associations between subsidiary and principal subjects.

Finally, there are any number of metaphors in academic IT contexts for characterizing technologies. In *Multiliteracies for a Digital Age* (2004), I discuss computers as tools and hypertextual media and introduce a third metaphor—computers as cultural artifacts—to round out the operative subsidiary subjects from a pedagogical perspective. I advise students and teachers to hold this particular set of metaphors in productive tension in teaching and learning settings. One of the reasons the tool metaphor is potent is because it evokes cultural connections that help demystify computers. As a tool, the computer is simply another apparatus for expanding the capacities of users, functioning as a prosthetic device that increases efficiency, enhances cognition, and spans temporal and spatial boundaries.

Computers are just a means to an end, so the logic goes; they are tools with practical utility that users manipulate for their own (often immediate) purposes. A keyword search for "tools" in the EDUCAUSE library database returns titles with phrases such as "collaboration tools," "social networking tools," and "antiplagiarism tools." There is no shortage of titles in the database that involve the tool metaphor.

The second metaphor I want to discuss, computers as hypertextual media, is something of a dialectical partner to the tool metaphor. If the tool metaphor positions students and teachers as users of technologies, the media metaphor positions them as producers of technologies. One touchpoint for this metaphor is Marshall McLuhan (1964), who questions communication theories that distinguish between the how and what of communication. His famous adage—the medium is the message—has become palpable in academic IT contexts (Tom, Voss, and Scheetz 2008) even as the tool metaphor encourages the design goal of making human-computer interfaces transparent. McLuhan holds that the mode of transmission (the medium) can determine the content of communication (the message) as much as the intention of senders. In other words, the way people obtain information influences them as much as the information itself. "The medium is the message" remains an important aphorism because it encourages academic IT specialists to consider the imprint of technologies on thought and action and positions students and teachers as media designers whose work overlaps with that of academic IT specialists. I mediate the dialectical pairing of tools and media with the metaphor of computers as cultural artifacts in order to highlight reflection and critique; the subsidiary subject foregrounds the ways computers instantiate values and belief systems (Selber 2004, 86–95). All institutional actors should be able to leverage these metaphors (tools, media, and artifacts) in specific situations, textualizing technologies in appropriate and productive ways.

Metaphors impose extensions or changes of meaning as people attempt to make sense of the juxtapositions created by principal and subsidiary subjects. My examples for institutions illustrate how metaphors textualize relationships between teachers and academic IT units, my examples of literacies illustrate how human-computer interfaces are not so much intuited as interpreted in teaching and learning contexts, and my examples for technologies illustrate how metaphors textualize assumptions about the roles of computers in sociotechnical articulations. By foregrounding a variety of subsidiary subjects, including opposing ones, these metaphors dramatize the ambiguous nature of institutional practices, opening spaces for a multiplicity of metaphors that can be mobilized for specific audiences and purposes.

Subjectivities

For my purposes here, subjectivities are institutional modes of thinking about and structuring what workers do and how they do it. Formed, to a significant extent, by interactions between workers and institutional environments, subjectivities help define what is permissible and possible within the boundaries of specific situations. Although institutional subjectivities regulate and influence behaviors, they do not determine them all on their own: in academic institutions, causal relationships have many factors and dimensions, which change over time. Thus subjectivity formation could be thought of as an ongoing institutional process. In addition, there is not a single totalizing scheme for imagining or structuring institutional subjectivities. I have already provided one example of a metaphorical scheme that formulates three subject positions in academic IT environments: students and teachers as users of technologies, which is encouraged by the tool metaphor; students and teachers as producers of technologies, which is encouraged by the media metaphor; and students and teachers as questioners of technologies, which is encouraged by the artifact metaphor. These metaphors, as a scheme, textualize a set of computer-related subject positions that organizes how work is or could be performed and how institutions understand or could understand worker roles and responsibilities. In an important sense, subject positions are effects of institutional discourses.

In the scheme I want to discuss here, subjectivities are structured relationally in contexts that range from job classifications to collectives of people who share professional interests. My distinction is an organizational one: collectives can be as consequential as anything else but operate outside the normal boundaries of institutional practice. Although I have already said something about job classifications, I want to make additional comments about their nature and meaning for understanding subject formation. I will then discuss project teams and collectives as other structuring variations that shape subjectivities in academic IT units.

A textual exemplar for representing job classifications is the organizational chart. I have already mentioned that IT managers can view them as either depictions of reporting lines or human arrangements that must be trustworthy and respectful. I have also noted that although organizational charts rank people according to levels of institutional authority, in specific situations there can be other types of hierarchies, such as access and experience hierarchies, that respatialize organizational charts, at least momentarily or unofficially. So organizational charts, in interpretation and in practice, are contingent representations of institutional relationships. They are also unstable and incomplete. The unstableness of organizational charts is a function of the turnover rate in academic IT units—turnover in the sense of people coming and going but also in the sense of opportunities and reorganizations. Since I started writing this book, numerous academic IT specialists have taken new positions at Penn State and elsewhere, and there have been key hires for leadership positions; academic IT units have taken on large, high-stakes projects that have shifted priorities and responsibilities; and the entire IT enterprise has been reorganized on two separate occasions. As a result, the organizational chart is often out of date, misrepresenting job classifications. Insofar as teachers pay attention to organizational charts and their role in helping structure institutional subjectivities, they are not always accurate or reliable maps for academic IT units. In addition, the incompleteness of organizational charts also reduces their value as learning resources. In organizational charts that are typical to academic IT units, everything flows upward and downward in a hierarchical fashion, which means the lateral relationships between academic IT specialists and teachers are either not represented at all or represented inadequately by job classifications like "faculty programs manager" or "director of campus engagement." Organizational charts do little to instruct teachers about some of the most relevant institutional subjects in academic IT units. This is not a criticism of organizational charts per se but a suggestion to look elsewhere for more informative learning resources.

Academic IT specialists also organize into project teams that help structure subjectivities. Although project teams can be based on organizational charts, hierarchies of authority also give way to other institutional configurations for specific purposes and situations, allowing academic IT units to assemble the most productive workers for a task at hand. Anders Jensen, Christian Thuesen, and Joana Geraldi (2016) trace factors that have given rise to project teams as a strategy for organizational problem solving. These researchers compare and contrast what they call disciplinary societies with project societies, discussing how changes in historical understandings of the nature of activities, relations, spaces, and time have encouraged institutions to work across silos and traditional boundaries. These changes include the realization that in certain contexts and cases, project activities become a first-order driver of innovation and change, shaping relations, spaces, and time in consequential ways. To paraphrase Jensen, Thuesen, and Geraldi, in project-based approaches, activities are relational, meaning that connecting with others is more important than relying on traditional institutional relationships; activities shape spaces, meaning that institutional spaces are designed to be flexible and adaptive; and activities shape time, meaning that institutional time is arranged around project activities and milestones and not thought of as a linear progression of hours in a workday. I would argue that the perspectives of project approaches should be considered to be tendencies rather than absolute positions, for project teams are not immune from larger institutional forces.

The textual exemplar for project teams is the use case. Use cases are reports about the experiences people have with academic IT. They range from quickly prepared informal reports to formal reports with extensive discussion and evaluation. The point of preparing a use case is to study interactions in a sociotechnical context, to determine how well a system is succeeding or would succeed if purchased by the university. In this way, use cases support planning and implementation phases. The process of preparing a use case usually begins with scenario development. Academic IT specialists at the University of Rochester articulate scenarios in which institutional actors might want to employ a virtual desktop, which allows various people to connect to a desktop environment over the internet: teachers who want to use Windows-only software with students who prefer Apple and other non-Windows products; students who want to access institutionally licensed software without having to go to campus labs; and academic IT specialists who want to provide users with secure remote access to university systems while traveling for work (https://tech.rochester.edu). Informal reports often simply explain the scenarios and provide reflections from the institutional actors. A good example are the brief Penn State use cases for VoiceThread, a collaboration platform that allows people to hold group conversations by commenting on images, videos, documents, and slide decks (https://voicethread.psu.edu). In a page or two, they discuss the case, its outcomes, and future possibilities. Formal reports, as Ashley Williams (2003) notes, tend to follow a rough template that has evolved for the genre. The template includes sections for naming the case, articulating its purposes and goals, describing sociotechnical conditions that must be satisfied for the case to begin and end, explaining the basic actions and interactions, and explaining alternative actions and interactions to accommodate errors, exceptions, and other modes of working (14). Although formal reports can be published as external primary research, they are usually shared on websites as institutional documents.

Project teams for use cases encompass various subject positions that are then occupied by specific institutional actors. Consider the case of an online module designed to help students integrate library research into written work. The academic IT specialist managing the project could imagine a range of relevant subject positions, including librarians, teachers, students, and academic IT specialists. What these subject positions entail is open to an extent, but the project manager will employ criteria for selecting team members that reflect institutional considerations, such as ability, or skills and experiences appropriate to the module; positionality, or institutional conditions that affect labor practices; availability, or openings for participation; personality, or characteristics and qualities of workers; and diversity, or differences in perspectives.

In applying these criteria to teachers, the project manager would consider work histories and how they have prepared teachers to be team members, especially interests and abilities in the teaching of writing research; institutional positions and how they have prepared teachers to be team members, especially when it comes to status and power issues and how those affect what people teach and the influence they have in departments; job commitments and the level of participation they afford, especially for excess work that can go unnoticed; personal qualities such as enthusiasm and professionalism and what they contribute to project teams; and personal differences such as age, gender, race, and physical ability and what they contribute to project teams. The subject position of teacher is thus conditioned by institutional priorities, and this conditioning, in turn, has implications for how project teams write use cases. For example, if the library module has already been developed, the project manager will likely look for faculty champions who are in a position to advocate for academic IT initiatives and help prepare a use case that foregrounds pedagogical affordances. If the library module is meant to be used in both general education and advanced writing courses, the project manager will likely look for teachers who can provide input from across academic ranks. And if the library module is running behind schedule, the project manager will likely prioritize the availability of teachers over other institutional criteria in order to improve the chances of meeting a deadline. Subject positions for project teams shift with institutional circumstances.

I stated that specific institutional actors occupy subject positions but did not elaborate on what then occurs. What happens next depends on the relationships and tendencies in sociotechnical articulations. Project team members are regulated to varying degrees by institutional forces, and they are never fully free to act without reference to their formal job classifications. But in the third structuring variation I want to discuss—collectives—institutional actors tend to have more leeway in representing themselves to others, and thus more potential to affect subject positions. I am not saying that collectives are inherently more liberating than formal job classifications or project teams but that they offer other possibilities for institutional engagement.

Collectives are composed of groups of individuals who share mutual interests and a desire to advance those interests through cooperation and coordinated activities. Collectives can range from formal to informal. I am interested in formal collectives because they are initiated by institutions, have discernible organizational structures, and are governed by charters or other authorizing documents. Collectives can be initiated for any number of reasons, including helping establish new institutional directions, supporting special projects, and addressing cross-institutional challenges. In all of the reasons, there is a sense that alternative work configurations would be more effective than conventional ones.

People can be invited to participate in collectives, or there can be calls for participation. I was invited to join the Learning Innovation Forum Team (LIFT) at Penn State, a collective initiated to help advance endeavors related to teaching and learning with technologies. LIFT is cochaired by an academic IT specialist and an innovation specialist from the online education unit. According to the charter, they look for people who are making a difference in the lives of students and teachers. The charter also explains that the charge for the collective involves identifying opportunities for innovation and economic growth, auditing emerging trends in higher education, and evangelizing the adoption of innovations. In the project I want to discuss, collective members prepared a written report for the provost of outreach and online education that contained recommendations for capital campaign themes, which the provost shared with the university president. The report frames the themes as fundable ideas, and the discussion for each one includes an overview description, a list of current investments in the area, and a list of campaign opportunities. For example, for the theme of "Spaces and Learning Experiences," the report defines the domain of learning spaces, describes the different types of learning spaces at Penn State, and lists things that could be funded by the capital campaign, such as renovations, teaching fellowships, and student awards. Through this project, the collective effectively operated as a special assistant to the provost, conducting institutional research and making investment recommendations.

I was invited to join LIFT because of my work on institutions, literacies, and technologies. I have become visible on campus as a faculty member who is willing to participate in cross-functional teams that aim to solve teaching and learning problems. At times I have occupied a token subject position, representing the liberal arts in academic IT contexts to meet a diversity goal, but I have also been able to leverage that tokenism to have an influence on institutional projects. Although my subject position in LIFT is not ahistorical—people who know me know about my administrative work in a campus writing program—collective members encounter continuing opportunities for self-definition that can be productive. For example, I want people in the collective to think of me as an engaged faculty member who is interested in exploring the possibilities in all things digital for writing and the teaching of writing, who is appropriately skeptical about technological hype in institutions, who takes a contextual approach to developing and evaluating academic IT, and who believes that under the right circumstances, change can be made from within institutions. During the capital campaign project for the provost, I attempted to perform my qualifications to a subject position for faculty members through various discursive activities, including maintaining an online presence to promote my own view of myself; playing devil's advocate to probe the assumptions and values underlying our deliberations; and posing broad questions to situate our investment recommendations in social, political, and historical contexts. I was not the only collective member who actively worked to shape institutional subjectivities.

In academic IT units, job classifications, project teams, and collectives help structure institutional modes of thinking about what workers do and how they do it. The textual exemplar for job classifications is the organizational chart, which tends to ignore the lateral relationships teachers have with academic IT specialists. Organizational charts can also be less than useful for learning about subject positions if they are inaccurate or vague. The textual exemplar for project teams is the use case, which traces interactions in sociotechnical contexts to determine how well a system is succeeding. Project teams are composed of subject positions that reflect institutional considerations for positionality, availability, diversity, and more. Such considerations affect how use cases are prepared and written. Although there is no textual exemplar for collectives, recommendation reports are a routine example. In preparing recommendation reports, collective members encounter unusually good opportunities for self-definition. Maintaining an online presence, playing devil's advocate, and posing broad questions are useful strategies for shaping institutional subjectivities.

Genres

I have referenced numerous genres used in academic IT settings, including policies, procedures, proposals, reports, literature reviews, memos, mission statements, meeting minutes, press releases, presentations, tutorials, websites, and blog entries. Genres, as I have discussed, help textualize activities and relationships in institutional contexts and contribute to processes of institutionalization. This section brings order to my treatment of genres by categorizing them according to rhetorical considerations and suggesting how those categories can be enlightening for teachers who want to influence academic IT units. The categories come from Carolyn Miller (2017), who offers a "preliminary classification" for genres—administered, institutional, marketed, and vernacular—in order to "begin to account for the different ways that genres emerge and evolve within their communities" (23). This preliminary classification is, in essence, a heuristic for thinking through the work that genres do across disciplinary boundaries. The elements of the heuristic include settings or situations, exigencies, and power relations. Although Miller is interested in what this heuristic can illuminate about genres, I am interested in what it can illuminate about academic IT. My appropriation embeds her heuristic into my own and reorients the agenda.

In previous work, Miller (1984) defines genres as social action, complicating more traditional perspectives that stress the formal characteristics of texts, such as format and style, and encouraging the field to think of genres as elements of rhetorical situations that help communities solve communication problems in recurring situations. As Charles Bazerman (1997) puts it, "Genres are not just forms. Genres are forms of life, ways of being. They are frames for social action. They are environments for learning. They are locations within which meaning is constructed" (19). For Miller, Bazerman, and others in the North American tradition, genres are stable enough to serve coordinating functions in communication situations and unstable enough to serve invention functions in discourse communities. Both aspects are relevant to analyzing the rhetorical dimensions of administered, institutional, marketed, and vernacular genres in academic IT units.

Administered genres are found in "corporate and organizational, government and bureaucratic settings, including education; such genres are social interactions that are formalized in particular ways, often literally through forms; they occur in situations where those with institutional authority (such as government regulators, teachers, or managers) can impose or require certain ways of doing things" (Miller 2017, 23). Administered genres, as Miller explains, are governed by guidelines or criteria introduced by legal or institutional demands, emerging to "suit those in power, those with the authority to regulate the social and symbolic interactions of others" (24). Common examples include annual reports, medical records, and work orders, but let me return to policy documents and training materials because they are prevalent in teaching and learning contexts.

In academic IT units, the legal demands motivating interactions and relationships that are formalized by administered genres have to do with such matters as complying with accessibility standards, data privacy regulations, copyright laws, and records requests. These interactions and relationships involve staff attorneys who interpret the law for institutions, administrators who make decisions about compliance and implementation, and academic IT specialists who execute action plans. For accessibility standards, for example, staff attorneys interpret the federal statutes and regulations for accessible website design, administrators use these legal interpretations to write policy documents, and academic IT staff create training materials to explain the policies to students and teachers. The policy documents formalize these interactions and relationships in conventional textual elements that define terms, state policies, list procedures, and outline consequences for noncompliance. Sections that define terms quote and interpret laws: What does accessibility mean, and why is it important? Sections that state policies articulate governing principles and understandings: What are the standards for accessibility? Sections that list procedures describe how the policies should be implemented: What are the steps for accomplishing the tasks governed by the policies? And sections for noncompliance define the boundaries for compliance and implications—institutional and legal—for failing to comply with the policies. The training materials are designed to teach people about the policies but also to support institutional relationships that involve reporting: training materials with login requirements, quizzes, and other trackable features provide data and information that can be used by institutions to demonstrate compliance or progress toward goals. I should note that the level of discursive regulation associated with administered genres does not have to be viewed in negative terms: as teachers know firsthand and practice themselves in syllabus writing, there can be good reasons for regulating symbolic interactions.

Institutional genres are more "regularized" than "regulated" as structures for invention and communication, being "held in place less by overt, authoritative regulation than by the power of tradition, social status, and mutual expectation" (Miller 2017, 24). This category includes genres that teachers would consider to be disciplinary modes of discourse, as in research articles, reports, and press releases: for many in the field, institutions have become synonymous with disciplinary systems, especially those that govern academic fields. A key distinction between institutional and administered genres, which are closely linked, is that "tacitly known strategies emerge largely from practice, not from stricture" (24). Customs rather than mandates are the central articulation for the constitution and formulation of institutional genres.

A good illustration is my example of a failed institutional proposal. The elements of the proposal textualize and formalize a variety of interactions and relationships based on traditions and expectations. For one, there is the expectation that institutions will invest in their own learning. Academic IT units have a history of running faculty development programs and funding the investigation of what they determine to be promising ideas. Proposals, as institutional genres, provide a competitive mechanism for inventing or communicating investment directions. Stabilizing these directions is the expectation that they will evolve in congruence with broader institutional priorities: a section explicitly calls for strong alignment statements. In addition, there are sections that enlist customs of building on and sharing ideas by asking proposal writers to specify how their seed money could attract external funding and lead to the dissemination of knowledge. Other sections of the proposal reinforce institutional assumptions about technologies. Recall that my proposal failed because of mismatches in assumptions about the nature of innovation. Still other sections reinforce institutional assumptions about literacies—for example, collaborative efforts are prized and encouraged over individual efforts. The interactions and relationships formalized by institutional genres can certainly accommodate the projects of teachers (if not always, then often enough). In fact, responding to calls for proposals from academic IT units is an available means of making the case for new and different approaches. Genre stability does not mean stasis or the absence of change, and there is always a degree of interpretive flexibility in textual practices. If my proposal had addressed institutional notions of innovation, even in resistant ways, my guess is that it would have been funded.

Miller (2017) associates marketed or commercial genres with film, television, and literary studies. For the genres in these disciplines—books, films, television programs, and music recordings—the "exigence is some cultural expectation or desire that is satisfied by the product category: in other words, these genres emerge and survive if they offer something that 'sells,' either to a mass market or to an audience with more specialized aesthetic criteria" (23). When it comes to audience-producer relationships, there is a particular power dynamic: "Producers exert their influence over genre emergence through their access to and manipulation of the means of production; audiences exert their influence through their ability to reward the decisions of producers" (23). Although user-generated content now plays a role in the production of marketed or commercial genres, I hear what Miller is saying about dynamics in a marketplace: there are winners and losers based on positioning and competitive outcomes.

In academic IT contexts, there are two levels to the exigence for marketed or commercial genres. On one level, institutions purchase academic IT from third-party vendors, satisfying expectations from many different constituencies about what a twenty-first-century education ought to entail. Using faculty testimonials, product demonstrations, white papers, and feature articles written for newsletters and magazines, institutions then market those systems to students and teachers in an attempt to secure buy-in from people beyond the pilot testers. In many situations, working to secure buy-in is a more effective route than mandating behaviors, for mandates can be difficult to enforce, and anyway, an important goal is encouraging participatory practices that yield learning opportunities for everyone.

For the genre of faculty testimonials, teachers themselves are asked to market academic IT to other teachers and students. What is an appropriate role for teachers as marketers of technologies? Faculty testimonials can have an almost evangelical feel to them, and there is something of an assumption in academic IT units that engaged teachers are advocates and institutional champions. Teachers should promote what they consider to be in the interests of students and education as a whole, but being an advocate is not really about sales: it is about encouraging teachers to invest the time needed to investigate possibilities and test ideas, no matter the result. This alternative viewpoint can be accommodated by the genre of testimonials, which uses experts to confirm the merits of products or services. The idea is that testimonials can be reassuring in contexts in which a lack of trust or understanding is a problem, but in the institutional contexts I am addressing, trust and understanding are likely to be enhanced by transparency and a healthy dose of skepticism. Faculty testimonials for academic IT should endorse the purposes and goals of pedagogical invention.

Vernacular genres are the least stable of the preliminary classifications, emerging in "situations where users have few institutional or administrative constraints and can collectively create a way of addressing shared exigence" (Miller 2017, 24). Miller emphasizes information technologies and their role in the democratization of production and distribution activities: "People have the means to do new kinds of things and to do them collectively, so that they can rapidly become joint modes of social action— holistically identifiable, socially meaningful, and reproducible" (25). She also notes that although the exigencies for vernacular genres can be less than obvious to those outside of discourse communities, they are nonetheless communally recognized as pertinent and important. Earlier in this chapter, I mentioned Cole Camplese's blog. Among its many purposes are elaborating the workings of institutions and communicating the roles and responsibilities of academic IT specialists. Camplese is not required to use a particular publishing platform or even to write a blog, but it helps him articulate the interactions and relationships that constitute processes of institutionalization. The blog is an unofficial resource for making the world of academic IT more visible and accessible to students and teachers, which is a goal for countless others in higher education. The genre features that support this task include subscribing, searching, commenting, and archiving systems. Although directories become quickly outdated, there is a rich informal network of academic IT blogs that can be instructive for students and teachers. Like others who read blogs, I build my own folksonomies one link at a time as I discover writers with whom I share intellectual interests. These folksonomies express bottom-up approaches to knowledge production that complement more traditional institutional approaches.

Miller (2017) emphasizes that the categories in her scheme are not exclusive or exhaustive and that genres can exhibit features from multiple categories and even change categories. She uses the scheme to illustrate dynamics that contribute to how genres emerge and evolve in a variety of different domains, concluding that the broad appeal of genres can be attributed to their status as boundary objects. Boundary objects, according to Susan Leigh Star and James Griesemer (1989), are artifacts or theories capable of establishing common ground between people with varied perspectives. These artifacts or theories can be interpreted and configured for specific purposes, but their overall structures remain relatively coherent, enabling coordinating activities without the need for intellectual or functional consensus. On the one hand, then, teachers can explore the applications and implications of genres for particular domains. On the other hand, academic IT units can employ administered, institutional, marketed, and vernacular genres to foster the cooperation needed for integrating academic IT systems into teaching and learning contexts. Genres can formalize interactions and relationships that cross institutional boundaries, blurring distinctions between the centralization efforts of academic IT units and the decentralization efforts of academic departments and programs.

Stories

Storytelling has become a standard practice for messaging and strategic communication (Gabriel 2000). A powerful aspect of storytelling is its ability to create bridges between the general propositions of institutions and the concrete experiences of audiences. By propositions, I mean the narratives institutions adopt to advance their agendas. People often use the terms *narratives* and *stories* interchangeably, but there is a distinction worth noting for my project: narratives are the broad themes that guide institutional planning and design; stories, in contrast, are constituted by events and experiences and play a reinforcing role. Consider the disruption narratives that many institutions have adopted. These narratives claim that disruption is a powerful engine for change in higher education and rely on stories to show how disruption leads to pedagogical innovation (Magana 2017). Narratives and stories are thus related but not identical, functioning together as a discursive unit in textual processes of institutionalization. I focus on storytelling because it is more within the purview of academic IT units: upper-level administrators tend to establish institutional narratives, which are then codified in vision documents.

How exactly do stories, as reinforcing elements, illuminate institutional narratives, especially those that involve technologies? Three of the more conspicuous ways include amplifying identities, contextualizing artifacts and practices, and substantiating claims. All universities use narratives to assert and convey identities, projecting strategic versions of themselves through selective self-representation and its constitutive possibilities for production. In chapter 1, I discussed Penn State's strategic plans and the thematic goals of enhancing student success, advancing academic excellence and research prominence, maintaining affordability and enhancing diversity, and controlling costs and generating additional efficiencies. I also noted that my institution understands technologies to be central to achieving overarching objectives. Phrased as goals for the genre of strategic plans, these themes or narratives are action oriented and organized around an integrated sense of what Penn State hopes to become in the future. The narratives, however, are also one-dimensional and rather bureaucratic in tone, failing to appeal to students and teachers on a concrete level.

Stories illuminate the identities projected by institutional narratives, bringing them to life in identifiable ways and helping communicate their meaning and implications. For example, the University of California hosts an information center on the web that storifies the narratives driving their identity-formation processes (https://www.universityofcalifornia.edu /infocenter). From a dashboard view, users select stories about social mobility, diversity, affordability, undergraduate student research, and other key themes; the stories elaborate the themes with dynamic visual data and various prose elements. The story for the impact the university system has on the state of California emphasizes the numerous start-up companies that have spun off from academic research. A slider at the top tells the basic story in five sequential parts. As users select parts of the story, a storyboard reveals statistics about growth and impact, which can be sorted by campus, field, and other variables. The storyboard also reveals prose paragraphs that explain and illustrate what the statistics mean and why, telling the stories behind the stories. The part about graduate students provides an overview of the winning projects in a campus-wide competition for innovative ideas. Although universities make measurable contributions to local economies, which are crucial to pedagogical themes and goals, students and teachers often misunderstand the role of universities as partners in economic development. The stories interpret the narrative of economic development from an academic perspective and situate technologies as central to this task.

A second way stories illuminate narratives is by contextualizing artifacts and practices. The purpose of this book is to offer a heuristic teachers can use to contextualize academic IT units, with an eye toward influencing institutional decision-making. I am taking a decidedly rhetorical perspective, but academic IT specialists also recognize the general importance of situating technologies in institutions and engendering awareness about factors that can affect teaching and learning. In fact, academic IT specialists often enlist teachers to help them storify institutional narratives and advance them in pedagogical communities. An academic IT unit at the University of British Columbia hosts a website that includes over two dozen instructional stories from teachers across the liberal arts (https://isit.arts.ubc.ca/). The purpose of this site is to help teachers "discover teaching tools, new ideas, and strategies" that they can employ in their classrooms, presumably in support of the narrative theme of advancing and sharing institutional knowledge, which is a value listed in the university's vision statement. There are stories about any number of technologies, but what is worth noting is that all of them explicitly discuss background and foreground contexts. The background contexts include details about the teachers, courses, and instructional problems being addressed; the foreground contexts include details about the projects themselves, including who and what was involved, what happened and where, and what was learned or accomplished.

Consider the story from Laurie McNeill about her uses of blogs in courses on academic writing. McNeill asks students to blog five times per term, read peer blogs, and comment on peer blogs three times per term. She explains the benefits of blogging for student writers, such as helping them negotiate genres and write for public audiences. And she offers advice for people who might want to try blogs in the classroom, such as using rubrics to help keep up with the commenting and grading workload. Her story is insightful and contextualizes blogs in a manner that should be useful to other teachers at her school, advancing and sharing knowledge in ways that support a key institutional narrative. The only comment I would make is to encourage people to be more thoroughgoing in their coverage of background contexts. In addition to sharing details about the teachers, courses, and instructional problems being addressed, I would also include assumptions about institutions, literacies, and technologies. McNeill, for example, uses the institutional blogging platform. How does it organize student writers and writing? How do the policies and procedures shape writers and writing? Are there other resources for teaching and learning with blogs? If so, what do they emphasize? What do people need to know about the institution in order to work effectively with blogs? Answers to such questions are essential to contextualizing institutional artifacts and practices for students and teachers.

Stories also illuminate institutional narratives by substantiating claims. In a certain sense, institutional narratives function as claims about what institutions are capable of doing now and in the future. The mission statement from San Jose State University claims that the institution values a general set of educational goals for all students (http://www.sjsu.edu /learninggoals/university/). Students who graduate from the university will have developed specialized knowledge in a degree area, mastering the learning outcomes from particular academic programs; broad integrative knowledge of research methods or creative processes, including an appreciation for the challenges of public communication and for societal implications; intellectual skills with technologies and tools for lifelong learning; applied knowledge for integrating theory and practice, solving problems, and collaborating in groups; and social and global perspectives, fostering an ability to think historically, act ethically, and be accountable to society. These general educational goals reflect the institutional narrative that San Jose State is a distinctive university, blending tradition and exploration in the heart of Silicon Valley. Although San Jose State is the oldest state university in California, many if not most universities trade on the narrative possibilities in the dialectical tensions between stasis and change.

A website for San Jose State embeds videos about how academic IT is enabling the university to deliver on its goal of preparing students to be effective professionals in the twenty-first century (http://www.sjsu.edu/it/). These stories substantiate the claims associated with institutional narratives by providing evidence in various forms and from different sources. For example, the video about how San Jose State partnered with Cisco to enhance campus infrastructures uses technical specifications as institutional evidence, arguing that increases in network connectivity speeds from 100 megabits per second to 10 gigabits per second have improved the ability of students to work in dorms. The video about the Virtual Desktop Infrastructure (VDI) uses cost savings and other efficiencies as institutional evidence, arguing that these savings and efficiencies afford access to a consistent, up-to-date environment for teaching and learning, one that is better able to handle the demands of mobility and distance education. And the video about WebEx uses quality measures as institutional evidence, arguing that online meetings afford access to workplace practitioners, integrating their expertise into courses and thus improving student experiences. The evidence provided in stories is developed on an ongoing basis as institutions strive to reflect and relate their evolving narrative themes.

Institutions employ narratives in order to maintain and advance their agendas, and an essential part of this process is constructing and circulating stories that can play a reinforcing role. Stories reinforce institutional narratives by amplifying identities, contextualizing artifacts and practices, and substantiating claims. Stories enliven institutional self-representations in ways that students and teachers can identify and that help communicate narrative meaning and implications. Stories have background and foreground elements that engender awareness about factors that can affect teaching and learning. Elaborating background elements in institutional terms is particularly important to contextualizing artifacts and practices for students and teachers. And stories substantiate the claims associated with institutional narratives, using technical specifications, cost savings, quality measures, and other forms of institutional evidence as components of an argument. Academic IT units often enlist teachers to help them storify narratives and advance them in pedagogical communities. Such moments represent useful opportunities for teachers to advance their own perspectives and shape institutional projects.

CONCLUSION

Nelson Phillips, Thomas Lawrence, and Cynthia Hardy (2004) argue that "institutions are constituted in discourse, and to understand the process of institutionalization and how institutions enable and constrain action, we need to understand the discursive dynamics underlying them" (646). In academic IT units, the dynamics associated with metaphors, subjectivities, genres, and stories have real and tangible effects on institutional processes and products. These textual elements are present in any and all situations and represent productive sites for engagement. The enduring questions for this chapter—which ask about the similarities that can be drawn between information technologies and texts, the assumptions in textual depictions of technologies, the textual practices involved in developing technologies, and the documentation practices for technologies—advocate for such engagement on professional grounds by showing what is at stake for the field. The final chapter integrates the parts of my heuristic—historical, spatial, and textual—and illustrates how they function together as a working whole.

5

ENGAGING ACADEMIC IT

The hard part comes in the wake of critique, because it is here that one must choose a course of action, invent solutions, and then fabricate the conditions that generate the life-sustaining sensation of forward movement.
RICHARD MILLER (1999)

The heuristic discussed in the previous chapters conceptualizes the enterprise of academic IT so that teachers of writing and communication can see how it works and why it matters to education. The dimensions of the heuristic are relevant to any and all institutions and to teachers working in any type of program. All academic IT units have historical, spatial, and textual dimensions, which shape current and future developments in significant ways. In addition, as the enduring questions illustrate, teachers have an abiding interest in historicizing, spatializing, and textualizing literacy technologies. As a result, the heuristic dimensions function as both nouns and verbs. As nouns, the dimensions can be thought of as rhetorical commonplaces: histories, spaces, and texts are touchstones for understanding institutional contexts. As verbs, the dimensions can be thought of as modes of investigation: historicizing, spatializing, and textualizing are rhetorical approaches to analyzing institutional contexts. Both forms of the heuristic—noun oriented and verb oriented—are central to the task of institutional engagement.

This final chapter integrates my heuristic into a larger approach that teachers can use in their own programs. It includes phases of problem posing and problem solving that can guide teachers as they work to make decisions about how and where to spend their time on academic IT matters. I want to reiterate that my heuristic and the approach introduced here are meant to be suggestive, not exhaustive. It is impossible to anticipate how the elements in sociotechnical articulations might interact and shape each other in specific moments of institutionalization: local settings will determine the particular nature of problems and engagement solutions. Although I will perform the approach with different types of examples, my interpretations and conclusions will necessarily reflect the contexts from which they emerge and my own sense of priorities. I expect others to arrive at solutions that fit their own circumstances.

I also want to reiterate that I view institutions as rhetorical systems that can be changed from within by people who cooperate across the silos that divide universities. Teachers and academic IT specialists wrestle with many of the same issues. However, they often look at each other through a distorted lens, stereotyping work roles and failing to understand the complexities of those roles. In addition, and for reasons not always of their own making, teachers often lack a vision for how to participate in academic IT endeavors and of the possibilities for change. The result is projects and processes that would have benefited from more of a collaborative approach. The other aspect I want to restate has to do with the durability of change. Teachers should aspire to create lasting institutional change, but I would also encourage them to think about the momentary change that can result from micropolitical action. All classrooms are situated in time and space: What is possible now? What can I control and manage? How can I improve things for the students in front of me? Change may be best thought of as a multifaceted undertaking with both short-term and long-term goals.

My approach to engagement has three parts. First, I ask teachers to situate academic IT as a project—that is, as a system or service—or process and as a formal or informal proposition. A positioning chart is useful here because many instances of academic IT confound these binary oppositions and because institutional locations affect resourcing, visibility, and more. I then ask teachers to use my heuristic for analysis to historicize, spatialize, and textualize the project or process at hand, to identify institutional forces at work in shaping decision-making. Finally, in my approach, I ask teachers to consider the type of institutional engagement they want to pursue in particular situations, from relatively passive to active roles. I illustrate the approach with examples from pedagogical and administrative contexts. My expectation is that the examples will serve as accessible models for institutional engagement.

APPROACHING INSTITUTIONAL ENGAGEMENT

Although institutional critique is a varied intellectual terrain with no single controlling method, most approaches involve positioning the objects of study in some fashion or another and then analyzing them to illuminate social dynamics and cultural meanings. In my approach, these steps can produce the institutional know-how needed to turn critique into action.

Positioning Academic IT

The first step asks teachers to locate academic IT on a positioning chart with horizontal and vertical axes. The horizontal axis runs from processes on the left to projects—systems or services—on the right. The vertical axis runs from formal settings on the top to informal settings on the bottom. The result is four quadrants that differently position academic IT as an institutional formation: processes in formal settings, projects in formal settings, processes in informal settings, and projects in informal settings (I populate an example of the chart at the end of this subsection). It is important to stress that the chart does not situate entries in a rigid fashion, defining them into absolute positions. Instead, the chart enables entries to be positioned along institutional continua with different points of emphasis. An entry can certainly be aligned neatly with a quadrant of the chart: strategic planning is a formal institutional process in any situation. Entries, however, can also confound distinctions between processes and projects and between formal and informal settings. Help desks, for example, provide services but are typically experienced as a process. Likewise, strategic planning is experienced as a product to those who simply read the final plan. Or consider the positioning of institutional grants for processes or projects: the size of a grant will help determine the level of formality. The positioning of entries is always relative to contexts.

But before I illustrate this point, let me explain the quadrants of the chart by considering questions of resourcing, reviewing, implementing, managing, and documenting academic IT. Formal processes and projects tend to be well resourced in terms of money and people, require inclusive stakeholder reviews, involve significant scales of implementation, exhibit discernible managerial control, and include comprehensive documentation practices. As noted earlier, a ubiquitous example of a formal process is strategic planning. This process is expensive and time consuming, taking

months if not years to complete; includes stakeholders from many different levels of an institution; affects the operations of an entire institution; is
overseen by upper-level administrators; and is document intensive, calling for procedural memos, meeting minutes, research reports, and more.
A ubiquitous example of a formal project—in this case, a product—is a
course-management system. Course-management systems are expensive
and time consuming, require significant ongoing resources, are governed
from above in centralized hierarchical systems, and are document intensive, particularly when it comes to specifications, use cases, and help
materials. In addition, course-management systems are designed to support teaching and learning across the disciplines and to elicit stakeholder
feedback. I am only speaking generally here because not every formal
process or project will exhibit all of these characteristics. For instance, an
institution could invest heavily in a system for a small subset of the university population if that system promises to be highly visible or have a
high-impact outcome.

Informal processes and projects do not always amount to the complete
inverse of formal ones, but they vary enough to warrant distinctions as institutional formations. On the minimum end of the spectrum, informal processes and projects can run on a shoestring budget and involve just a handful of academic IT specialists, rely on stakeholder advocates rather than on
stakeholders themselves, address the needs of just a handful of teachers or
even a single person, exhibit loose if any real managerial control, and involve a limited set of documentation practices, perhaps only a recommendation memo. An example of an informal process is a paperless grading
initiative at Penn State. The Teaching and Learning with Technology unit
encourages teachers to use electronic annotation programs for responding
to assignments. The motivation comes from a desire to reduce the environmental footprint of academic IT and test the performance of the software.
The TLT unit advertised small grants of up to four thousand dollars. The
studio I direct—the Penn State Digital English Studio—applied for a grant
that asked us to write a one-page proposal about what we wanted to learn
and how we would spend the money. We proposed purchasing Chrome-
books for twelve instructors who would spend a semester using Google
Docs to respond to assignments. The instructors would keep a diary of reflections, and we would meet with them periodically to discuss their experiences. We won the grant and delivered on the promises in our proposal,
including communicating our insights to the TLT unit, which used them
to inform a white paper about annotation software. Note that we were not
obligated to design a study, write for publication, or implement a program.

In exchange for a small grant, all we needed to do was provide organized feedback for institutional purposes.

There are numerous examples of informal projects, but I want to discuss this book because it would not have been possible without informal institutional access and because it illustrates the power of teacher-initiated engagement. Academic IT units are often charged with research agendas, so they collaborate with teachers on externally funded grants and contracts. My book was not externally funded or even typical of academic IT research, but I was taken seriously as an institutional actor who wanted to study literacies and technologies. I approached Cole Camplese about shadowing him during my sabbatical; at the time, Camplese was senior director of the TLT unit and an influential decision maker at Penn State. As I noted in my sabbatical proposal, shadowing would involve meeting one-on-one with Camplese to ask questions and learn more about the institutional agenda for academic IT; attending business meetings to learn more about the management side of things; attending technical meetings to learn more about requirements, infrastructures, and workflows; meeting with financial officers to learn more about budgets, overhead, and the like; and meeting with human resources to learn more about job classifications and staffing issues. In addition, Camplese added me to email lists and document repositories and suggested that I attend meetings external to the unit, in which TLT collaborates with campus constituencies.

My project was informal in that it was exploratory in nature, addressed the needs and interests of a single person, involved just a handful of academic IT specialists in a direct fashion, was loosely managed in a peer network, and only required a final sabbatical report. Although I initiated the project for my own research purposes, it rather quickly became a productive two-way street: I was treated as an active participant in meetings, and Camplese and others routinely sought my input on their ideas. In addition, I was asked to share my thinking at an annual all-staff meeting and serve on a search committee for a senior leadership position. These developments did not surprise me because academic IT units are always looking for ways to engage teachers and learn about their interests. What is notable is that I introduced the project. Faculty engagement programs are a crucial source of institutional access, but teachers can and should approach academic IT units with their own proposals. Academic IT units are receptive to, and even count on, teachers who show initiative.

The areas I use to characterize processes and projects as formal or informal suggest questions that position academic IT initiatives in institutional contexts. In terms of resources, is there a budget for the process or project? If so, what does it look like? Is there a budget line for encouraging teacher involvement? Are there other resources for teachers? How many academic IT specialists are aligned with the process or project? What are their positions and capacities? Do they have the ability to make institutional decisions? In terms of reviews, who are the stakeholders? What are their needs? Does the process or project mandate that stakeholders be involved in reviews? If so, how? In terms of implementation, what is the scale of the process or project? Is it meant to serve an entire university population? A subset of the population? Does the implementation plan draw on conventional institutional parameters, or is there something new or different about the process or project? In terms of management, what is the governing structure for the process or project? Is there a strict hierarchical structure? A more loosely configured approach? In terms of documentation, what is required? Who reads the documentation? What are its purposes? These questions are not meant to be used to make general value judgments about academic IT processes and projects, for such judgments can only be made with reference to particular situations: in the abstract, no one approach to resourcing, reviewing, implementing, managing, or documenting is inherently better or worse than the others. Instead, the point of the questions is to help teachers position academic IT processes and projects in institutional contexts, to set the stage for engagement by thinking about the levels of formality involved in key aspects of invention and production.

I have located the examples from this subsection on the positioning chart in figure 5.1. Recall that the positioning of entries is always relative to

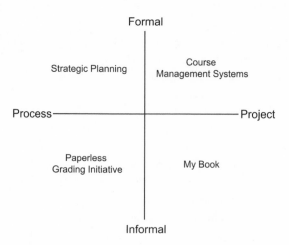

FIGURE 5.1 Modes of positioning for academic IT

contexts and can change in different situations. If the paperless grading initiative had required my studio to implement a program, for instance, then I would relocate this initiative as more of a formal institutional process. Also, if I had received an external grant for my research and partnered with an academic IT unit, then I would relocate my book as more of a formal institutional project. These moves are based on material changes in institutional conditions, but they could also be based on lived experiences: I would relocate strategic planning toward the project side of the process-project continuum if my involvement had been limited to filling out a survey and reading the final plan. The less-more distinctions illustrated by the chart are useful because they help teachers imagine the priorities in institutions and position their own work. Although my book project was well received by the TLT unit, in the scheme of things, it was positioned as a low-priority project. I therefore needed to make sure that it remained visible and that I had ongoing access to pertinent resources.

Analyzing Academic IT

The second step of the approach asks teachers to use my heuristic to conduct a multidimensional analysis. Once a process or project has been located on the positioning chart, teachers can historicize, spatialize, and textualize it as an artifact of institutionalization. As I discussed in chapter 2, historicizing academic IT involves considering how standards, legacies, conventions, and rituals shape institutional thought and action. As I discussed in chapter 3, spatializing academic IT involves considering how hierarchies, processes, methods, and bodies shape institutional thought and action. And as I discussed in chapter 4, textualizing academic IT involves considering how metaphors, subjectivities, genres, and stories shape institutional thought and action. Although all of these dimensions are significant, not all of them will turn out to be equally important to all analysis activities. A reality of sociotechnical articulations is that they operate asymmetrically in specific situations, with certain elements exerting more influence than others.

To aid the task of historicizing, I have generated questions from the discussion in chapter 2 that prompt teachers to consider the effects of standards, legacies, conventions, and rituals. Recall that standards enable interconnection and sharing by establishing procedures and specifications that serve as the basis for development activities. Although standards can become invisible or transparent, they should be considered impossible to ignore or avoid. What standards were adopted to develop the process or project? What is the source for the standards? Do they come from central organizing bodies, or are they the products of grassroots efforts? What is the scope of the standards? Local, as in institutional? National or international? How were the standards created? What was the method? Was it inclusive of stakeholders? Is there a mechanism for revision? Are the standards flexible or rigid? Open or closed or a combination of both? What is political about the standards? In other words, what do they make possible or impossible? How might the standards enable or constrain future options for institutional thought and action? These are not the only questions to ask about standards, but they are fundamental to all analyses.

Legacies are academic IT systems that have been outdated and surpassed by technical improvements but still serve to support teaching and learning activities. Legacies encompass more than just software and hardware: they reflect a wide range of institutional practices and structures, including compliance structures, business and administrative practices, and pedagogical practices. All academic IT processes and projects will eventually become legacies. What is the current status of the process or project? Does it involve legacies? If so, should they be abandoned? Maintained? Reengineered? Replaced? No matter the approach, how are the legacies indebted to precedent and to received notions of institutional structures and practices? There are always future implications in how legacies are treated.

Conventions are social rules or norms that guide actions and activities on local and global scales. They are instruments for making meaning that go beyond the realms of individual workers and particular situations. What conventions are at work in the process or project? Where do they come from? What are their levels of scale? Are they being used by a small group of workers? A large group? A group (of any size) that extends beyond institutional boundaries? Is the group modifying the conventions? What are the complex problems of institutional coordination that the conventions address? Are they writing problems? Academic IT problems? Are the conventions having a slowing effect on new technologies? If so, how? Is this slowing effect necessarily bad? How do the conventions constitute actions and activities? What do they define and delimit? Make possible in the first place? Conventions and their histories are always present as active expressions of social rules and norms.

Rituals serve socializing functions and embody knowledge practices. By paying attention to the ritualized activities in institutions, people can learn a great deal about the historical dimensions of university commitments, worker roles, and work processes. Does the process or project involve rituals of passage, degradation, enhancement, renewal, conflict reduction, or integration? If the process or project involves ritualized activities, do they embody institutional lore, an important body of knowledge that addresses practical questions of what to do on the job? Ritualized activities involving lore help people manage the demands of knowledge and professional development.

To aid the task of spatializing, I have generated questions from the discussion in chapter 3 that prompt teachers to consider the effects of hierarchies, processes, methods, and bodies. Recall that hierarchies are a primary organizing structure in institutions. As spatial forms of organization, hierarchical structures both solve and create problems. Does a managerial control hierarchy govern the process or project? Is there a chain of command specifying who is responsible for what? Does the process or project involve a formal communication channel, with messages flowing downward from individuals at higher levels to those in lower levels? What is the managerial style of the process or project? Are there feedback loops to augment communication and learning for managers and others? Does the process or project make use of access hierarchies? Experience hierarchies? Expertise hierarchies? Are there networks within hierarchies? Hierarchies within networks? Hierarchies always exist in the midst of institutional tensions that open up fields of possibilities for interaction and communication.

Processes are phased tasks or activities that organize work in institutions. They are meant to lead to the development and implementation of products and services for university communities or generate data and information about university business practices. Much of the work in academic IT units is process driven and iterative by design. Does a systematic development process drive the process or project? If so, is it a macrolevel process anchored to broader institutional structures? A microlevel process that is more insulated from broader institutional structures, targeting tasks and activities at the unit level? Is more than one organizing process involved? Does the development process for the process or project provide people with a holistic view of institutional practices, allowing them to more easily contextualize and troubleshoot the phased tasks or activities for which they are responsible? Does the development process provide a sense of spatial continuity that is independent of individual capabilities? And does the development process heighten sensitivity to fundamental rhetorical considerations? One of the key distinctions of process-driven approaches is that all the phased tasks or activities share the common objective of meeting the needs of audiences.

Research methods are used by academic IT specialists to produce knowledge and understanding about teaching and learning with technologies. Is there a formalized research component to the process or project? If so, is it meant to produce internal secondary research? Internal primary research? External secondary research? External primary research? Institutional needs, which can be understood in spatial terms as either internal or external, are key factors in determining methodological choices and setting expectations for research.

Bodies are themselves (at least in part) an institutionally constructed element of academic IT contexts and central to the spatial practices that constitute human-machine interactions in teaching and learning settings. How does the process or project understand and represent embodied spatial practices? Is it meant to automate, mediate, augment, or hybridize the embodied spatial practices of students and teachers? These different views can coexist in the same process or project and serve a variety of purposes.

To aid the task of textualizing, I have generated questions from the discussion in chapter 4 that prompt teachers to consider the effects of metaphors, subjectivities, genres, and stories. Recall that metaphors help construct and constitute knowledge, mainly by shaping how people make sense of and experience institutions, literacies, and technologies. What are the metaphorical dimensions of the process or product? How do they textualize relationships between teachers and academic IT units? How do the metaphorical dimensions of the process or project textualize the literate activities associated with learning and using human-computer interfaces? And how do the metaphorical dimensions of the process or project textualize assumptions about the roles of computers in sociotechnical articulations? All institutional actors should be able to mobilize a variety of metaphors in specific situations, textualizing institutions, literacies, and technologies in appropriate and productive ways.

Subjectivities are institutional modes of thinking about and structuring what workers do and how they do it. Formed to a significant extent by interactions between workers and institutional environments, subjectivities help define what is permissible and possible within the boundaries of specific situations. For the process or project, what are the subject positions made available by job classifications? Where do the job classifications fall on the organizational chart? Does the organizational chart account for the work academic IT specialists do with teachers? How is the organizational chart informative for teachers? Does the process or project organize people into project teams? If so, what are the subject positions made available by the teams? Do they follow the organizational chart, or are they based on another type of structuring approach? Does the process or project organize people into collectives? What are the opportunities for self-representation? Maintaining an online presence, playing devil's advocate, and posing broad questions are useful strategies for affecting institutional subjectivities.

Genres are features of language use that textualize and formalize recurring institutional interactions and relationships. They are stable enough to serve coordinating functions in communication situations and unstable enough to serve invention functions in discourse communities. Does the process or project include administered, institutional, marketed or commercial, or vernacular genres? And does the process or project include genres with features from more than one category? Genre categories are not exhaustive or exclusive: genres can exhibit features from multiple categories and even change categories.

Stories create bridges between the general propositions of institutions and the concrete experiences of students and teachers. By propositions, I mean the narratives institutions adopt in order to maintain and advance their agendas. Does the process or project include stories that function as reinforcing elements for institutional narratives? If so, do the stories amplify institutional identities? Contextualize institutional artifacts and practices? Substantiate institutional claims? And does the process or project enlist teachers to help storify narratives and advance them in pedagogical communities? Teachers who involve themselves in institutional storytelling create opportunities to advance their own perspectives and shape institutional processes and projects.

In the second step of my approach, the questions for institutional analysis ask teachers to consider historical, spatial, and textual dimensions. The historical questions reflect the facts that academic IT units adopt standards to enable processes and projects to be interconnected and shared by users, contend with technologies as outdated legacies, adopt conventions that both constitute and regulate institutional rules and norms, and participate in institutional rituals that serve socializing functions and embody knowledge practices. The spatial questions reflect the facts that academic IT units reside in hierarchies that institutionalize actions and activities and organize sociotechnical relationships, employ systematic work processes at macro and micro levels, use research methods to produce knowledge and understanding about teaching and learning, and embrace perspectives on bodies that assign different roles and capacities to technologies. And the textual questions reflect the facts that academic IT units employ metaphors that filter understandings and experiences, include subject positions that are effects of institutional discourses, employ genres that textualize and formalize institutional interactions and relationships, and construct and circulate stories that play a reinforcing role in the advancement of institutional narratives. Analyzing historical, spatial, and textual dimensions is a critical antecedent to engaging academic IT.

Engaging Academic IT

The third step of the approach asks teachers to think about levels or modes of engagement. It is not possible or even desirable to engage all academic IT processes and projects in the same fashion or with the same mindset. Although there are implications for literacy in nearly every decision and action in academic IT settings, teachers need to be able to determine on a case-by-case basis why, when, and how to proceed as institutional actors depending on priorities and the stakes for writing and communication instruction.

Figure 5.2 presents six modes of institutional engagement available to teachers: maintaining awareness, using systems and services, mediating for audiences, participating as user advocates, working as designers, and partnering as researchers. They are ordered on a continuum from passive to active engagement, with the dashed line between the third and fourth modes representing an inflection point for working more directly with academic IT units. As the figure illustrates, engagement can involve both accommodation and resistance, including both in the same project or process. Teachers should be neither cheerleaders nor cynics in the contexts for

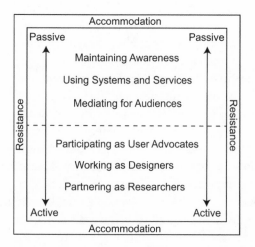

FIGURE 5.2 Modes of engagement for academic IT

literacies and technologies but curious people who bring a healthy dose of skepticism to institutionalization efforts.

Maintaining awareness is the most passive mode on the engagement spectrum. It only assumes that teachers will stay abreast of academic IT initiatives as consumers of institutional information. I hesitate to say "only" here because keeping up with an academic IT landscape can start to feel like a full-time job. But this task can be managed, for example, by curating informative institutional resources and then paying attention to them on an ongoing basis. At Penn State, this would mean subscribing to a newsletter from the Office of the Vice President for Information Technology, which provides the most comprehensive view of what is happening on campus; subscribing to a newsletter from the TLT unit, which provides information about teaching and learning initiatives; following relevant social media streams, such as those for the Penn State Media Commons and Maker Commons, two physical spaces for creating multimodal projects; and subscribing to RSS feeds for relevant websites, such as those for Classroom and Lab Computing and Accessibility and Usability, to get notifications of updates. If after positioning and analyzing an academic IT process or project teachers determine that maintaining awareness is a suitable level of engagement, they can then consider the extent to which that awareness needs to include critical as well as informational understandings. Is it enough to keep a general eye on things, or do the stakes or potential opportunities call for closer scrutiny? Maintaining awareness is a variable practice that can be tailored to fit the circumstances of individual processes and projects.

As a mode of engagement, the decision to use academic IT systems is a decision to work from within institutions rather than from without. I am sympathetic to some of the reasons people have for turning away from institutionally supported systems, including finding simpler solutions or solutions with fewer restrictions to user experiences. My commitment stems from the assumption that turning away from institutionally supported systems will only serve to marginalize teachers by ceding decision-making to others and forgoing the learning opportunities and economies of scale that accrue from pooling knowledge and resources in local communities. In addition, my commitment assumes that writing programs often lack the resources needed to provide workable and sustainable alternatives. As a default position, most programs will be better off by opting in (versus opting out) and then seeing what is possible as users of institutionally supported systems.

Mediating for audiences is a mode of engagement in which teacher-users see themselves as institutional communicators who have knowledge and experience to share with others, particularly other teachers and administrators. Mediating for audiences could be understood as part of a formal assignment: directors of writing programs should probably view this task as an aspect of their leadership positions. It could also be viewed more informally, as an expectation of institutional citizenship for people with expertise in the area. In fact, it is not unusual for early adopters to share their projects locally and illustrate how academic IT systems can be applied in disciplinary settings.

At times, mediating for audiences involves explaining purposes and functions to provide basic information or dispel misunderstandings. For example, I worked to dispel misunderstandings about a new institutional system for two-factor authentication because my colleagues both overestimated the complexity of the system and underestimated its importance for securing data and information. They were surprised to learn that users are not subject to double authentication each time they check their email or run a library search. They were also surprised to learn that a server attack compromised the dissertation research of several graduate students. Once my colleagues actually understood the why and how, they became sympathetic to the idea of the system and even supportive of it. At other times, mediating for audiences involves not just explaining purposes and functions but also taking positions on value-laden issues. In meetings with upper-level administrators, I have campaigned for the legitimacy of remix projects as original academic contributions and against the use of plagiarism detection programs in writing-intensive courses. The argumentative grounds for these positions were pedagogical and ethical, and in the case of plagiarism detection programs, my stance broke with an institutional direction that is expensive by most measures. Mediating for audiences has persuasive as well as informative objectives.

Participating as user advocates is a mode of engagement in which teachers see themselves as institutional feedback agents for academic IT units. Academic IT specialists can sometimes function as advocates for students and teachers, standing in for them at key moments in the development process and attempting to represent their priorities to other academic IT specialists and administrators. I am thinking not of persona-playing team members here but of actual teachers who are actively working to respond as users, in large part by providing feedback and helping interpret the results of institutional research. Providing feedback involves not only sharing the experiences of using systems but also contextualizing those experiences in richly textured ways so that academic IT specialists can learn about how writing is taught in universities. Helping interpret the results of institutional research involves telling the stories behind the numbers and explaining what they mean for classroom practices. Participating as user advocates can take many different forms or a combination of forms, including submitting help tickets with requests for new or revised systems, filling out surveys, attending symposia and workshops, contributing to online knowledge bases, joining usability tests, taking part in strategic-planning cycles, serving on advisory committees, volunteering for pilot projects, and requesting consultations with software trainers to explain course objectives, requirements, and assignments. In all of these advocacy tasks, teachers are first and foremost educator colleagues who want to assist academic IT specialists with a fundamental goal of their job: understanding users in context.

Working as designers is a mode of engagement in which teachers collaborate with academic IT specialists on the look, feel, and operation of institutional systems and services, including policies and help resources. Although I do not imagine the need for a strict linear progression through the modes of engagement, designing is often an extension of participating as user advocates, one in which teachers help turn feedback into action. Advisory committees, pilot projects, and usability tests present occasions for teachers to become designers by begging questions about next steps, about what to do to solve concrete problems. In a classic example of designing as a mode of engagement, teachers participating in usability tests identify problems with a course-management system that impede writing or the teaching of writing. In follow-up sessions, the teachers collaborate with academic IT specialists to redesign the course-management system, rethinking its look, feel, or operation in order to solve the problems. I have been involved in follow-up sessions that reimagined how a course-management system handles reading and writing privileges, organizes the content of electronic conversations, and assembles reports about student performance. The sessions resulted in revised features that are more in alignment with the perspectives of writing and communication teachers.

Partnering as researchers is a mode of engagement in which teachers collaborate with academic IT specialists to produce institutional knowledge. Either academic IT specialists or teachers can initiate these collaborations. In addition, they can be focused on either internal or external research, primary and secondary. Research partnering makes a good deal of sense from an institutional standpoint: academic IT units need access to methodological expertise and consequential sites for studying literacy practices, and teachers need access to resources and decision-making processes. Partnering as researchers serves the collective need for responsible and informed action. Because this mode of engagement can be especially time consuming and demanding, teachers need to be sure that the payoff is proportionate to the investment. Striking a balance will mean different things to different people, but it is important to controlling careers and being valued institutionally.

In the best examples of research partnering, the results would not have been possible without the contributions of everyone involved. I have partnered with academic IT specialists to investigate the integration of tablet devices and e-books into writing courses. In a study of the Apple iPad, I was the principal investigator on a project team that included other teacher-researchers, academic IT specialists, and textbook publishers. Although I envisioned and managed the project, the other teacher-researchers helped implement the study across multiple course sections, the academic IT specialists purchased and supported the iPads, and the textbook publishers purchased and supported the e-books. In a study of the Sony Reader, university librarians were the principal investigators on a project team that included teacher-researchers, academic IT specialists, and representatives from Sony USA. In my role here, I designed a graduate seminar that incorporated the devices into reading and writing activities, interviewed students about their experiences, and analyzed the devices to understand how students used them. Both studies yielded publishable insights for the teacher-researchers, who played an essential part in the production of knowledge about tablet devices and e-books as institutional platforms for literacy education.

The modes of engagement I discuss present opportunities for learning about academic IT initiatives and making positive pedagogical change. My passive-active scale is meant to communicate that engagement does not have to begin and end with time-consuming efforts. Indeed, small actions can have big effects. Moreover, time-consuming efforts can be devised to dovetail with administrative responsibilities or research expectations. The modes of engagement, in addition, can involve both accommodation and resistance, both adopting and subverting institutional orders. Engagement, as I understand it here, is grounded in reciprocal relationships that advance success in many directions.

INSTITUTIONAL TOUCHPOINTS AND INTERVENTIONS

Let me now turn to the final examples that illustrate my approaches to positioning, analyzing, and engaging academic IT. The examples are organized by everyday institutional touchpoints in the lives of writing and communication teachers. By everyday institutional touchpoints, I mean points of contact between teachers and institutions that occur quite naturally in the contexts of routine work—that is, in the contexts of teaching courses and administering programs. These contexts share some of the same activities, such as setting objectives, designing interactions, and evaluating outcomes, although at the program level, there are somewhat different considerations and concerns. The examples I use are not meant to be exclusive to teaching or administration but are meant as familiar illustrations that are accessible across institutions and encompass many of the dimensions of my heuristic. The goal is to show teachers how to pull everything together into a rhetorically functioning whole. Although my examples come from the technical writing service course, I could just as easily draw on the scenes for other writing courses. My examples come from technical writing not because it makes more or better use of academic IT but because I have an institutional responsibility for this general education requirement, which has led me to contend with an endless array of touchpoints: the positioning, analyzing, and engaging moves I discuss come from lived experiences in concrete situations, not abstract understandings of the relationships among institutions, literacies, and technologies.

My work with the technical writing service course is also a useful framework because it has required me to think about teacher training and professional development. All new technical writing teachers, including people with a lot of other teaching experience, must enroll in my weekly practicum, which provides a common syllabus, assignment sheets, lesson plans, and more. And because all the sections meet in computer classrooms and assign e-books, I have to address the curricular integration of information technologies. There is, in effect, a double-layered challenge here, for the vast majority of new technical writing teachers in our program are also new to teaching in computer classrooms and with e-books. In terms of professional development, experienced teachers rely on me to help them follow pedagogical and technological developments. I am constantly considering how to evolve the course for an ever-changing workplace.

I also want to emphasize that teachers can position, analyze, and engage academic IT at all phases of pedagogical and programmatic development, from brainstorming to maintenance. The "when" of my heuristic is anytime, and the "where" is anyplace that involves literacy and literacy education. I have tried to conceptualize the approaches that can be employed to help teachers respond substantively to institutional processes and projects and solve academic IT problems in professionally useful ways. Teachers, however, often find themselves coming in on the tail end of academic IT workflows and responding to minor aspects of institutional processes and projects, playing small ball with academic IT units and working more reactively than proactively or strategically. I encourage teachers to work proactively and strategically in areas of pedagogical and programmatic significance and to do so in a sustainable and worthwhile fashion.

Touchpoints in Teaching Activities

As with all teachers of writing and communication, I divide my time between a number of recursive activities—among them planning, preparing, and teaching classes and reflecting on how things went. Planning for classes includes selecting a textbook; creating a syllabus, assignment sheets, and lesson plans; and designing the macrolevel structures of the course-management system. Preparing for classes includes reviewing the textbook, reading and responding to student work in formative stages, creating materials to support in-class activities, and designing the microlevel structures of the course-management system. Teaching classes includes conducting minilectures, facilitating student discussions, and running writing workshops. And reflecting on how things went includes soliciting student feedback, responding to student work in summative stages, and reviewing analytics from the course-management system. Teaching activities are manifold and range from the simple to complex, but I have noted recurring activities that most people would expect to perform.

Performing such activities can put teachers into contact with numerous institutional touchpoints that involve academic IT. In planning for the technical writing service course, I have to reserve a computer classroom whose design configuration is sympathetic (enough) to my own priorities, identify e-books that are accessible to everyone in the course, imagine multimodal assignments that can be produced in the computer classroom, and customize the course-management system to reflect my own approaches. In preparing for classes, I have to create slide decks to support minilectures on key concepts, respond to proposals and drafts, and create workflows to support production and collaboration activities. In teaching classes, I have to explain and demonstrate how course technologies work for our assignments, address acceptable use and fair use policies, and model approaches for solving academic IT problems. And in reflecting on how things went, I have to respond to final versions of work and consider drafts, peer reviews, and course evaluations.

I want to elaborate by returning to the enduring textual question of how to document technologies for users and analyze how the establishment of a university makerspace presented an occasion for considering something new and different in my classroom. Makerspaces are physical institutional spaces where students and teachers can use a wide range of technologies—including things like soldering irons, sewing machines, and laser cutters—to prototype concepts and ideas. Makerspaces can be located in academic IT units, libraries, student centers, and elsewhere on a campus, and they can also be situated in off-campus sites. There are even mobile makerspaces used to stage pop-up educational events in both university and community locations. Makerspaces can be managed by academic IT specialists, faculty members, and students, and depending on the circumstances, there can be different levels of access for different users. Ironically, university makerspaces are indebted to the do-it-yourself (DIY) ethos prevalent in arts-and-crafts movements, youth culture movements, and various other counterculture movements that aim to resist institutional norms for practice and expression. This indebtedness is echoed by an emphasis on innovating, tinkering, hacking, and repurposing and in pedagogical approaches that value the principles of constructivism. University makerspaces blend old and new notions of invention and production.

At Penn State, the makerspace with open access is located on the first floor of the main library and operated by academic IT specialists. It includes an invention studio for conceptualizing and prototyping projects, a computer classroom for training and working sessions, and areas for doing collaborative work and housing equipment and resources. In the invention studio, there are custom standing desks with built-in whiteboards for brainstorming and note taking; the desks, which can be moved up and down electronically, also include iPads on articulating arms for documenting projects in pictures and videos. In addition, there are electronic building blocks (littleBits), programmable robots (Makeblock and Techykids), microcontrollers (Arduino), single-board minicomputers (Raspberry Pi), and more. In the computer classroom, there are forty iMacs with software applications to support design and production activities. The software includes Final Cut Pro, Adobe Creative Cloud, and Microsoft Office 365. The instructor workstation is connected to two large monitors and three large screens so that students sitting anywhere can see projected materials. Whiteboards also line the classroom walls. In the areas for collaboration, furniture can be rearranged, and there are large monitors for projecting materials. In the areas for housing equipment and resources, there are thirty-two 3D printers (MakerBot) and a library with reference materials.

The makerspace is an exploratory institutional space for thinking and doing.

Although I heard about the makerspace from a manager in the TLT unit, it was publicized on university email lists, websites, and social media platforms. Early press releases invited students and teachers to tour the space, schedule an appointment, or simply drop in with questions or concerns. As with most institutional initiatives that involve teaching and learning activities, I began to wonder what might be in it for my own students and program. How might we use the makerspace in the technical writing service course? My first idea was to create a new assignment. Following the work of David Sheridan (2010) and Jody Shipka (2011), students could fabricate three-dimensional objects and explore their potential as rhetorical compositions. But part of me worried about asking first-time teachers to participate in an experimental project. My second idea was to revise an existing course assignment, the instruction set, reconsidering its materials and methods in light of the features and benefits of an academic IT platform—in this instance, the electronic building blocks, or littleBits, in the invention studio (https://littlebits.com/). Students could use the littleBits to document instructions for building small inventions. I was drawn to this second idea and to the prospect of evolving my thinking about a hallmark assignment but needed to decide if I even wanted to use the makerspace in the first place and to what extent and how. In the discussion that follows, I share how I used my approach to position, analyze, and engage the Penn State makerspace as an institutional formation for the study and practice of writing and communication.

In my approach, academic IT initiatives can be positioned as processes in formal settings, projects in formal settings, processes in informal settings, and projects in informal settings. I would position the makerspace as a formal institutional project that involves both systems and services. The formal character of the project can be seen in how the makerspace is resourced and in how it reviews, implements, manages, and documents work. The makerspace is a project that falls within the scope of the Penn State Media Commons, which helps teachers integrate a variety of media technologies into their courses; it is thus a new project for an already established unit, extending its reach into the realm of DIY cultural production. The staff includes a manager, who provides leadership and oversees the budget; a coordinating manager, who oversees daily operations; consultants, who assist students and teachers and run training sessions; and work-study students, who wrangle equipment and otherwise pitch in where needed. The operating budget is stable, coming from student IT fees and other centralized sources. Although there is no budget line to encourage teacher involvement, teachers have ample access to equipment and the personnel needed to help make sense of the possibilities. The makerspace is well resourced in terms of money and people.

Because the makerspace was designed as a workspace for exploring pedagogical ideas, reviews are inclusive of stakeholder perspectives—that is, teachers drive how the makerspace is taken up and applied, so their priorities and experiences form an important basis for evaluation. The success of the makerspace can only really be measured by involving teachers in review processes. The formal character of the makerspace as an institutional project is conspicuous in the scale of implementation: it is meant to support all Penn State courses. According to reports on the makerspace website, each semester hundreds of students and teachers use the makerspace as a classroom, and thousands of objects are printed on the 3D printers (I am not thinking of using the printers, but this capacity is significant, signaling a sizable investment).

All of this work is managed at two levels. At the macro level is a hierarchy that indicates who has institutional responsibility for which aspects of the operation. At the micro level, teachers and staff members collaborate to determine a governing structure for instruction. Teachers, for example, can elect to outsource instruction not only in software and hardware applications but also in theories and practices of prototyping and design thinking. There is documentation to support such instruction and also to help students work independently to solve their own problems. As a user of the makerspace, I would have access to considerable institutional resources while still maintaining reasonable control over my course.

In moving from the positioning step to the analyzing step, I next considered how historical, spatial, and textual dimensions contribute to the processes of institutionalization that constitute the makerspace. As for histories, standards are at issue on both general and specific levels. On a general level, the invention studio and computer classroom employ the same standards that enable processes and projects to be interconnected and shared within Penn State and beyond. For example, the iPads in the invention studio save videos as MOV files, which can be easily converted to MP4 files; MP4 files use a widely supported international standard for compressing video content. And the software in the computer classroom, for example, is licensed for all students, who can install it on multiple personal devices and export content in various standard file formats. Furthermore, all the digital content created in the makerspace can be stored on and shared from a Penn State cloud server (Box) and integrated into an institutional platform (WordPress) for creating websites and e-portfolios.

On a specific level, the littleBits themselves are aligned with additional sets of standards. Brick adapters, for example, allow students to connect littleBits to LEGO bricks, providing an accessible and inexpensive approach to building out inventions, and the code used for programming littleBits circuits is open source and free to use and modify. Also, the educator guide that comes with littleBits emphasizes Common Core State Standards for writing and communication and Next Generation Science Standards to convey that littleBits are designed to support problem-based learning and help students and teachers document learning. I did not anticipate finding mentions of flexible and rhetorically minded writing and communication standards prioritizing audiences, organizing frameworks, and multimodal analyses. Although there are layers of different types of standards in the makerspace, none of them would create barriers in our courses: the standards function together readily in interoperative networks of sociotechnical practices.

Legacies, likewise, would not create any issues for my students or me. Although the hardware platforms in the invention studio and computer classroom are not the latest and greatest platforms, the operating systems and software programs are robust and up to date, and they are kept current and properly patched by academic IT specialists (campus computers are replaced every three to four years). And if students were to integrate a littleBits app into their inventions, they would simply need to be sure to install any app updates.

In terms of conventions, an institutional problem of coordination for the invention studio is providing access to the littleBits components. Although the invention studio has a rack of littleBits, there are not enough of them to allow the creation of individual inventions in a class of twenty-four or to allow students to extend their invention-making sessions beyond a single class period. In this case, then, an academic IT problem would regulate pedagogical activities, establishing short-term group work as the institutional norm. I would need to rethink my single-authored approach to the instruction set assignment.

On a more local level, design conventions for the littleBits components aim to assist teaching and learning. For example, the four types of components are color coded to help students visualize sequencing patterns: blue is for power components, which must initiate inventions; pink is for input components, such as sensors and buttons; green is for output components, such as lights and motors; and orange is for wire components, which expand the reach of circuits by adding options for physical spacing and enabling virtual connectivity, including to the internet of things. Such design conventions are specific to littleBits and would not affect or be affected by institutional conventions.

Finally, a ritualized endeavor in the makerspace is MAKEiT 2.0, a one-day workshop that socializes new users into appropriate activities and roles. This ritual of passage provides introductions to printing 3D objects, making 360-degree videos, and prototyping with littleBits. Attending the littleBits workshop would allow me to experience institutional instruction in creating inventions—instruction that reflects the educational perspectives of makerspace staff members. I could then better anticipate the implications of histories and what teachers would need to do to ensure a balance of perspectives in the project.

All the spatial dimensions of my heuristic are discernible in the sociotechnical articulations that influence the disposition of the makerspace. The makerspace is governed by a control hierarchy that specifies who is responsible for what, but the managerial approach is a soft approach that emphasizes people and their talents and relationships. The manager, who is also responsible for the Penn State Media Commons, relies on a coordinating manager to oversee daily operations, who in turn relies on consultants and work-study students to ensure a positive experience for users. This primary concern requires staff members to work closely with users, providing the support they need to be successful. I would anticipate my students and I needing help with designing littleBits inventions that involve virtual connectivity. Fortunately, the soft managerial approach would provide makerspace staff members with the ability to leverage the most useful types of spatial organizations—hierarchies, networks, or both—in specific situations. I could imagine a work-study student being repositioned as a teacher to help us connect littleBits inventions to the internet of things.

The institutional processes that organize work in the makerspace are systematic and transparent. There is a microlevel process for teachers that includes three phases: registering projects, designing assignments, and anticipating support needs. In the first phase, teachers tell makerspace staff members about their plans and specify basic project parameters, such as time frames, due dates, and numbers of students; this phase also calls for project descriptions. In the second phase, teachers meet with makerspace staff members to design or review assignments. Although this phase is optional, makerspace staff members can share assignments that have been successful in the past and offer pedagogical and institutional suggestions.

In the third phase, teachers anticipate their needs and consider how maker-space resources might be integrated into teaching and learning activities so that everyone can plan accordingly; these resources include workshops and tutorials.

There is also a microlevel process for inventing with littleBits, which people can learn about by either taking the makerspace workshop on design thinking or using the educator guide that comes with littleBits. Developed by researchers from the Hasso Plattner Institute of Design at Stanford University, this microlevel process encourages inventors to first empathize with users to understand their contexts and concerns and then define, ideate, prototype, and test design solutions for concrete situations, heightening sensitivities to fundamental rhetorical considerations. Teachers would be responsive to a context-centered process for inventing with littleBits, which resonates with how the field approaches writing and communication as design activities.

Staff members in the makerspace conduct external secondary research to inform their workshops and tutorials with state-of-the-art information and to aid purchasing decisions. For the computer classroom, this research focuses on ways to design educational spaces for both short-term group work and large-group discussions. What is the latest thinking on computer classroom design? On designing flexible educational spaces that can accommodate different types of activities? On how network infrastructures can facilitate collaboration? Such questions need to be revisited from time to time by makerspace staff members: the design of educational spaces is a dynamic topic that is ever changing and growing. For the invention studio, external secondary research focuses on design thinking and rapid prototyping and on expanding and upgrading the littleBits components. How are design thinking and rapid prototyping evolving as fields of study? How do other university makerspaces operationalize design thinking and rapid prototyping as heuristics for invention? How are they incorporating littleBits or other materials for physical computing projects? What are their processes for supporting students and teachers? External secondary research is a key to success for the makerspace, and it would help ensure that our experiences would not be too idiosyncratic to be meaningful or of interest to others.

For the final spatial dimension in my heuristic—bodies—the dominant perspective in the makerspace is that machines enhance or amplify their capacities, making them more effective in the world. This augmentation perspective is noticeable on two levels. On a narrower level, many of the basic inventions created with littleBits are themselves augmentation machines, things like monitoring and lighting systems. In fact, in the introductory workshop in the makerspace, teachers and students learn how to create a basic flashlight. A major assumption in the world of littleBits is that people invent their way out of problems, using technologies to unlock human potential and advance progress. On a broader level, a major assumption is that machine-inventing activities augment education, emphasizing active processes of meaning making that engage higher-order thinking skills. Learning by doing is one of several constructivist principles that shapes the actions of academic IT units as they work to imagine, develop, and manage campus spaces—material and virtual—for teaching and learning. As I mentioned in chapter 3, constructivism as a framework for thinking about the relationships between literacies and technologies is effective to an extent, foregrounding the social construction of knowledge. But I would need to be alert to the ways apolitical strains of constructivism can mystify processes of institutionalization that instill patterns of authority and influence in learning settings.

All the textual dimensions of my heuristic are also discernible in the sociotechnical articulations that influence the disposition of the makerspace. Although a number of popular metaphors are associated with the makerspace, the following definitional formulation (of my own making) incorporates some of the key ones that are likely to be relevant across a range of institutions: in makerspaces, students are creators who use a variety of tools and materials to rapidly prototype design solutions to real-life problems. The creator metaphor constructs students as people who actively participate in the production of culture, including classroom culture, drawing on their own perspectives and experiences to help make meaning and solve problems in communities of practice. One of the potential benefits of the creator metaphor is that teachers could extend it to writing and communication tasks to emphasize the epistemic functions that discursive activities perform and to illustrate how they perform them.

In something of a contradiction, the tool metaphor constructs the technologies in the computer classroom and invention studio as effective means to an end, as effective means for getting things done in educational settings. As I discussed in chapter 4, the tool metaphor has a certain upside, but I would need to counterbalance its functional orientation with both critical and rhetorical perspectives. The prototype metaphor constructs processes of making as low-risk explorations of concepts or ideas that result in working models of inventions; these models are meant to be critiqued by audiences and iterated by creators. Making as prototyping, which involves deliberating, experimenting, and trial-and-error tinkering, would be an approach that is compatible with how teachers think about the invention and drafting stages for multimodal texts.

Lastly, the problem-solution metaphor constructs education as a process of inquiry that uses problems as starting points and organizing frameworks for teaching and learning. Problem contexts can be rich and complex, challenging students to contend with a tangle of rhetorical issues. One of the potential benefits of the problem-solution metaphor is that it could help teachers emphasize the ill-defined nature of technical writing problems, especially their capacity to elicit multiple, even contradictory, solutions. A possible downside is that the metaphor could serve to diminish the vital role of emotions, feelings, sensations, and visceral reactions in educational processes. It would therefore be important to avoid presenting problem-solution frameworks as relatively mechanistic or overly rational. Assuming careful planning, the popular metaphors in my definitional formulation could textualize the makerspace in productive ways for students and teachers.

In the case of an instruction set assignment with littleBits, subjectivities in the makerspace could be effects of both job classifications and project teams. Because the makerspace employs a soft managerial approach, it would follow that the coordinating manager would view the organizational chart as a depiction of human arrangements that must be trustworthy and respectful. Although the organizational chart does not represent the lateral relationships between academic IT specialists and teachers, many of the academic IT specialists inhabit the job classification of consultant, which in institutional terms defines support for teachers and students as a major responsibility. In fact, all the job classifications that fall below the top spot in the hierarchy involve supporting students and teachers. The consultants and other workers are meant to facilitate the successful functioning of the makerspace for courses.

In terms of project teams, my analysis has already indicated that I would need to rethink my single-authored approach to the instruction set assignment in order to solve an access problem in the makerspace. In my discussion in chapter 4, I focused on how institutions assemble project teams by referencing organizational charts and using institutional considerations such as the positionality, availability, and diversity of workers. Members of my project team would be assigned by the coordinating manager, who reviews project descriptions and confers with teachers about their assignments in order to match them with academic IT specialists. Because the makerspace is a busy institutional space, staff availability would be a factor in assembling my project team, which is fine for a teacher without personnel preferences.

Another influence on subject formation would be the roles assigned to students in project teams. The littleBits educator guide suggests five roles: creatives, or students who think creatively about problem solving; engineers, or students who understand how to assemble the littleBits components; mechanics, or students who are good at troubleshooting problems; organizers, or students who can group and sort the littleBits components; and cleaners, or students who understand how to clean the littleBits components. These roles represent modes of being and learning that constitute a sense of self in the makerspace, regulating what is possible within the assignment. Although regulation can serve a positive agenda in institutions, in this case, I would view it as limiting and even problematic. First, the roles define human capacities as a property of subject positions, asserting, for instance, that engineers are not good (or as good) at being creative or that creatives are not good (or as good) at troubleshooting problems. Second, I would worry about assigning students to the role of cleaners. Although the littleBits components must be cleaned according to a special protocol to preserve the functioning of the circuits, cleaning is a downstream maintenance task that is marginal to learning. I would need to imagine an approach to assembling project teams, to textualizing institutional subject positions, that avoids these pitfalls.

In order to advance its mission, the makerspace employs institutional and marketed or commercial genres. The institutional genres include reports and training materials and the marketed or commercial genres include teacher testimonials. The reports, which can be downloaded from the Media Commons website, are infographics that provide descriptive statistics about things that can be easily measured for a period of time and communicated to audiences, such as how many classes have used the makerspace or how many staff hours have been dedicated to in-person training. The training materials are procedural documents that show people how to do things, such as connecting the different types of littleBits circuits or sending jobs to the MakerBot printers (again, I am not thinking of using the printers, but students could decide to print 3D objects to incorporate into their inventions). The marketed or commercial genres are video-based testimonials from teacher-champions, who use their own experiences to help explain the value of the makerspace. All the genres serve to textualize and formalize recurring institutional interactions and relationships that involve reporting, training, and marketing activities.

For an instruction set assignment, the most relevant materials for students would be the procedural documents, but the only option is the module cards packaged with littleBits, which list steps for activating and connecting the components. Although the module cards are useful, it would also be helpful to have procedural documents that formalize recurring interactions and institution-specific relationships. I am thinking, for example, of documents that address how to collaborate in the makerspace or scaffold its various help resources. A possibility is that some of my students could prepare such documents for their assignments. For teachers, the reports with descriptive statistics could also be relevant, but I would want to see qualitative feedback from students and teachers to contextualize the statistics. The testimonials would likely include qualitative feedback, and they would alert me to teacher-champions who have developed productive relationships with the makerspace. I could approach these teachers for input and advice, focusing less on the outcomes of projects and more on the prospects for critical explorations. In my approach to academic IT contexts, a healthy dose of skepticism is compatible with the genre of teacher testimonials.

Stories—the final textual dimension in my heuristic—are used by the Maker Commons to create bridges between general institutional propositions and the concrete experiences of students and teachers. Although the section of the Media Commons website titled "Faculty Stories" does not (yet) include any entries about the makerspace, the stories about the Penn State One Button Studio—the video production system I analyzed in chapter 3—are instructive and reinforce several institutional narratives by amplifying identities and contextualizing artifacts and practices (the makerspace testimonials discussed in the previous section appear in a video report for the New Media Consortium). The faculty stories on the Media Commons website are presented as videos of teachers explaining how they incorporate the One Button Studio into their courses and the value it creates in several contexts. A teacher for a course in sustainability leadership discusses how assigning video projects helps advance the institutional identity theme of making university activities public and visible, a teacher for a course in geosciences discusses how assigning video projects helps advance the institutional identity theme of increasing student engagement, and a teacher for a course in social studies education discusses how assigning video projects helps advance the institutional identity theme of preparing future workers with an education that is relevant to twenty-first-century life. I could leverage these narrative themes, which are equally germane to writing and communication courses, to help position the instruction set as an especially fitting assignment for the makerspace.

The teachers in the videos contextualize the artifacts and practices in their courses by responding to questions provided by the Media Commons: What educational goals did you hope to reach by assigning your students a video project? How did this video project help your students learn more about the topics of the course than a traditional project? How did working with the Media Commons help facilitate the delivery of this project to your students? And in what ways have your experiences with this project shaped your plans for future assignments in this and other courses? Putting aside the leading nature of some of the questions, I would take advantage of the opportunity to tell an institutional story that textualizes littleBits as a platform for writing and communication and advances my own perspectives on what it means to work productively in academic IT settings.

In step three of my approach, I decided on a suitable level of engagement with the makerspace: using systems and services, the second mode on my continuum from passive to active engagement. To reiterate and elaborate, the first step in my approach led me to position the makerspace as a formal institutional project, but in the best sense of the phrase: I will have access to considerable resources while still maintaining reasonable control over my course. The second step led me to historicize, spatialize, and textualize the makerspace as an institutional formation. This critique produced a relatively positive view of the prospects for engagement. My historicizing efforts showed that the standards for the makerspace enable it to interoperate with more general institutional spaces for teaching and learning and that the standards for littleBits support problem-based learning, a typical approach to teaching technical writing, and even align with literacy standards with rhetorical dimensions. The legacies in the makerspace will not pose any pedagogical problems, assuming normal institutional maintenance. And a ritual of passage in the makerspace—a workshop that socializes new users into appropriate activities and roles—will help me anticipate the implications of histories and how I can ensure a balanced range of perspectives. The only historical issue involves conventions, which help solve institutional problems of coordination. Because the supply of littleBits is limited for a class of twenty-four students, I will need to adopt the institutional norm of short-term group work in the makerspace, rethinking my single-authored approach to the instruction set. This adjustment is workable and could even enhance the assignment: collaboration is a defining feature of technical writing contexts.

My spatializing efforts showed that the hierarchies in the makerspace are softened by managers who emphasize the talents and relationships of staff members, allowing them to leverage the most useful types of spatial organizations in specific situations. The processes in the makerspace are systematic and transparent and resonate with how the field approaches writing and communication as design activities. And the methods in the makerspace, specifically external secondary research, help ensure that the experiences of students and teachers are not too idiosyncratic to be meaningful or of interest to others. The only spatial issue involves bodies and the perspectives on constructivism that guide academic IT approaches to learning by doing and to augmenting practices, especially pedagogical practices. I will need to pay attention to the role apolitical strains of constructivism can play in helping mystify institutional patterns of authority and influence that have negative consequences for education.

Finally, my textualizing efforts showed that the genres in the makerspace formalize recurring institutional interactions and relationships associated with reporting, training, and marketing activities and that students themselves have the opportunity to produce institution-specific procedural documents; this opportunity affords a rich and complex context for problem-based learning. The testimonials, in addition, will alert me to teacher-champions who I can approach for advice about working both effectively and critically in the makerspace. The stories presented on the Media Commons website reinforce several institutional narratives that I will leverage to position the instruction set as an especially fitting assignment for the makerspace. I will also take advantage of the chance to advance my own story about what it means to engage productively with academic IT units.

The textual issues of concern involve aspects of institutional metaphors and subjectivities. The subsidiary subjects for the creator and prototype metaphors should filter learning experiences in productive ways, but I will need to counterbalance the tool metaphor with critical and rhetorical perspectives and frame the problem-solution metaphor so that it does not diminish the vital role of emotions, feelings, sensations, and visceral reactions in processes of educational inquiry. And in assembling student project teams, I will need to avoid approaches that define human capacities as a property of institutional subject positions or that construct institutional subject positions that are marginal to learning. Being able to recognize such pitfalls ahead of time is invaluable to planning but also to step three of my approach, to determining levels or modes of institutional engagement.

Let me conclude this example by elaborating on my decision to engage the makerspace in a relatively modest fashion as a user of its systems and services. Although my critique produced a positive view of the prospects for engagement, the makerspace is a comparatively new institutional project, especially for teachers of writing and communication. The makerspace was designed to support teaching and learning across the curriculum, but most of its users are from outside the humanities. I am anticipating a worthwhile experience for students and can even imagine a more ambitious relationship with the makerspace, assuming that being an early adopter from the humanities turns out to be a good idea. But it makes sense to first test the waters without making the commitments involved in mediating for audiences, participating as user advocates, working as designers, or partnering as researchers to see if the makerspace actually matches up (enough) with my own expectations, interests, and professional values.

Touchpoints in Administering Programs

The touchpoints for administrators of writing and communication programs are no less prevalent or significant. Administrators also plan and reflect on pedagogical practices, but they adopt a programmatic ethos that is more broadly sensitive to institutional dynamics. They occupy a middle ground between teachers and institutions, helping both to achieve their objectives, which are not so much incompatible as categorically different. If teachers spend much of their time planning, preparing, and teaching classes and reflecting on how things went, administrators spend much of their time designing and managing macrostructures to organize individual efforts into a coherent system and to produce a social order that is congruent with the values of the profession. As a coherent system, programs define parameters and procedures for teaching and learning and for evaluating efforts and outcomes; an important consideration is whether students are receiving a consistent, high-quality experience in all course sections. As a social order, programs attempt to govern behavior in ways that align with research findings and position statements from the field. Administrators spend a fair amount of time negotiating the tensions between institutional and professional contexts.

The service course in technical writing puts administrators into contact with numerous institutional touchpoints that involve academic IT. The touchpoints are associated with a variety of planning, managing, and evaluating activities and are inflected by issues of scope and scale. My planning activities include scheduling access to computer classrooms for dozens of sections, providing an approved list of e-books that can be integrated into institutional infrastructures and workflows, creating a standard syllabus for new teachers that specifies multimodal assignments in digital media, and annotating this syllabus to provide new teachers with starting points for employing academic IT. My managing activities include running a weekly teaching practicum that emphasizes integrating literacies and technologies in institutions, explaining relevant academic IT policies, and maintaining a program website that has a portal for distributing and archiving pedagogical and administrative documents. My evaluating activities include analyzing usage analytics from the program website and course-management system and analyzing course evaluations, both individually and in the aggregate. Retrieving useful data and information from institutional systems can be harder than expected and a time sink for administrators.

Let me elaborate on the academic IT touchpoints in administering programs by employing my approach to position, analyze, and engage the online version of our technical writing service course. Because all our online courses are treated as an institutional portfolio that operates under a unified framework, this example is more encompassing than my teaching example, having wider implications for the program. Before I begin, however, I want to return to something I said earlier: the "when" of my approach is anytime, and the "where" is anyplace that involves literacy and literacy education. In my previous example for touchpoints in teaching activities, I considered the pedagogical feasibility of initiating a new institutional relationship with a university makerspace. Although the instruction set assignment is an old one, the makerspace version is novel and different, contributing to efforts at keeping the program relevant and up to date. In contrast, my next example for touchpoints in administering programs will revisit a well-established institutional relationship for the purpose of revaluation. My approach supports the view that the status quo should always be questioned to ensure its efficacy and success.

In 1998, I received an internal grant to create the online version of our technical writing service course, the first English department course in our institutional portfolio for distance education (we now offer seventeen online courses). The funding for the grant came from the university president, who at the time was developing the World Campus, the centralized unit that supports online courses and programs. As I noted in chapter 1, the World Campus was considered to be the twenty-fifth Penn State campus, but this designation has always puzzled me because it does not hire faculty or do many of the other things a college campus is expected to do. The

World Campus, in reality, functions as a delivery unit, and this fact helps explain its perspectives, processes, and relationships.

As opposed to hiring faculty, the World Campus collaborates with academic departments to develop online courses and programs. Although delivery platforms have evolved since 1998, the process for course development has remained relatively constant over the years. Assuming that an academic department, the dean of its college, and the World Campus have all agreed to develop an online course, the World Campus assigns an instructional designer and the department assigns a (tenure-track or non-tenure-track) faculty member, establishing the basic project team; faculty members receive a course reduction for their work on the team. In a nutshell, the faculty member is responsible for authoring the content, and the instructional designer is responsible for structuring that content into a course. This process constructs a form/content binary that has consequences for the status quo—not all negative, by any means—in academic programs. My discussion will reason through these consequences as it positions, analyzes, and engages the World Campus as an institutional formation.

I structure my discussion by comparing how we currently work with the World Campus to an alternative arrangement for the program. In the alternative arrangement, which all stakeholders would need to approve, the department would become responsible for both authoring content and structuring it into online courses. In other words, the department would assume ownership over the entire development process, including instructional design. In a sense, this alternative arrangement would not be an unprecedented change for the World Campus, for there are already instructional design units within colleges that help departments produce online courses. In these situations, colleges receive additional revenue for doing the instructional design work, with the World Campus still carrying out essential institutional functions, such as admitting students, advertising courses, and running a help desk. What would be unique is that a department with regular academic faculty would have complete control over the look, feel, and operation of a distance education portfolio. I am exploring this possibility because the status quo situation is less than ideal, but change is not necessarily a continuous succession of improvements. I will need to weigh the pros and cons in deciding whether or not to pursue complete control over the portfolio.

To begin, I would position the World Campus as a formal institutional process. Although the World Campus could be positioned as an institutional project in that it provides systems and services for students and teachers, including learning platforms for online students and training programs for online teachers, administrators tend to experience it as a process, spending most of their time working with staff members to develop and maintain a coherent portfolio of online courses. As with the makerspace, the formal character of the World Campus can be seen in how it is resourced and in the ways work is reviewed, implemented, managed, and documented. The internal grant I received in 1998 was for twenty-five thousand dollars, a substantial amount of money for developing a single online course. I used the money to buy six course releases: two for me and two each for two graduate students. We used the time away from teaching to review the literature on distance learning and draft and test the course content. But personal experience is not my only gauge for measuring institutional investments. The World Campus has been highlighted as a priority in all the Penn State strategic plans since the 1990s, and it receives budgetary infusions from central administration. For example, in 2013 there was an infusion of twenty million dollars to support the goal of more than tripling enrollment numbers. And revenue from online courses is used to support residential programs, motivating program administrators to maintain an online portfolio. The World Campus is well resourced and backed by high-level institutional commitments.

Because the World Campus collaborates closely with academic departments, reviews are inclusive of stakeholder perspectives. Program administrators must accept the final versions of online courses, signing off on an approval form, and even then courses are considered pilot versions until student feedback has been incorporated. Small revisions to existing courses are also subject to administrative review—not to police course authors but rather to ensure coherence in online portfolios. The formal character of the World Campus as an institutional process is also evident in the scale of implementation: it offers over 150 degrees and certificates, all of which must be developed, updated, and assessed in a systematic fashion. In addition to our general education courses, my department offers an online English minor that students in any online major can add. If the minor continues to grow, we may need to hire, train, and support remote teachers, an undertaking that would require us to create new institutional processes.

All this course development is managed at two levels. At the broadest level, the World Campus is a unit within Outreach and Online Education, which is headed by a vice provost who is also responsible for MOOCs, professional development programs, and adult learning programs. Outreach and Online Education is a large operation, relying on a hierarchical structure to indicate who is responsible for what. More relevant to teachers is the micro level and how online portfolios themselves are managed. As I already noted, portfolios are comanaged by academic departments and the World Campus, using a strict approach that divides responsibilities for content and form according to job roles. For people on both sides of the divide, there are institutional requirements for documentation, and there is also extensive documentation to help students and teachers employ a variety of systems. As an administrator of a World Campus portfolio, I have access to considerable institutional resources but do not control the look, feel, or operation of online courses.

In moving from the positioning step to the analyzing step, I next considered the historical, spatial, and textual dimensions from my heuristic, analyzing the processes of institutionalization that constitute the World Campus. As for histories, the relevant standards issues are associated with authoring platforms and instructional design practices. Course authors can use any platform that saves multimodal content in standard file formats — that is, formats that can be read easily by a wide range of software in educational settings. My campus has institutional licenses for Microsoft Office 365 and Adobe Creative Cloud, so these platforms are among the advisable choices. The World Campus imports content from course authors into Evolution, the content-management system used for instructional design work; course authors do not have access to Evolution. Evolution, in turn, integrates with Canvas, the student-facing platform for distance education, by way of Learning Tools Interoperability (LTI) standards. The institutional thought behind these layers is that it makes sense to use the right tools for the tasks at hand: Microsoft and Adobe products for content development, Evolution for instructional design, and Canvas for online learning. A panoply of compatible standards enable this layered approach, but we would not have access to Evolution if we assumed complete control over the portfolio, creating the need to secure a platform for instructional design.

The World Campus has adopted several sets of standards to guide instructional design activities. I mentioned the Sloan-C Quality Framework in chapter 1. Following this framework, instructional designers are guided by standards used to judge the success of online education: learning effectiveness, cost-effectiveness and institutional commitment, access, faculty satisfaction, and student satisfaction. For each standard, the Sloan-C Quality Framework provides goals, metrics, and progress indices, making it actionable in concrete ways. Although I would want to reexamine how the framework defines effectiveness, access, and satisfaction to be sure that the definitions align with how the field thinks about those terms, it would make sense for us to continue to consider instructional design standards that address (in some fashion) learning effectiveness, cost-effectiveness and institutional commitment, access, faculty satisfaction, and student satisfaction.

A second set of standards adopted by the World Campus comes from Quality Matters, a nonprofit organization founded with a Fund for the Improvement of Postsecondary Education (FIPSE) grant from the US Department of Education. The goal of this organization is to provide national benchmarks for online course design. There are eight general standards in the Quality Matters framework: course overview and introduction, learning objectives, assessment and measurement, instructional materials, course activities and learner interaction, course technology, learner support, and accessibility and usability (https://www.qualitymatters.org/). Each general standard includes a number of specific review standards that operationalize instructional design activities. For example, there are five specific review standards that help instructional designers evaluate course technologies, such as making sure they support learning objectives, promote active learning, and are readily obtainable. A simple but often missed point about all of these standards is that enacting them effectively requires expertise in both content development and instructional design, confounding perspectives that assume a binary opposition between form and content and helping make the case that teachers have an essential role to play in academic IT initiatives.

More to the point for the question of assuming complete control over the portfolio, we could drill down on the specific review standards in the Quality Matters framework to make them more applicable to our own situation. Returning to my example of specific review standards, what does it mean for course technologies to support learning objectives in writing and communication programs? For course technologies to promote active learning for writing and communication students? And for course technologies to be readily obtainable to writing and communication students? A positive step would be to refine the instructional design standards to better suit our contexts.

Legacies would not likely create any issues for the program or portfolio and in fact could present opportunities for moving in a new direction. Although the hardware platforms in offices and computer labs are not always the latest ones, the operating systems and software programs are robust and kept up to date by academic IT specialists. For content development, we always have access to more recent versions of Microsoft Office 365 and Adobe Creative Cloud, including from home offices: the institutional licenses for these software suites allow people to install them on multiple devices and on personal devices. In terms of instructional design, questions about the effects of legacies would be open questions until we secured a platform to replace Evolution, but we would certainly work to answer them in our decision-making process.

The course content itself is an institutional legacy with deep historical roots. The standard online version of our technical writing service course matches the standard face-to-face version in fundamental ways, using more or less the same syllabus, assignments, and resources. We landed on this approach for two reasons. On our side of the equation, we wanted to be able to leverage our existing teacher training program, which is well established and sustained by significant institutional investments. Mirroring the face-to-face course gave us a running start with experienced technical writing teachers, enabling us to train them relatively quickly for an online environment. On the World Campus side of the equation, the content development workflow emphasized the elements of a syllabus. As opposed to asking us to imagine designing online content from the ground up, the workflow encouraged us to think about transferring our face-to-face content to an online environment. We have updated the content several times over the years, but assuming complete control over the portfolio would allow us to use a development workflow that is more born-digital in nature, especially now that we have a sizable pool of experienced online teachers.

An institutional problem of coordination for the World Campus is designing online courses that can be taken by nontraditional students from anywhere in the world. By nontraditional students, I mean working adults, returning students, and students serving in the military. The World Campus accommodates the daily lives of nontraditional students and addresses the challenges of multiple time zones by employing conventions that govern the pace of online learning and the character of online interactions. One convention we were able to resist from the start is the institutional norm of designing online courses to be self-paced and self-directed experiences. For students, the advantages include flexibility in studying and completing assignments and a more personal feel to education. Although institutions value such advantages, they are also attracted to rolling enrollments, which allow students to start and finish courses at any time rather than adhering to a set schedule, for rolling enrollments can increase student numbers overall. For pedagogical reasons, we insisted on a cohort model, with classes limited to twenty-four students, matching the pace and course cap for residential instruction. To date, we have not been overly pressured to increase online enrollments, but assuming complete control over the portfolio would put us in an even better position to maintain our priorities in times of institutional strain.

A convention we did not consider carefully enough is the institutional norm of emphasizing student-teacher interactions. Distance education at Penn State began in 1892 with correspondence courses, and in certain contexts and cases, a correspondence model has been difficult to overcome. I noted previously that the content development workflow for the World Campus stresses the elements of a syllabus. Institutionally speaking, a syllabus is understood as something of a contract between students and teachers, but in the context of instructional design, it was rearticulated as a guide for mapping interactions. First and foremost, we were encouraged to think of the role of teacher presence in an online course. However, this important concept was interpreted as being about the aspects of teacher presence that are discernible in a syllabus, such as information about satisfying course expectations, completing and turning in assignments, attending (virtual) office hours, and grading practices. The result was a series of instructional design patterns that centered more on the teacher and content than on student interaction and learning. For example, online courses begin with an overview of requirements and deadlines. Although the overviews are useful, they do not warrant a central location in the design of the template grid. Assuming complete control over the portfolio would allow us to redesign the template to foreground student interaction and learning.

The ritualized behaviors relevant to our decision-making about the portfolio are associated with professional development activities. The World Campus has an Office of Online Faculty Development that aims to create order and continuity in distance education environments by helping teachers understand and manage the specificities of online teaching and learning. For example, there are rituals of passage that introduce the World Campus to teachers who are new to online environments, socializing them into the culture of distance education at Penn State, and there are rituals of renewal that target experienced teachers who want to take their careers to the next level. These rituals are instantiated in experience by asking teachers to complete a series of self-paced online courses and create professional development plans. In addition, a ritual of enhancement enables teachers to strengthen their social identities at Penn State by earning up to four online teaching certificates. No matter our decision about the portfolio, we would continue to have access to all of these professional development activities. However, if we were to assume complete control over the portfolio, we might want to create new institutional rituals to reflect our own approaches to instructional design, including rituals that value lore as a form of institutional knowledge that can help teachers manage the demands of their jobs.

All the spatial dimensions of my heuristic are discernible in the socio-technical articulations that influence the disposition of the online version of our technical writing service course. The World Campus is governed by a control hierarchy with many institutional levels, but most relevant to our situation are the governing structures for the basic project team and final approvals. In the current approach, there are separate hierarchies for form and content considerations, with the World Campus controlling instructional design and the academic department controlling course content. Both units are free to mobilize any type of spatial organization that is useful to a task at hand, but the formal lines of responsibility are clearly drawn by the institution. Assuming complete control over the portfolio would redraw these lines, making us responsible for all aspects of the course. We would need to decide how to govern the responsibilities for instructional design and what the relationship should be between its governing structures and those for content development. Would it make sense for us to continue to use separate structures, or should we instead use one structure for both operations? What about an overlapping approach? And who would be responsible for what? These are open questions with numerous possible answers.

The institutional processes that organize work on the portfolio are systematic and transparent. I have already introduced phases of the macrolevel process for developing a portfolio: a department, its dean, and the World Campus all agree to create an online course or program, a basic project team is established, the instructional designer provides a workflow for content development, and the department head or program director approves the final content. Although we would intend to continue to have systematic and transparent processes to help inform our colleagues about what we are doing and why, at a micro level we would employ processes that are more congruent with our pedagogies. I am thinking of the approach offered by Scott Warnock and Diana Gasiewski (2018), which is meant to be used for designing online courses organized around discussions of readings, student-centered conversations, peer-review workshops, and student-teacher conferences. I am also thinking of the approach offered by Kristine Blair (2015), which addresses the challenge of transitioning an online writing class from a "text-centric composing space for our students to one that integrates multimodal elements for students and instructors in as viable, accessible, and introductory a way as possible" (474). Although the processes used by the World Campus are mature and take advantage of the strengths of academic IT specialists, the processes cannot possibly address all the various different contexts of all the departments with distance education portfolios. I suspect this reality is not lost on the World Campus.

Staff members in the World Campus conduct internal and external research to produce knowledge and understanding about distance education. The internal research, both primary and secondary, supports the tasks of benchmarking, strategic planning, establishing and evaluating practices, managing people and projects, and making purchasing decisions. The external research, both primary and secondary, also contributes to these tasks, but the goal is to create value beyond institutional reporting and decision-making by sharing findings with colleagues at other universities and working to advance the Penn State brand. World Campus staff members are encouraged to publish and present research at instructional design conferences. In addition, the World Campus funds research on distance education. The only research directly tied to the online version of our technical writing service course is the external secondary research conducted by instructional designers to keep up with their field. Assuming complete control over the portfolio would require us to commit to keeping up with relevant aspects of the field of instructional design, which already overlaps with the disciplinary domain of writing and communication teachers in important ways (cf. Mehlenbacher 2010).

Two perspectives on embodied spatial practices are discernible in World Campus contexts: mediation and augmentation. The vast majority of interactions in online courses occur in frequent acts of writing, formal and informal, and these writing acts take place in course-management systems. These layers of mediation are not the only ones in institutions, but instructional designers tend to concentrate on their roles in helping connect thought and action in learning situations. How does the instructional design for the online version of our technical writing service course serve as an intermediary between students and teachers? Between students and students? Between students and course content? And what claims does the instructional design make about the capacities of bodies? These would be important questions for us to consider if we become responsible for instructional design. We could start with a pedagogical audit of the navigation and feedback systems to see how they value interactions constituted by writing and normalize bodily capacities.

In terms of augmentation, the World Campus shares the institutional perspective that can be found in the makerspace: technologies amplify the capabilities of bodies, making them more productive in the world. But in this case, the focus is on how distance learning shrinks spatial and temporal boundaries for nontraditional students, allowing them access to education. Although I appreciate this focus and would want to continue to promote it in our own instructional design, I also know that our online courses include traditional students who had trouble scheduling a residential section. Assuming adequate demand, we could use the pedagogical audit to explore the idea of designing different versions of the online course for different student populations.

All the textual dimensions of my heuristic are also conspicuous in the sociotechnical articulations that influence the disposition of the online version of our technical writing service course. A number of popular metaphors are associated with the World Campus, including academic IT specialists as instructional designers, teachers as content developers, students as nontraditional learners, courses as learning communities, and technologies as tools. Such metaphors help textualize how Penn State thinks about distance education and its institutional management and performance. The subsidiary subjects for several of these metaphors are appropriate and productive. For example, the metaphorical contexts for courses emphasize quality educational experiences in which students are expected to contribute to knowledge production and learning.

The metaphors that give me the greatest pause textualize technology as a tool and the delivery unit for distance education as a (world) campus. As I discussed in my analysis of the makerspace, the tool metaphor constructs technologies as effective means to an end. The tool metaphor has a certain upside, but I would need to counterbalance its functional orientation with both critical and rhetorical perspectives. In addition, the campus metaphor is puzzling because it suggests that the World Campus is as autonomous as any other Penn State campus, which is not the case. In reality, the World Campus is a delivery unit that partners with academic departments, dividing responsibilities and sharing revenues. My view of our partnership is relatively positive, even as I contemplate becoming responsible for the instructional design of our portfolio, but most of my colleagues have an inaccurate sense of what the World Campus does as an institutional formation. The campus metaphor is not the only problem here, but it is a big one. To help clarify the situation, we should shift to partnership metaphors.

Subjectivities in World Campus contexts could be effects of job classifications and project teams, both of which instantiate the form/content binary that regulates development activities. Although the organizational chart does not represent the lateral relationships between academic IT specialists and teachers, the World Campus employs over fifty people who inhabit the institutional subject position of instructional designer. On the program side, any faculty member with approval from a department head could inhabit the institutional subject position of course author. The relationship between these two positions is based on an expert-novice model of work, but the model is not linear in a strict sense, shifting directions depending on the task. On a project team, the World Campus staff member is considered the expert in instructional design and a novice in the academic domain. The faculty member, in contrast, is assumed to be the expert in the academic domain and a novice in instructional design. This expert-novice model works well in certain cases, especially when a course author is new to online learning or to how online courses are created at Penn State.

According to institutional descriptions of their job classification, instructional designers guide faculty in the overall design of an online course, drawing on learning theory and research; collaborate with faculty to create learning objectives and activities; review course content to make suggestions for improvements; recommend assessment options that are appropriate for the learning objectives; recommend educational technologies that can support the learning objectives; ensure that the content is accessible and adheres to copyright guidelines; and manage the development process, including planning and testing phases and making and meeting deadlines. Although instructional designers add value to the course development process, in our case their focus on establishing and assessing learning objectives dissolves institutional distinctions between expert and novice, conflating the subject positions of instructional designer and course author to a considerable degree.

Our program already has a lot of experience with establishing learning objectives, designing courses around them, and assessing the extent to which students are able to achieve learning objectives. In addition, our program knows a great deal about employing educational technologies, following accessibility guidelines, and following copyright laws. In the most important senses, then, we are already doing the work of instructional designers, defying job classifications as we attend to not only fundamental programmatic concerns but also enduring field questions. Assuming complete control over the portfolio would require us to reconstitute the basic project team and adopt institutional processes for making and meeting deadlines and managing other logistics.

The genres relevant to our decision-making about the portfolio are institutional genres for documenting the development of an online course: a time line, budget, detailed course outline, sample lesson, status reports, and approval forms. These institutional genres serve to textualize and formalize recurring interactions and relationships between instructional designers and course authors. As I previously noted, the content development workflow for the World Campus emphasizes the elements of a syllabus, which form the basis for the detailed course outline. We would need to rethink our approach to a planning document to guard against the impulse to simply transfer face-to-face content to an online environment. The sample lesson is a mock-up that demonstrates the look, feel, and operation of the online course. It does not include all the course elements but provides a prototype walk-through that illustrates the student experience. Developing a sample lesson is crucial to iterative processes of instructional design: it is reviewed and approved by everyone involved in the project. If we were to assume complete control over the portfolio, we might want to revise the genre of the sample lesson to include formal written minutes from review meetings in order to capture important if fleeting conversations.

The time line, budget, status reports, and approval forms are all useful in their current modes. The time line includes steps and milestones in the project, such as a kickoff meeting, a halfway-point check-in with managers and other leaders, and a go/no-go date, which is the date by which a course must be completed in order for it to be offered in the schedule. The budget is really a document about the scope of work, about who is responsible for which aspects of the project. At some point we might want to rename this document to better reflect its purpose (budget is not really an issue anyway). Status reports are monthly progress memos written from instructional designers to managers. This is a useful practice for taking stock of development progress but also of institutional partnerships. The approval forms are sign-off sheets for the sample lesson and final version of the course; a department head must sign both of these forms. In the short term, we would not need to revise or replace the approaches used by the World Campus to produce time lines and budgets, report progress, or document approvals.

The World Campus uses stories to create bridges between general institutional propositions and the concrete experiences of students. The World Campus website includes over three dozen stories in which students explain the value of online courses to their professional and personal lives (https://www.worldcampus.psu.edu/). A student in an online graduate program in youth literature illustrates the institutional identity theme of transforming education by discussing how teachers in the program went the extra mile to develop meaningful relationships beyond the classroom. A student in an online undergraduate program in nursing illustrates the institutional identity theme of enhancing health by discussing how the program has helped him improve the quality of the care he provides to patients and their families. And a student in an online graduate program in geographic information systems illustrates the institutional identity theme of driving digital innovation by discussing how the program integrates the most advanced technologies into both courses and field practices. Although these stories are instructive in that they provide insights into student perspectives and experiences, they do not really help us make decisions about our portfolio. What we need instead are institutional stories from teachers and program directors who have assumed complete control over their portfolios, but those people do not yet exist as far as I can tell. We would become the first adopter of such an alternative arrangement with the World Campus.

In step three of my approach, I decided on a suitable level of engagement with the World Campus: working as (instructional) designers, the fifth mode on my continuum from passive to active engagement. In a real sense, we are already working as designers in our role as experts in content development, but the decision to go ahead and pursue a proposal to assume complete control over the portfolio intensifies this mode of engagement in significant ways. In order to stabilize the conditional nature of the rest of my discussion, I will go ahead and assume that our proposal has been accepted. Because the World Campus is an increasingly busy operation, it welcomes reasonable proposals from departments and programs. In my proposal, the World Campus still receives an attractive share of the revenue.

The first step in my approach led me to position the World Campus as a formal institutional process, but one that divides responsibilities for form and content according to job roles. Although our program controls academic content and has access to considerable institutional resources, we do not control the look, feel, or operation of our online courses. The problems with this situation became clearer and more concrete in step two of my approach, which led me to historicize, spatialize, and textualize the World Campus as an institutional formation.

My historicizing efforts showed that we will need to adopt a platform for instructional design but also that we will be free to refine the instructional design standards to better suit our contexts. The instructional design platform we adopt will need to be compatible with the platforms our program uses for content development (Microsoft and Adobe products) and online learning (Canvas). Legacies would not likely create any issues for the program or portfolio and in fact could present opportunities for moving in a new direction. In terms of instructional design, questions about the effects of legacies will remain open until we secure a platform to replace the World Campus platform. The online course content itself actually presents the biggest legacy issue, for it fundamentally matches the content in the standard face-to-face version of the course and uses more or less the same syllabus, assignments, and resources. We are free to shift to a development workflow that is more born-digital in nature, especially now that we have a sizable pool of experienced online teachers.

The problems of coordination have to do with designing online courses that can be taken by nontraditional students from anywhere in the world. Although we have insisted on a cohort model, it is less profitable than models allowing for rolling enrollments. To date, we have not been overly pressured to increase our online numbers, but by assuming complete control over the portfolio we are in an even better position to maintain our priorities. In addition, we are now in a position to reconsider instructional design conventions that center more on the teacher and content than on student interaction and learning. One place to begin is with the main content area of the course template grid. Finally, we will continue to have access to the rituals of passage and enhancement from the World Campus that socialize teachers and strengthen their social identities, but we will need to create new rituals that reflect our own approaches to instructional design.

My spatializing efforts showed that by assuming complete control over the portfolio, we are redrawing formal lines of institutional responsibility. We will need to decide how we want to manage the duties for instructional design and what the relationship should be between its governing structures and those for content development. This is an important and open question about hierarchies for the program. Although we intend to continue to have systematic and transparent institutional processes, we will employ microlevel processes that are more congruent with our pedagogies. The only research directly tied to our portfolio is the external secondary research conducted by World Campus instructional designers to keep up with their field. We will now need to keep up with relevant aspects of the field of instructional design, which already overlaps with the disciplinary domain of writing and communication teachers. For the final spatial dimension—bodies—we will begin with a pedagogical audit of the navigation and feedback systems to look at how the course values interactions constituted by writing and normalizes bodily capacities. We will also use the audit to explore the idea of designing different versions of the online course for different student populations. This may not be a good idea, but it is an idea worth exploring.

My textualizing efforts showed how metaphors shape how the World

Campus thinks about distance education and its management and performance. We will counterbalance the functional orientation of the tool
metaphor with both critical and rhetorical perspectives and shift to using
partnership metaphors that more accurately reflect our relationship with
the World Campus. In addition, the institutional subject positions in our
relationship are dissolved to a considerable degree by an emphasis on establishing and assessing learning objectives, employing educational technologies, following accessibility guidelines, and following copyright laws.
Our program already has a lot of experience in these areas, but we will
need to reconstitute the basic project team and adopt processes for making
and meeting deadlines and managing other logistics.

The genres that are relevant to our situation are institutional genres for
documenting the development of an online course. In the short term, we
would not need to replace the approaches used by the World Campus to
produce time lines and budgets, report progress, or document approvals.
However, we will need to rethink our approach to documenting planning
in order to guard against the impulse to simply transfer face-to-face content to an online environment and revise the genre of the sample lesson to
include formal written minutes from review meetings. Finally, although the
stories on the World Campus website are instructive and interesting, creating bridges between general institutional propositions and the concrete
experiences of students, they will not help us design or manage the portfolio. What we need instead are relevant stories from teachers and program
directors, but we will be the first department with regular academic faculty
to have complete control over the look, feel, and operation of a distance
education portfolio.

Let me finish this example by elaborating on my decision to engage
the World Campus in an ambitious fashion. I structured my discussion by
comparing how we have been working with the World Campus to an alternative arrangement, one in which our program becomes responsible for
both authoring content and structuring that content into online courses. I
explored this possibility because the status quo situation has been less than
ideal, but the steps in my approach helped me understand and evaluate this
situation in specific and concrete ways. Although the analysis shows that
our program will be able to appropriate certain rituals, processes, methods, metaphors, genres and more, we will want to reinvent much of the
work and its institutional support systems, both social and technical. My
approach also produced several starting places for the program and identified salient issues requiring attention, and it raised open questions that will
need to be answered. I anticipate that assuming complete control over the

portfolio will be a heavy lift for the program. We will need ongoing forms of support from the World Campus and also new forms of support from our department and dean. But in the end, getting to the root of the institutional problems by dismantling the form/content binary is the best way for us to improve the implementation of the portfolio and the experiences of students and teachers in our distance education courses.

CONCLUSION

In response to the opportunities and challenges of using technology in educational contexts, universities have created academic IT units that are meant to serve the needs and interests of students and teachers. These units contribute to many critical activity areas on a campus, including determining pedagogical requirements, providing and maintaining technologies that can meet those requirements, designing learning spaces that integrate technologies, assessing the outcomes of computer-based learning activities, creating academic IT policies and procedures, providing software training services, supplying consulting services for pedagogical projects, piloting pedagogical projects that explore new applications of technologies, and a great deal more. In all higher education settings, academic IT units are planning, designing, and maintaining institutional environments that enable, constrain, and shape the teaching and learning of writing and communication. These environments are technical and social, physical and virtual, and internal and external to traditional university boundaries. Their implications for students and teachers are significant and far-reaching and not to be taken lightly by the field.

Although teachers of writing and communication have a rich history of engagement with information technologies and their myriad contexts, the field has yet to develop a deep and thorough understanding of the workings and implications of academic IT units. In this book, I have made the case for paying attention to these units, conceptualized and illustrated the ways in which they function, and provided an approach to participating productively in their activities. My aim has been to encourage teachers to cultivate a voice on academic IT matters and to use that voice to help enact a vision on campus that is informed by their own disciplinary perspectives.

I have advanced this aim with a heuristic comprising rhetorical commonplaces for analyzing historical, spatial, and textual dimensions, which are conspicuous in both enduring field questions and academic IT units, to help teachers of writing and communication discern how processes of institutionalization affect teaching and learning. In addition, I have integrated the heuristic into a larger approach that turns critique into action by defining and illustrating available modes of engagement. My hope is that teachers will employ the approach to make sense of and influence the complex relationships among institutions, literacies, and technologies in their own work settings. This project is well worth the time and effort it entails.

REFERENCES

Alberti, John. 2008. "The Game of Reading and Writing: How Video Games Reframe Our Understanding of Literacy." *Computers and Composition* 25 (3): 258–69.

Alexander, Jonathan. 2009. "Gaming, Student Literacies, and the Composition Classroom: Some Possibilities for Transformation." *College Composition and Communication* 61 (1): 35–63.

Alexander, Jonathan, and William P. Banks. 2004. "Sexualities, Technologies, and the Teaching of Writing: A Critical Overview." *Computers and Composition* 21 (3): 273–93.

Anschuetz, Lori, and Stephanie Rosenbaum. 2002. "Expanding Roles for Technical Communicators." In *Reshaping Technical Communication: New Directions and Challenges for the 21st Century*, edited by Barbara Mirel and Rachel Spilka, 149–63. New York: Routledge.

Apple, Michael W. 1990. *Ideology and Curriculum*. New York: Routledge.

Arend, Carl E. 2009. *Teacher Empowerment through Curriculum Development: Theory into Practice*. 3rd ed. Claremont, South Africa: Juta Academic.

Aspray, William, and Peter A. Freeman. 2002. "The Supply of IT Workers in the United States." In *Technology Everywhere: A Campus Agenda for Educating and Managing Workers in the Digital Age*, edited by Brian L. Hawkins, Julia A. Rudy, and William H. Wallace Jr., 6:1–23. EDUCAUSE Leadership Strategies. San Francisco, CA: Jossey-Bass.

Azevedo, Alisha. 2012. "In Colleges' Rush to Try MOOC's, Faculty Are Not Always in the Conversation." *Chronicle of Higher Education*, September 26.

Baker, Margaret Ann, and Carol David. 1994. "The Rhetoric of Power: Political Issues in Management Writing." *Technical Communication Quarterly* 3 (2): 165–78.

Banks, Adam J. 2006. *Race, Rhetoric, and Technology: Searching for Higher Ground*. Mahwah, NJ: Lawrence Erlbaum and National Council of Teachers of English.

———. 2011. *Digital Griots: African American Rhetoric in a Multimedia Age*. Carbondale: Southern Illinois University Press.

Bartholomae, David. 1986. "Inventing the University." *Journal of Basic Writing* 5 (1): 4–23.

Barton, Ellen L. 1994. "Interpreting the Discourses of Technology." In *Literacy and Computers: The Complications of Teaching and Learning with Technology*, edited by Cynthia L. Selfe and Susan Hilligoss, 56–75. New York: Modern Language Association.

Bazerman, Charles. 1997. "The Life of Genre, the Life in the Classroom." In *Genre and Writing: Issues, Arguments, Alternatives*, edited by Wendy Bishop and Hans Ostrom, 19–26. Portsmouth, NH: Heinemann.

Beaumont, Peter. 2010. "Rwanda's Laptop Revolution." *Guardian*, March 27, sec. Technology. http://www.theguardian.com/technology/2010/mar/28/rwanda-laptop-revolution.

Berger, Carl. 2002. "Surveys Support IT Decision Making in Higher Education." *ECAR Research Bulletin*, no. 11: 1–14.

Bernhardt, Stephen A. 1993. "The Shape of Text to Come: The Texture of Print on Screens." *College Composition and Communication* 44 (2): 151–75.

Bérubé, Michael. 1998. "Why Inefficiency Is Good for Universities." *Chronicle of Higher Education*, March 27, 1998.

Bjork, Olin, and John Pedro Schwartz. 2009. "Writing in the Wild: A Paradigm for Mobile Composition." In *Going Wireless: A Critical Exploration of Wireless and Mobile Technologies for Composition Teachers and Researchers*, edited by Amy C. Kimme Hea, 223–37. Cresskill, NJ: Hampton Press.

Black, Max. 1981. "Metaphor." In *Philosophical Perspectives on Metaphor*, edited by Mark Johnson, 63–82. Minneapolis: University of Minnesota Press.

Blair, Kristin L. 2015. "Teaching Multimodal Assignments in OWI Contexts." In *Foundational Practices of Online Writing Instruction*, edited by Beth L. Hewett and Kevin Eric DePew, 471–91. Fort Collins, CO: WAC Clearinghouse.

Bodenhamer, David J. 2010. "The Potential of Spatial Humanities." In *The Spatial Humanities: GIS and the Future of Humanities Scholarship*, edited by David J. Bodenhamer, John Corrigan, and Trevor M. Harris, 14–30. Bloomington: Indiana University Press.

Bolter, Jay David. 1991. "Topographic Writing: Hypertext and the Electronic Writing Space." In *Hypermedia and Literary Studies*, edited by Paul Delany and George P. Landow, 105–18. Cambridge, MA: MIT Press.

Boonruang, Sasiwimon. 2013. "This Line of Thinking Simply Won't Wash." *Bangkok Post*, August 20. http://m.bangkokpost.com/opinion/365458.

Boswell, Dustin, and Trevor Foucher. 2011. *The Art of Readable Code*. Sebastopol, CA: O'Reilly Media.

Bouwma-Gearhart, Jana L., and James L. Bess. 2012. "The Transformative Potential of Blogs for Research in Higher Education." *Journal of Higher Education* 83 (2): 249–75.

Bowen, William G. 2013. *Higher Education in the Digital Age*. Princeton, NJ: Princeton University Press.

Boyle, Casey. 2015. "The Rhetorical Question Concerning Glitch." *Computers and Composition* 35 (March): 12–29.

Bradbury, Kelly S. 2014. "Teaching Writing in the Context of a National Digital Literacy Narrative." *Computers and Composition* 32 (June): 54–70.

Brandt, Deborah. 1995. "Accumulating Literacy: Writing and Learning to Write in the Twentieth Century." *College English* 57 (6): 649–68.

Bricken, Meredith. 1992. "Virtual Worlds: No Interface to Design." In *Cyberspace: First Steps*, edited by Michael L. Benedikt, 363–82. Cambridge, MA: MIT Press.

Britton, W. Earl. 1978. "The Trouble with Technical Writing Is Freshman English." In *Directions in Technical Writing and Communication*, edited by J. R. Gould, 131–35. Farmingdale, NY: Baywood.

Brooke, Collin Gifford. 2009. *Lingua Fracta: Toward a Rhetoric of New Media*. Cresskill, NJ: Hampton Press.

Brown, James J. 2012. "Composition in the Dromosphere." *Computers and Composition* 29 (1): 79–91.

Burke, Kenneth. 1989. *On Symbols and Society*. Edited by Joseph R. Gusfield. Chicago: University of Chicago Press.

Camplese, Cole. 2011. "Organizational Frameworks." *Cole Camplese: Learning and Innovation* (blog), August 19. http://www.colecamplese.com/2011/08/organizational-frameworks/.

Carroll, John M. 1990. *The Nurnberg Funnel: Designing Minimalist Instruction for Practical Computer Skill*. Cambridge, MA: MIT Press.

Carroll, John M., and Mary Beth Rosson. 1992. "Getting around the Task-Artifact Cycle: How to Make Claims and Design by Scenario." *ACM Transactions on Information Systems* 10 (2): 181–212.

Carter, Joyce Locke. 2003. "Argument in Hypertext: Writing Strategies and the Problem of Order in a Nonsequential World." *Computers and Composition* 20 (1): 3–22.

"CCCC Position Statement of Principles and Example Effective Practices for Online Writing Instruction (OWI)." 2013. National Council of Teachers of English. Last modified March 2013. http://www.ncte.org/cccc/resources/positions/owiprinciples.

"CCCC Position Statement on Principles and Practices in Electronic Portfolios." 2007. National Council of Teachers of English. Last modified March 2015. http://www.ncte.org/cccc/resources/positions/electronicportfolios.

"CCCC Position Statement on Teaching, Learning, and Assessing Writing in Digital Environments." 2004. *College Composition and Communication* 55 (4): 785–90.

Chandler, Sally, and John Scenters-Zapico. 2012. "New Literacy Narratives: Stories about Reading and Writing in a Digital Age." *Computers and Composition* 29 (3): 185–90.

Chester, Timothy. 2011. "Outsource the Transactional, Keep the Transformative." *EDUCAUSE Quarterly*, June. http://www.educause.edu/ero/article/outsource-transactional-keep-transformative.

———. 2015. "Leadership Lessons I Learned from Diana Oblinger." *EDUCAUSE Review*, May/June, 35–38.

Ching, Kory Lawson, and Cynthia Carter Ching. 2012. "Past Is Prologue: Teachers Composing Narratives about Digital Literacy." *Computers and Composition* 29 (3): 205–20.

Cohen, Michael E., and Richard A. Lanham. 1984. "HOMER: Teaching Style with a Microcomputer." In *The Computer in Composition Instruction: A Writer's Tool*, edited by William Wresch, 83–90. Urbana, IL: National Council of Teachers of English.

Condella, Craig. 2010. "Why Can't We Be Virtual Friends." In *Facebook and Philosophy: What's on Your Mind?*, edited by D. E. Wittkower, 111–21. Chicago: Open Court.

Cooper, Marilyn M. 1986. "The Ecology of Writing." *College English* 48 (4): 364–75.

———. 2010. "Biology, Technology, and Writing." In *Rhetorics and Technologies: New Directions in Writing and Communication*, edited by Stuart A. Selber, 15–32. Columbia: University of South Carolina Press.

Couldry, Nick. 2003. *Media Rituals: A Critical Approach*. New York: Routledge.

Croton, Bethany, James E. Willis, and Jason Fish. 2014. "PassNote: A Feedback Tool for Improving Student Success." *EDUCAUSE Review*, September. http://www.educause.edu/ero/article/passnote-feedback-tool-improving-student-success.

Curry, Barbara K. 1991. "Institutionalization: The Final Phase of the Organizational Change Process." *Administrator's Notebook* 35 (1): 1–5.

Davidson, Cathy N. 2000. "Them versus Us (and Which One of 'Them' Is Me?)." *Profession*, 97–108.

Day, Michael. 2000. "Teachers at the Crossroads: Evaluating Teaching in Electronic Environments." *Computers and Composition* 17 (1): 31–40.

Denning, Peter J. 2001. "The Profession of IT: The IT Schools Movement." *Communications of the ACM* 44 (8): 19–22.

deWinter, Jennifer, and Stephanie Vie. 2008. "Press Enter to 'Say': Using Second Life to Teach Critical Media Literacy." *Computers and Composition* 25 (3): 313–22.

Dewitt, Scott Lloyd. 1996. "The Current Nature of Hypertext Research in Computers and Composition Studies: An Historical Perspective." *Computers and Composition* 13 (1): 69–84.

De Young, Raymond. 2013. "Environmental Psychology Overview." In *Green Organizations: Driving Change with IO Psychology*, edited by Ann H. Huffman and Stephanie Klein, 17–33. New York: Routledge.

Dicks, Stan. 2009. "The Effects of Digital Literacy on the Nature of Technical Communication Work." In *Digital Literacy for Technical Communication: 21st Century Theory and Practice*, edited by Rachel Spilka, 51–81. New York: Routledge.

Dolmage, Jay. 2009. "Disability, Usability, and Universal Design." In *Rhetorically Rethinking Usability: Theories, Practices, and Methodologies*, edited by Susan K. Miller-Cochran and Rochelle L. Rodrigo, 167–90. Cresskill, NJ: Hampton Press.

Dolphin, Ian. 2014. "Open Source in Higher Education: Building a Life Raft for the Perfect Storm." *EDUCAUSE Review*, May/June, 50–51.

Dougherty, Jennifer Dowling, William Clebsch, and Greg Anderson. 2004. "Management by Fact: Benchmarking University IT Services." *EDUCAUSE Quarterly* 1:14–25.

Dragga, Sam. 1991. "Responding to Technical Writing." *Technical Writing Teacher* 18 (3): 202–21.

Dray, Susan. 1994. "Taming the Sticky GUI: New Roles for Technical Communicators in Graphical User Interface Design." In *Proceedings of the 41st Annual Conference of the Society for Technical Communication*, 157–59. Arlington, VA: Society for Technical Communication.

Duffelmeyer, Barbara Blakely. 2000. "Critical Computer Literacy: Computers in First-Year Composition as Topic and Environment." *Computers and Composition* 17 (3): 289–307.

Duffy, Thomas M., James E. Palmer, and Brad Mehlenbacher. 1992. *Online Help Systems: Design and Evaluation*. Norwood, NJ: Ablex.

Dutkiewicz, Keri, LuAnne Holder, and Wayne D. Sneath. 2013. "Creativity and Consistency in Online Courses: Finding the Appropriate Balance." In *Online Education 2.0: Evolving, Adapting, and Reinventing Online Technical Communication*, edited by Kelli Cargile Cook and Keith Grant-Davie, 45–72. Amityville, NY: Baywood.

Eble, Michelle F. 2009. "Digital Delivery and Communication Technologies: Understanding Content Management through Rhetorical Theory." In *Content Management: Bridging the Gap between Theory and Practice*, edited by George Pullman and Baotong Gu, 87–102. Amityville, NY: Baywood.

Eeles, Peter. 2009. *The Process of Software Architecting*. Boston, MA: Addison-Wesley Professional.

Faigley, Lester. 1986. "Competing Theories of Process: A Critique and a Proposal." *College English* 48 (6): 527–42.

———. 1992. *Fragments of Rationality: Postmodernity and the Subject of Composition*. Pittsburgh: University of Pittsburgh Press.

———. 1997. "Literacy after the Revolution." *College Composition and Communication* 48 (1): 30–43.

Faris, Michael J., and Stuart A. Selber. 2011. "E-book Issues in Composition: A Partial Assessment and Perspective for Teachers." *Composition Forum* 24 (Fall). http://compositionforum.com/issue/24/ebook-issues.php.

———. 2013. "iPads in the Technical Communication Classroom: An Empirical Study of Technology Integration and Use." *Journal of Business and Technical Communication* 27 (4): 359–408.

Farman, Jason. 2011. *Mobile Interface Theory: Embodied Space and Locative Media*. New York: Routledge.

Felix, Elliot, and Malcolm Brown. 2011. "The Case for a Learning Space Performance Rating System." *Journal of Learning Spaces* 1 (1). http://libjournal.uncg.edu/index.php/jls/article/view/287/137.

Fenn, Jackie, and Mark Raskino. 2008. *Mastering the Hype Cycle: How to Choose the Right Innovation at the Right Time*. Boston, MA: Harvard Business Review Press.

Fountain, T. Kenny. 2014. *Rhetoric in the Flesh: Trained Vision, Technical Expertise, and the Gross Anatomy Lab*. New York: Routledge.

France, Jacques La. 1972. "Comments on the Administrative/Academic Interface." In *Proceedings of the Annual ACM SIGUCCS Symposium on the Administration and Management of Small-College Computing Centers*, 48. SIGUCCS '72. New York: ACM. https://doi.org/10.1145/800273.809360.

Friedman, Thomas L. 2013. "The Professors' Big Stage." *New York Times*, March 5,

2013, sec. Opinion. http://www.nytimes.com/2013/03/06/opinion/friedman-the
-professors-big-stage.html.

Frith, Jordan. 2015. "Writing Space: Examining the Potential of Location-Based Composition." *Computers and Composition* 37 (September): 44–54.

Fulkerson, Richard. 2011. "The Epistemic Paradox of 'Lore': From the Making of Knowledge in Composition to the Present (Almost)." In *Changing of Knowledge in Composition: Contemporary Perspectives*, edited by Lance Massey and Richard C. Gephardt, 47–62. Logan: Utah State University Press.

Gabriel, Yiannis. 2000. *Storytelling in Organizations: Factions, Fictions, Fantasies*. New York: Oxford University Press.

Galin, Jeffrey R. 2009. "Own Your Rights: Know When Your University Can Claim Ownership of Your Work." In *Composition and Copyright: Perspectives on Teaching, Text-Making, and Fair Use*, edited by Steve Westbrook, 190–216. Albany: State University of New York Press.

Galin, Jeffrey R., and Joan Latchaw. 2010. "From Incentive to Stewardship: The Shifting Discourse of Academic Publishing." *Computers and Composition* 27 (3): 211–24.

Gee, Lori. 2006. "Human-Centered Design Guidelines." In *Learning Spaces*, edited by Diana G. Oblinger, 10.1–10.13. Boulder, CO: EDUCAUSE.

George, Diana, and Diane Shoos. 1993. "Issues of Subjectivity and Resistance: Cultural Studies in the Composition Classroom." In *Cultural Studies in the English Classroom*, edited by James A. Berlin and Michael Vivion, 200–210. Portsmouth, NH: Heinemann.

Giroux, Henry A. 1997. *Pedagogy and the Politics of Hope: Theory, Culture, and Schooling*. Boulder, CO: Westview Press.

———. 2011. *On Critical Pedagogy*. New York: Continuum International.

Glen, Paul, and Maria McManus. 2013. "Geeks and Non-geeks: From Contraxioms to Collaboration in Higher Education." *EDUCAUSE Review*, June. http://www.educause.edu/ero/article/geeks-and-non-geeks-contraxioms-collaboration-higher-education.

Gold, Edward. 1989. "Bridging the Gap: In Which the Author, an English Major, Recounts His Travels in the Land of the Techies." In *Worlds of Writing: Teaching and Learning in Discourse Communities of Work*, edited by Carolyn Matalene, 335–42. New York: Random House.

Goodliffe, Pete. 2006. *Code Craft: The Practice of Writing Excellent Code*. San Francisco, CA: No Starch Press.

Grundy, Chas. 2015. "User Advocate: Product Management in Higher Ed." *EDUCAUSE Review*, May. http://er.educause.edu/articles/2015/5/user-advocate-product-management-in-higher-ed.

Gruwell, Leigh. 2015. "Wikipedia's Politics of Exclusion: Gender, Epistemology, and Feminist Rhetorical (In)Action." *Computers and Composition* 37 (September): 117–31.

Gurak, Laura J. 1997. "Technical Communication, Copyright, and the Shrinking Public Domain." *Computers and Composition* 14 (3): 329–42.

Haas, Christina. 1996. *Writing Technology: Studies on the Materiality of Literacy*. Mahwah, NJ: Routledge.

———. 1999. "On the Relationship between Old and New Technologies." *Computers and Composition* 16 (2): 209–28.

Halpern, Jeanne W. 1986. "An Electronic Odyssey." In *Writing in Nonacademic Settings*, edited by Lee Odell and Dixie Goswami, 157–89. New York: Guilford Press.

Hart-Davidson, William. 2013. "What Are the Work Patterns of Technical Communication?" In *Solving Problems in Technical Communication*, edited by Johndan Johnson-Eilola and Stuart A. Selber, 50–74. Chicago: University of Chicago Press.

Hawkins, Brian L. 2006. "Twelve Habits of Successful IT Professionals." *EDUCAUSE Review* 41 (1): 56–67.

Hawkins, Brian L., and Carole A. Barone. 2003. "Assessing Information Technology: Changing the Conceptual Framework." In *Organizing and Managing Information Resources on Your Campus*, edited by Polley A. McClure, 129–45. San Francisco, CA: Jossey-Bass.

Head, Karen. 2013. "Inside a MOOC in Progress." *Chronicle of Higher Education. Wired Campus* (blog), June 21. http://chronicle.com.ezaccess.libraries.psu.edu/blogs/wiredcampus/inside-a-mooc-in-progress/44397.

Heckel, Mark. 2009. "Classrooms in the Cloud: Adobe Connect Pro in the Penn State Learning Community." In *Proceedings of the 37th Annual ACM SIGUCCS Fall Conference*, 185–88. SIGUCCS '09. New York: ACM.

Heilker, Paul. 1997. "Rhetoric Made Real: Civic Discourse and Writing beyond the Curriculum." In *Writing the Community: Concepts and Models for Service Learning in Composition*, edited by Linda Adler-Kassner, Robert Crooks, and Ann Watters, 72–73. Washington, DC: AAHE and NCTE.

Hesse, Doug. 2013. "Grading Writing: The Art and Science—and Why Computers Can't Do It." *Washington Post*, May 2. https://www.washingtonpost.com/news/answer-sheet/wp/2013/05/02/grading-writing-the-art-and-science-and-why-computers-cant-do-it/?utm_term=.e4ffabdd0570.

Hofstadter, Douglas, and Emmanuel Sander. 2013. *Surfaces and Essences: Analogy as the Fuel and Fire of Thinking*. New York: Basic Books.

Holdstein, Deborah H., and Cynthia L. Selfe. 1990. *Computers and Writing: Theory, Research, Practice*. New York: Modern Language Association.

Horton, S., and D. Sloan. 2014. "Accessibility in Practice: A Process-Driven Approach to Accessibility." In *Inclusive Designing: Joining Usability, Accessibility, and Inclusion*, edited by P. M. Langdon, J. Lazar, A. Heylighen, and H. Dong, 105–15. Cham, Switzerland: Springer International.

Howard, Tharon W. 1998. "Four Designs for Electronic Writing Projects." In *The Dialogic Classroom: Teachers Integrating Computer Technology, Pedagogy, and Research*, edited by Jeffrey R. Galin and Joan Latchaw, 210–40. Urbana, IL: National Council of Teachers of English.

Hughes, Jessica. 2015. "Can the Apple Watch Enhance Student Achievement?" *Government Technology*, July 7. http://www.govtech.com/education/Can-the-Apple-Watch-Enhance-Student-Achievement.html.

International Reading Association and National Council of Teachers of English. 2009. *Standards for the Assessment of Reading and Writing.* Newark, DE: International Reading Association and National Council of Teachers of English.

Jasso, John J. 2013. "Merging Pedagogies and Converging Media: Classical Meets Critical in the Digital Age." *Explorations in Media Ecology* 12 (1–2): 121–34.

Jay, Joelle K., and Kerri L. Johnson. 2002. "Capturing Complexity: A Typology of Reflective Practice for Teacher Education." *Teaching and Teacher Education* 18 (1): 73–85.

Jensen, A., C. Thuesen, and J. Geraldi. 2016. "Projectification of Everything: Projects as Human Condition." *Project Management Journal* 47 (3): 21–34.

Johnson, Matthew S. S. 2008. "Public Writing in Gaming Spaces." *Computers and Composition* 25 (3): 270–83.

Johnson, Robert R. 1995. "Romancing the Hypertext: A Rhetorical/Historiographical View of the 'Hyperphenomenon.'" *Technical Communication Quarterly* 4 (1): 11–22.

Johnson-Eilola, Johndan. 1996. "Relocating the Value of Work: Technical Communication in a Post-industrial Age." *Technical Communication Quarterly* 5 (3): 245–70.

———. 2010. "Among Texts." In *Rhetorics and Technologies: New Directions in Writing and Communication,* edited by Stuart A. Selber, 33–55. Columbia: University of South Carolina Press.

Johnson-Eilola, Johndan, and Stuart A. Selber. 1996. "Policing Ourselves: Defining the Boundaries of Appropriate Discussion in Online Forums." *Computers and Composition* 13 (3): 269–91.

———. 2007. "Plagiarism, Originality, Assemblage." *Computers and Composition* 24 (4): 375–403.

Kalmbach, James. 1996. "From Liquid Paper to Typewriters: Some Historical Perspectives on Technology in the Classroom." *Computers and Composition* 13 (1): 57–68.

Kemp, Fred. 1992. "Who Programmed This? Examining the Instructional Attitudes of Writing-Support Software." *Computers and Composition* 10 (1): 9–24.

Kimball, Kathleen R. 2011. "Security 2010: Breaches and Malware and Phish (Oh, My!)." Presented at the Faculty Advisory Committee on Academic Computing, University Park, PA, March 1.

Kirtley, Susan. 2012. "Rendering Technology Visible: The Technological Literacy Narrative." *Computers and Composition* 29 (3): 191–204.

Knuth, Donald E. 1992. *Literate Programming.* Stanford, CA: Center for the Study of Language and Information.

Kolowich, Steve. 2013. "Faculty Backlash Grows against Online Partnerships." *Chronicle of Higher Education,* May 6, 2013. http://chronicle.com.ezaccess.libraries.psu.edu/article/Faculty-Backlash-Grows-Against/139049/.

Konkel, Frank. 2012. "Legacy Systems Still Power Much of Government." *FCW: The Business of Federal Technology,* December 10. http://fcw.com/articles/2012/12/10/legacy-systems.aspx.

Korn, Melissa. 2013. "Coursera Makes Case for MOOCs." *Wall Street Journal,* May 14, sec. Boss Talk. http://online.wsj.com/article/SB10001424127887324715704578483570761525766.html.

Kostelnick, Charles, and Michael Hassett. 2003. *Shaping Information: The Rhetoric of Visual Conventions.* Carbondale: Southern Illinois University Press.

Kotter, John P. 2011. "Hierarchy and Network: Two Structures, One Organization." *Harvard Business Review,* May 23. https://hbr.org/2011/05/two-structures-one-organization.

Krause, Steven D. 2013. "MOOC Response about 'Listening to World Music.'" *College Composition and Communication* 64 (4): 689–95.

Kreta, Chandler, and Karen Hyatt. 2003. *Customer-Centered Design: A New Approach to Web Usability.* Upper Saddle River, NJ: Prentice Hall.

Lakoff, George, and Mark Johnson. 1980. *Metaphors We Live By.* Chicago: University of Chicago Press.

Lang, Leah. 2015. "Benchmarking to Inform Planning." *EDUCAUSE Review,* May/June, 40–48.

Lanham, Richard A. 1995. *The Electronic Word: Democracy, Technology, and the Arts.* Chicago: University of Chicago Press.

Lauer, Claire. 2015. "High-Tech Invention: Examining the Relationship between Technology and Idea Generation in the Document Design Process." *Journal of Business and Technical Communication* 29 (4): 367–402.

Lewin, Tamar. 2012. "Instruction for Masses Knocks Down Campus Walls." *New York Times,* March 4, 2012, sec. Education. http://www.nytimes.com/2012/03/05/education/moocs-large-courses-open-to-all-topple-campus-walls.html.

Liang, Chen, Shuting Wang, Zhaohui Wu, Kyle Williams, Bart Pursel, Benjamin Brautigam, Sherwyn Saul, Hannah Williams, Kyle Bowen, and C. Lee Giles. 2015. "BBookX: An Automatic Book Creation Framework." In *Proceedings of the 2015 ACM Symposium on Document Engineering,* 121–24. DocEng '15. New York: ACM.

Lucas, Christopher, and Heather Huntsinger. 2009. "After the Class: Informal Training Support through the Penn State Technology Training Community." In *Proceedings of the 37th Annual ACM SIGUCCS Fall Conference,* 105–10. SIGUCCS '09. New York: ACM.

Lunsford, Andrea A., and Susan West. 1996. "Intellectual Property and Composition Studies." *College Composition and Communication* 47 (3): 383–411.

Madden, Shannon. 2014. "Obsolescence in/of Digital Writing Studies." *Computers and Composition* 33 (September): 29–39.

Magana, Sonny. 2017. *Disruptive Classroom Technologies: A Framework for Innovation in Education.* Thousand Oaks, CA: Corwin.

Mahoney, Michael S. 1996. "Issues in the History of Computing." In *History of Programming Languages, Volume 2,* edited by Thomas J. Bergin and Richard G. Gibson, 772–81. Reading, MA: Addison-Wesley Professional.

Mansfield, John. 2010. *The Nature of Change or the Law of Unintended Consequences: An Introductory Text to Designing Complex Systems and Managing Change.* Singapore: World Scientific.

Markoff, John. 2013. "Essay-Grading Software Offers Professors a Break." *New York*

Times, April 4, sec. Science. http://www.nytimes.com/2013/04/05/science/new
-test-for-computers-grading-essays-at-college-level.html.

Marmor, Andrei. 2014. *Social Conventions: From Language to Law*. Princeton, NJ:
Princeton University Press.

Maurya, Ash. 2012. *Running Lean: Iterate from Plan A to a Plan That Works*. Sebastopol, CA: O'Reilly Media.

McClure, Polley A. 2003. "Managing the Complexity of Campus Information Resources." In *Organizing and Managing Information Resources on Your Campus*,
edited by Polley A. McClure, 1–13. San Francisco, CA: Jossey-Bass.

McKee, Heidi A. 2005. "Richard Lanham's The Electronic Word and AT/THROUGH
Oscillations." *Pedagogy* 5 (1): 117–30.

McLuhan, Marshall. 1964. *Understanding Media: The Extensions of Man*. New York:
Penguin.

McLuhan, Marshall, and Quentin Fiore. 1967. *The Medium Is the Massage*. New York:
Bantam Books.

McMahon, Russell. 2007. "Researching Your Institution's Computer Past." In *Proceedings of the 8th ACM SIGITE Conference on Information Technology Education*, 191–
94. SIGITE '07. New York: ACM.

Mehlenbacher, Brad. 2010. *Instruction and Technology: Designs for Everyday Learning*.
Cambridge, MA: MIT Press.

Metros, Susan E., and Joan Falkenberg Getman. 2012. "Going the Distance: Outsourcing Online Learning." In *Game Changers: Education and Information Technologies*,
edited by Diana Oblinger, 229–51. Washington, DC: EDUCAUSE.

Miller, Carolyn R. 1979. "A Humanistic Rationale for Technical Writing." *College English* 40 (6): 610–17.

———. 1984. "Genre as Social Action." *Quarterly Journal of Speech* 70 (2): 151–67.

———. 2017. "Where Do Genres Come From?" In *Emerging Genres in New Media
Environments*, edited by Carolyn R. Miller and Ashley R. Kelly, 1–34. New York:
Palgrave Macmillan.

Miller, Richard. 1999. "Critique's the Easy Part: Choice and the Scale of Relative Op-
pression." In *Kitchen Cooks, Plate Twirlers and Troubadours: Writing Program
Administrators Tell Their Stories*, edited by Diana George, 3–13. Portsmouth, NH:
Heinemann.

Moeller, Henry B. 1999. "Student Employees—How to Make a Constantly Changing
Work Force Your Successful Backbone." In *Proceedings of the 27th Annual ACM
SIGUCCS Conference on User Services: Mile High Expectations*, 169–71. SIGUCCS
'99. New York: ACM.

Moore, Janet C. 2005. *The Sloan Consortium Quality Framework and the Five Pillars*.
Needham, MA: Sloan Consortium.

Moses, Myra G., and Steven B. Katz. 2007. "The Phantom Machine: The Invisible
Ideology of Email (A Cultural Critique)." In *Critical Power Tools: Technical Com-
munication and Cultural Studies*, edited by J. Blake Scott, Bernadette Longo, and
Katherine V. Wills, 71–105. Albany: State University of New York Press.

Murphy, Trevor. 2004. "Research Based Methods for Using PowerPoint, Animation, and Video for Instruction." In *Proceedings of the 32nd Annual ACM SIGUCCS Conference on User Services*, 372–74. SIGUCCS '04. New York: ACM.

"NCTE Position Statement on Machine Scoring." 2013. National Council of Teachers of English. Last modified April 2013. http://www.ncte.org/positions/statements /machine_scoring.

Nold, Ellen W. 1975. "Fear and Trembling: The Humanist Approaches the Computer." *College Composition and Communication* 26 (3): 269–73.

Norris, Donald M., Paul Lefrere, and Jon Mason. 2006. "Making Knowledge Services Work in Higher Education." *EDUCAUSE Review*, September/October, 84–100.

North, Steven M. 1987. *The Making of Knowledge in Composition: Portrait of an Emerging Field*. Upper Montclair, NJ: Heinemann.

Office of Computer and Information Systems, the Pennsylvania State University. 1995. "Observations on Benchmarking Information Technology Support." *CAUSE/ EFFECT*, Spring, 20–28.

Office of the Mayor of New York City. 2011. "Mayor Bloomberg Announces Request for Proposals for New or Expanded Engineering and Applied Sciences Campus in New York City." Press Release. July 19, 2011. https://www1.nyc.gov/office-of -the-mayor/news/261-11/mayor-bloomberg-request-proposals-new-expanded -engineering-applied#/0.

Ohmann, Richard. 1985. "Literacy, Technology, and Monopoly Capital." *College English* 47 (7): 675–89.

Ong, Walter J. 1988. *Orality and Literacy: The Technologizing of the Word*. New York: Routledge.

Pacheco, Beatriz de Almeida, Ilana A. Souza-Concílio, and Eliani Maria Kfouri. 2013. "Visual Metaphors in Learning Management Systems: How Professors Understand and Use This Feature." In *2013 IEEE Conference on E-Learning, e-Management and e-Services*, 34–39. Piscataway, NJ: IEEE.

Palmeri, Jason. 2006. "Disability Studies, Cultural Analysis, and the Critical Practice of Technical Communication Pedagogy." *Technical Communication Quarterly* 15 (1): 49–65.

Parker, Sherri. 2014. "Increase Your Influence: Culture Matters." *EDUCAUSE Review*, March. https://er.educause.edu/articles/2014/3/increase-your-influence-culture -matters.

Peaker, Alicia. 2015. "Crowdsourcing and Community Engagement." *EDUCAUSE Review*, November/December, 90–91.

Penrod, James I. 2003. "Building an Effective Governance and Decision-Making Structure for Information Technology." In *EDUCAUSE Leadership Strategies, Organizing and Managing Information Resources on Your Campus*, edited by Polley A. McClure, 15–28. San Francisco, CA: Jossey-Bass.

Pew Internet and American Life Project. 2008. "Teens, Video Games, and Civics." Washington, DC: Pew Internet & American Life Project. http://www.pew internet.org/2008/09/16/teens-video-games-and-civics/.

Phillips, Nelson, Thomas B. Lawrence, and Cynthia Hardy. 2004. "Discourse and Institutions." *Academy of Management Review* 29 (4): 635–52.

Porter, James E. 2003. "Why Technology Matters to Writing: A Cyberwriter's Tale." *Computers and Composition* 20 (4): 375–94.

———. 2010. "Rhetoric in (as) a Digital Economy." In *Rhetorics and Technologies: New Directions in Writing and Communication*, edited by Stuart A. Selber, 173–97. Columbia: University of South Carolina Press.

Porter, James E., Patricia Sullivan, Stuart Blythe, Jeffrey T. Grabill, and Libby Miles. 2000. "Institutional Critique: A Rhetorical Methodology for Change." *College Composition and Communication* 51 (4): 610–42.

Potts, Liza. 2013. *Social Media in Disaster Response: How Experience Architects Can Build for Participation*. New York: Routledge.

Prensky, Marc. 2001. "Digital Natives, Digital Immigrants Part 1." *On the Horizon* 9 (5): 1–6.

Purdy, James P., and Dánielle N. DeVoss. 2017. *Making Space: Writing Instruction, Infrastructure, and Multiliteracies*. Ann Arbor: University of Michigan Press.

Ratliff, Clancy. 2009. "'Some Rights Reserved': Weblogs with Creative Commons Licenses." In *Composition and Copyright: Perspectives on Teaching, Text-Making, and Fair Use*, edited by Steve Westbrook, 50–67. Albany: State University of New York Press.

Redish, Janice C. 1992. "Understanding Readers." In *Techniques for Technical Communicators*, edited by Carol M. Barnum and Saul Carliner, 14–41. New York: Longman.

Reid, Alex. 2008. "Portable Composition: iTunes University and Networked Pedagogies." *Computers and Composition* 25 (1): 61–78.

Reynolds, Nedra. 2007. *Geographies of Writing: Inhabiting Places and Encountering Difference*. Carbondale: Southern Illinois University Press.

Rice, Jeff. 2006. "Networks and New Media." *College English* 69 (2): 127–33.

———. 2013. "What I Learned in MOOC." *College Composition and Communication* 64 (4): 695–703.

Rice, Jenny Edbauer. 2008. "Rhetoric's Mechanics: Retooling the Equipment of Writing Production." *College Composition and Communication* 60 (2): 366–87.

Rickly, Rebecca. 2000. "The Tenure of the Oppressed: Ambivalent Reflections from a Critical Optimist." *Computers and Composition* 17 (1): 19–30.

Rife, Martine Courant. 2007. "The Fair Use Doctrine: History, Application, and Implications for (New Media) Writing Teachers." *Computers and Composition* 24 (2): 154–78.

Ritter, Kelly. 2005. "The Economics of Authorship: Online Paper Mills, Student Writers, and First-Year Composition." *College Composition and Communication* 56 (4): 601–31.

Roberts, Michael M. 2006. "Lessons for the Future Internet: Learning from the Past." *EDUCAUSE Review* 41 (4): 16–25.

Robidoux, Charlotte. 2007. "Rhetorically Structured Content: Developing a Collaborative Single-Sourcing Curriculum." *Technical Communication Quarterly* 17 (1): 110–35.

Rodrigues, Dawn, and Raymond J. Rodrigues. 1984. "Computer-Based Creative Problem Solving." In *The Computer in Composition Instruction: A Writer's Tool*, edited by William Wresch, 34–46. Urbana, IL: National Council of Teachers of English.

Rudolph, Frederick. 1990. *The American College and University: A History*. Athens: University of Georgia Press.

Ruecker, Todd. 2012. "Exploring the Digital Divide on the U.S.-Mexico Border through Literacy Narratives." *Computers and Composition* 29 (3): 239–53.

Russell, David S. 2015. "Writing Mediates Activity." In *Naming What We Know: Threshold Concepts of Writing Studies*, edited by Linda Adler-Kassner and Elizabeth Wardle, 26–27. Logan: Utah State University Press.

Sabatino, Lindsay. 2014. "Improving Writing Literacies through Digital Gaming Literacies: Facebook Gaming in the Composition Classroom." *Computers and Composition* 32 (June): 41–53.

Samson, Don. 1995. "Writing in High-Tech Firms." In *Professional Writing in Context: Lessons from Teaching and Consulting in Worlds of Work*, edited by John Frederick Reynolds, Carolyn B. Matalene, Joyce Neff Magnotto, Donald C. Samson Jr., and Lynn Veach Sadler, 97–127. Hillsdale, NJ: Lawrence Erlbaum Associates.

Schon, Donald A. 1990. *Educating the Reflective Practitioner: Toward a New Design for Teaching and Learning in the Professions*. San Francisco, CA: Jossey-Bass.

Schroeder, Tracy. 2014. "The IT Service Organization for a Post-enterprise World." *EDUCAUSE Review* 49 (4): 14–24.

Selber, Stuart A. 1994. "Beyond Skill Building: Challenges Facing Technical Communication Teachers in the Computer Age." *Technical Communication Quarterly* 3 (4): 365–90.

———. 2004. *Multiliteracies for a Digital Age*. Carbondale: Southern Illinois University Press.

———. 2010. "A Rhetoric of Electronic Instruction Sets." *Technical Communication Quarterly* 19 (2): 95–117.

Selfe, Cynthia L. 1999. "Lest We Think the Revolution Is a Revolution: Images of Technology and the Nature of Change." In *Passions Pedagogies and 21st Century Technologies*, edited by Gail E. Hawisher and Cynthia L. Selfe, 292–322. Logan: Utah State University Press.

Selfe, Cynthia L., Dawn Rodrigues, and William R. Oates. 1989. *Computers in English and the Language Arts: The Challenge of Teacher Education*. Urbana, IL: National Council of Teachers of English.

Selfe, Cynthia L., and Richard J. Selfe. 1994. "The Politics of the Interface: Power and Its Exercise in Electronic Contact Zones." *College Composition and Communication* 45 (4): 480–504.

Selzer, Jack. 1983. "The Composing Processes of an Engineer." *College Composition and Communication* 34 (2): 178–87.

Sheridan, David Michael. 2010. "Fabricating Consent: Three-Dimensional Objects as Rhetorical Compositions." *Computers and Composition* 27 (4): 249–65.

Sherwin, Katie. 2014. "Breaking Web Design Conventions = Breaking the User Experience." Nielsen Norman Group. July 20. http://www.nngroup.com/articles/breaking-web-conventions/.

Shipka, Jody. 2011. *Toward a Composition Made Whole*. Pittsburgh: University of Pittsburgh Press.

Siemens, George. 2008. "Learning and Knowing in Networks: Changing Roles for Educators and Designers." Paper 105. University of Georgia IT. http://it.coe.uga.edu/itforum/Paper105/Siemens.pdf.

Simon, Herbert A. 1972. "Theories of Bounded Rationality." In *Decision and Organization: A Volume in Honor of Jacob Marschak*, edited by C. B. McGuire and R. Radner, 161–76. Amsterdam: North Holland.

———. 1980. "The Consequences of Computers for Centralization and Decentralization." In *The Computer Age: A Twenty Year View*, edited by Michael L. Dertouzos and Joel Moses, 212–28. Cambridge, MA: MIT Press.

Sims, Chris, and Hillary Louise Johnson. 2011. *The Elements of Scrum*. Foster City, CA: Dymaxicon.

Sinclair, Bryan, and Glenn Gunhouse. 2016. "The Promise of Virtual Reality in Higher Education." *EDUCAUSE Review*, March. http://er.educause.edu/articles/2016/3/the-promise-of-virtual-reality-in-higher-education.

Skeen, Thomas. 2009. "The Rhetoric of Human-Computer Interaction." In *Rhetorically Rethinking Usability: Theories, Practices, and Methodologies*, edited by Susan K. Miller-Cochran and Rochelle L. Rodrigo, 91–104. Cresskill, NJ: Hampton Press.

Slack, Jennifer Daryl. 1989. "Contextualizing Technology." In *Rethinking Communication, Volume 2: Paradigm Exemplars*, 329–45. Newbury Park: SAGE.

Slade, Giles. 2007. *Made to Break: Technology and Obsolescence in America*. Cambridge, MA: Harvard University Press.

Smith, David L. 1995. "Estimating Costs for Documentation Projects." In *Publications Management: Essays for Professional Communicators*, edited by O. Jane Allen and Lynn H. Deming, 143–51. Amityville, NY: Routledge.

Souther, James W. 1989. "Teaching Technical Writing: A Retrospective Analysis." In *Technical Writing: Theory and Practice*, edited by Bertie E. Fearing and W. Keats Sparrow, 2–13. New York: Modern Language Association.

Spencer, Gene, and Jeannie Zappe. 2006. "A Comprehensive Approach to Professional Development for an IT Staff." In *Cultivating Careers: Professional Development for Campus IT*, edited by Cynthia Golden, 2.1–2.12. Washington, DC: EDUCAUSE.

Sproull, Lee, and Sara Kiesler. 1992. *Connections: New Ways of Working in the Networked Organization*. Cambridge, MA: MIT Press.

Star, Susan, and James Griesemer. 1989. "Institutional Ecology, 'Translations' and Boundary Objects: Amateurs and Professionals in Berkeley's Museum of Vertebrate Zoology, 1907–1939." *Social Studies of Science* 19 (3): 387–420.

Stein, Sarah R. 2002. "The '1984' Macintosh Ad: Cinematic Icons and Constitutive Rhetoric in the Launch of a New Machine." *Quarterly Journal of Speech* 88 (2): 169–92.

Strauss, Valerie. 2014. "Everything You Need to Know about Common Core—Ravitch." *Washington Post*, January 18. http://www.washingtonpost.com/blogs

/answer-sheet/wp/2014/01/18/everything-you-need-to-know-about-common
-core-ravitch/.

Subramaniam, Manimegalai M. 2005. "The Emergence of IT Degree Programs: When
Did It Happen?" In *Proceedings of the 6th Conference on Information Technology
Education*, 31–35. SIGITE '05. New York: ACM.

Sullivan, Patricia. 1991. "Taking Control of the Page: Electronic Writing and Word
Publishing." In *Evolving Perspectives on Computers and Composition Studies: Questions for the 1990s*, edited by Gail E. Hawisher and Cynthia L. Selfe, 43–64. Urbana, IL: National Council of Teachers of English.

Sullivan, Patricia, and James E. Porter. 1997. *Opening Spaces: Writing Technologies and
Critical Research Practices*. Greenwich, CT: Ablex.

Swarts, Jason. 2004. "Textual Grounding: How People Turn Texts into Tools." *Journal
of Technical Writing and Communication* 34 (1–2): 67–89.

———. 2015. "Help Is in the Helping: An Evaluation of Help Documentation in a
Networked Age." *Technical Communication Quarterly* 24 (2): 164–87.

Tebeaux, Elizabeth. 1988. "The Trouble with Employees' Writing May Be Freshman
Composition." *Teaching English in the Two-Year College* 15 (1): 9–19.

Tom, Jim, Kenneth Voss, and Christopher Scheetz. 2008. "The Space Is the Message: First Assessment of a Learning Studio." *EDUCAUSE Review*, May. http://
er.educause.edu/articles/2008/5/the-space-is-the-message-first-assessment-of
-a-learning-studio.

Toscano, Aaron A. 2011. "Using *I, Robot* in the Technical Writing Classroom: Developing a Critical Technological Awareness." *Computers and Composition* 28 (1): 14–27.

Toulmin, Stephen E. 1958. *The Uses of Argument*. Cambridge: Cambridge University
Press.

Trice, Harrison M., and Janice M. Beyer. 1984. "Studying Organizational Cultures
through Rites and Ceremonials." *Academy of Management Review* 9 (4): 653–69.

Trimbur, John. 1988. "Cultural Studies and Teaching Writing." *Focuses* 1 (2): 5–18.

Tyndall, John B. 2012. "Building an Effective Software Deployment Process." In *Proceedings of the 40th Annual ACM SIGUCCS Conference*, 109–14. SIGUCCS '12.
New York: ACM.

University of Cincinnati. 2006. "Computer Memory Project: Writing the History
of Computing at UC." Press Release. September 27, 2006. https://www.uc.edu
/news/articles/legacy/enews/2006/09/e4425.html.

———. 2008. "Celebration Set for June 4: Fifty Years Ago, UC Got Its First Computer." Press Release. May 25, 2008. https://www.uc.edu/news/articles/legacy
/enews/2008/05/e8443.html.

Vee, Annette. 2013. "Understanding Computer Programming as Literacy." *Literacy in
Composition Studies* 1 (2): 42–64.

Warnick, Barbara. 2005. "Looking to the Future: Electronic Texts and the Deepening
Interface." *Technical Communication Quarterly* 14 (3): 327–33.

Warnock, Scott, and Diana Gasiewski. 2018. *Writing Together: Ten Weeks of Teaching and Studenting in an Online Writing Course*. Urbana, IL: National Council of
Teachers of English.

Webb, Patricia. 2003. "Technologies of Difference: Reading the Virtual Age through Sexual (In)Difference." *Computers and Composition* 20 (2): 151–67.

Weber, Barbara. 1995. "Project Management: The Art of Managing Deadlines." In *Publications Management: Essays for Professional Communicators*, edited by O. Jane Allen and Lynn H. Deming, 107–15. Amityville, NY: Baywood.

Weimer, Maryellen. 2002. *Learner-Centered Teaching: Five Key Changes to Practice*. San Francisco, CA: Jossey-Bass.

Williams, Ashley. 2003. "Examining the Use Case as Genre in Software Development and Documentation." In *Proceedings of the 21st Annual International Conference on Documentation*, 12–19. SIGDOC '03. New York: ACM.

Williams, Sean D. 2002. "Why Are Partnerships Necessary for Computer Classroom Administration?" *Technical Communication Quarterly* 11 (3): 339–58.

Winsor, Dorothy A. 1990. "Engineering Writing/Writing Engineering." *College Composition and Communication* 41 (1): 58–70.

Wishon, Gordon, and John Rome. 2012. "Enabling the Data-Driven University." *EDUCAUSE Review*, August. http://er.educause.edu/articles/2012/8/enabling-the-datadriven-university.

Wolfe, Joanna. 2006. "Meeting Minutes as a Rhetorical Genre: Discrepancies between Professional Writing Textbooks and Workplace Practice Tutorial." *IEEE Transactions on Professional Communication* 49 (4): 354–64.

Wolfman-Arent, Avi. 2014. "How Do You Plan the Campus of the Future? Try Not To." *Chronicle of Higher Education*, July 18. http://chronicle.com/article/How-Do-You-Plan-the-Campus-of/147803/.

Wresch, William, ed. 1984. *The Computer in Composition Instruction: A Writer's Tool*. Urbana, IL: National Council of Teachers of English.

Yeo, Kee Meng, and A. Frank Mayadas. 2010. "The Sloan-C Pillars: Towards a Balanced Approach to Measuring Organizational Learning." *Journal of Asynchronous Learning Networks* 14 (2): 45–52.

Young, Jeffrey R. 2002. "Ever So Slowly, Colleges Start to Count Work with Technology in Tenure Decisions." *Chronicle of Higher Education*, February 22, 2002, sec. Technology. http://chronicle.com.ezaccess.libraries.psu.edu/article/Ever-So-Slowly-Colleges-Start/28557/.

Zappen, James P. 2005. "Digital Rhetoric: Toward an Integrated Theory." *Technical Communication Quarterly* 14 (3): 319–25.

Zuboff, Shoshana. 1985. "Automate/Informate: The Two Faces of Intelligent Technology." *Organizational Dynamics* 14 (2): 5–18.

INDEX